Maternity and Parental Rights

Employment Law Handbook

April 2015

IDS

THOMSON REUTERS

Maternity and Parental Rights

Employment Law Handbook

Previous edition 2012

IDS
Floor 5
Friars House
157-168 Blackfriars Road
London SE1 8EZ
Email: ids.sales.support@thomsonreuters.com
Website: www.incomesdata.co.uk

ISBN 978 0 414 04985 7

IDS Employment Law Handbook, 'Maternity and Parental Rights', is published by Thomson Reuters (Professional) UK Limited (Registered in England & Wales, Company No. 16790446). Registered Office: 2nd Floor, 1 Mark Square, London, EC2A 4EG.

© 2015 Thomson Reuters (Professional) UK Limited

The information contained in this journal in not intended to be a substitute for specific legal advice and readers should obtain advice from a qualified adviser in relation to individual transactions or matters.

No natural forests were destroyed to make this product: only farmed timber was used and re-planted.

A CIP catalogue record for this book is available from the British Library.

Typeset by DC Graphic Design Ltd, Swanley Village, Kent BR8 7PA
Printed by St Austell Printing Co Ltd, St Austell Business Park, Cornwall PL25 4FD

Contents

Abbreviations

Courts

ECJ	European Court of Justice
ECHR	European Court of Human Rights
PC	Privy Council
SC	Supreme Court
HL	House of Lords
CA	Court of Appeal
Ct Sess	Court of Session
NICA	Northern Ireland Court of Appeal
QBD	Queen's Bench Division
Div Ct	(Queen's Bench) Divisional Court
KBD	King's Bench Division
ChD	Chancery Division
NIRC	National Industrial Relations Court
EAT	Employment Appeal Tribunal
ET	Employment Tribunal

Case references

AC	Law Reports, Appeal Cases
All ER	All England Law Reports
Ch	Law Reports, Chancery Division
CMLR	Common Market Law Reports
COET	Employment Tribunal folio number
EAT	Employment Appeal Tribunal unreported case number
ECR	European Case Reports
ET	Employment Tribunal unreported case number
EWCA	Court of Appeal unreported case number
ICR	Industrial Cases Reports
IRLR	Industrial Relations Law Reports
ITR	Industrial Tribunal Reports
KB	Law Reports, King's Bench Division
QB	Law Reports, Queen's Bench Division
SCOET	Scottish Employment Tribunal folio number
SLT	Scots Law Times
TLR	Times Law Reports
UKSC	Supreme Court unreported case number
WLR	Weekly Law Reports

Legislation

DDA	Disability Discrimination Act 1995
EA	Employment Act 2002
EqA	Equality Act 2010
EqA 2006	Equality Act 2006
EqPA	Equal Pay Act 1970
ERA	Employment Rights Act 1996
ETA	Employment Tribunals Act 1996
PIDA	Public Interest Disclosure Act 1998
RRA	Race Relations Act 1976
SDA	Sex Discrimination Act 1975
SSCBA	Social Security Contributions and Benefits Act 1992
TULR(C)A	Trade Union and Labour Relations (Consolidation) Act 1992

Introduction

The law governing family-friendly rights – now contained in the Employment Rights Act 1996 (ERA) and the Social Security Contributions and Benefits Act 1992 (SSBCA) – has come a long way since the right not to be unfairly dismissed on the ground of pregnancy was first enacted by the Employment Protection Act 1975. That Act, which also provided for six weeks' maternity pay and introduced a right to return to work after maternity leave, was followed some five years later by the Employment Act 1980, which introduced the right to paid time off for ante-natal care. Rights to unpaid parental leave and time off work for dependants were brought into effect in 1999 by the Employment Relations Act 1999, and three years later the Employment Act 2002 introduced rights to paid paternity and adoption leave, and to request flexible working. Most recently, new rights to shared parental leave and time off work to attend pre-adoption appointments were enacted by the Children and Families Act 2014 and came into force in 2015.

These 'family-friendly' rights, which are discussed in depth in Chapters 1 to 11 of this Handbook, exist alongside employees' rights not to be discriminated against under the Equality Act 2010 or to suffer an unlawful detriment or be unfairly dismissed under the ERA – see Chapter 12, 'Detriment and unfair dismissal', and Chapter 13, 'Discrimination and equal pay'. They are also augmented by rights enjoyed by workers under European law, in particular the EU Pregnant Workers Directive (No.92/85) ('the Pregnant Workers Directive') and the EU Parental Leave Directive (No.2010/18), both of which are referred to extensively throughout this Handbook.

Proposals to extend Pregnant Workers Directive. Proposals to amend the EU Pregnant Workers Directive (No.92/85) to increase the rights and protections of new and expectant mothers were published by the European Commission in October 2008. The proposals included extending the minimum length of maternity leave under the Directive from 14 to 18 weeks, a recommendation that women be paid their full salary for the 18-week minimum maternity leave period (which could be capped at the level of statutory sick pay), and increasing compulsory maternity leave from two to six weeks.

However, in October 2010 the European Parliament voted in favour of more controversial amendments. Among other things, the proposed changes provided for 20 weeks' maternity leave on full pay (with some opaque exceptions); a right to time off for breastfeeding; a prohibition on night work and overtime in certain circumstances; and a compulsory period of fully paid maternity leave for at least six weeks after childbirth, regardless of the number of days worked prior to confinement.

The text of the Directive (as agreed by the European Parliament) needed to be approved by a qualified majority of the Council of the European Union to become law. However, it was made clear in a Polish Presidency report dated 21 November 2011 that 20 weeks of maternity leave on full pay, or even a shorter period, was unacceptable to the Council. There were no further developments until June 2014, when the European Commission indicated that the proposals were to be withdrawn. In a press release issued on 18 June 2014, the Commission stated that, following close scrutiny of all proposals before the legislator, it had identified some that were either 'outdated or without support' and which should therefore be withdrawn. These included proposals on pregnant workers. The Commission noted that the withdrawal would allow for 'a fresh start or for alternative ways to achieve the intended legislative purpose'.

Recent developments

The Children and Families Act 2014 made a number of important changes to the existing framework of family-friendly rights. These included:

- the introduction of a right to unpaid time off work to accompany a pregnant woman to ante-natal appointments

- the introduction of new rights to time off to attend pre-adoption appointments

- the extension of the right to adoption leave and pay to local authority foster parents in the 'fostering for adoption' scheme and to intended parents in a surrogacy arrangement

- the removal of the 26 weeks' continuous service requirement for the right to statutory adoption leave

- the enhancement of the rate of statutory adoption pay to mirror the rate for statutory maternity pay

- the introduction of shared parental leave, allowing mothers and adopters to bring their statutory maternity leave and pay/statutory adoption leave and pay to an early end and to share the balance with the father, spouse, civil partner or partner as shared parental leave and pay

- the abolition of the right to additional paternity leave (to make way for the new shared parental leave scheme)

- the extension of the right to request flexible working to all employees with 26 weeks' service (and the simplification of the rules governing how requests should be dealt with).

These changes are considered in the appropriate chapters of this Handbook, with the exception of those relating to flexible working, which are dealt with in IDS Employment Law Handbook, 'Atypical and Flexible Working' (2014), Chapter 4, 'Flexible working'.

Scheme of the Handbook

The scheme of this Handbook is as follows:

- Chapters 1 and 2 deal with the special provisions that apply to pregnant employees (and their partners) and to employees who have recently given birth. Chapter 1 covers the rights to take time off for ante-natal care and to accompany a pregnant woman to ante-natal appointments and Chapter 2 looks at the legislative regime governing their health and safety in the workplace, including the provisions relating to the suspension of employees on maternity grounds

- Chapter 3 looks at the law governing maternity leave (comprising 26 weeks' ordinary maternity leave, followed by 26 weeks' additional maternity leave). This chapter also considers compulsory maternity leave, the two-week period immediately following childbirth

- Chapter 4 explains an employee's right to return to work after taking maternity leave. It also examines the consequences of an employee being made redundant during her leave period

- Chapter 5 sets out the rules relating to statutory maternity pay (SMP). It deals with entitlement to, and payment of, SMP, and explains the situation in which an employee may become disentitled to SMP. It also briefly considers the rules relating to Maternity Allowance (which is a social security benefit payable to the self-employed and to women who do not satisfy the service requirement for SMP)

- Chapter 6 looks at the right to adoption leave and pay, which in many ways mirrors the right to maternity leave and pay and entitles eligible employees to 52 weeks' leave (comprising 26 weeks' ordinary adoption leave, followed by 26 weeks' additional adoption leave), of which 39 weeks is paid. This chapter also considers the new rights to time off work to attend pre-adoption meetings

- Chapter 7 is concerned with the right to paternity leave and pay. Under this right, new fathers (and other partners) are entitled to take up to two weeks' paid paternity leave on the birth or placement for adoption of a child

- Chapter 8 explains the detailed and complex rules that govern the new right to shared parental leave and pay, under which a mother or adopter can convert any unused maternity or adoption leave and pay into shared parental leave and pay

- Chapter 9 focuses on the rules governing the administration of statutory maternity, paternity, adoption and shared parental pay

- Chapter 10 describes the right to unpaid parental leave and examines the default scheme that will apply in the absence of any agreement to the contrary

- Chapter 11 is concerned with the right to take time off to care for dependants – 'dependant care leave'. It explains who has the right, the circumstances in which the right will apply, and the remedies available to employees who are refused the right to take time off

- Chapters 12 and 13 explain the rights enjoyed by all employees not to suffer a detriment, be unfairly dismissed, or be discriminated against for a reason connected with pregnancy; childbirth; maternity, parental, adoption or paternity leave; or time off to care for a dependant. Chapter 13 also considers the special protection afforded to part-time workers under the Part-time Workers (Prevention of Less Favourable Treatment) Regulations 2000 SI 2000/1551

- finally, Chapter 14 examines how employees specifically engaged to cover for maternity absence should be treated by their employer.

This Handbook replaces IDS Employment Law Handbook, 'Maternity and Parental Rights' (2012). The law is stated as at 5 April 2015.

This publication aims to provide accurate, authoritative information and comment on the subjects it covers. It is offered to subscribers on the understanding that the publisher is not in business as a lawyer or consultant.

1 Time off for ante-natal care

This chapter considers the statutory provisions contained in Part IV of the **1.1** Employment Rights Act 1996 (ERA) (Ss.55–57ZS) that afford employees and agency workers time off in advance of the birth of a child. The most important of these are the rights of pregnant employees and agency workers to paid time off work to attend ante-natal appointments ('Right to time off for ante-natal care' and 'Right to payment for time off for ante-natal care' below). These rights are unaffected by the various reforms to maternity and parental rights introduced by the Children and Families Act 2014. They have, however, been augmented by new rights for employees and agency workers to unpaid time off to accompany a pregnant woman to ante-natal appointments (see 'Right to time off to accompany pregnant woman' below). These new rights to accompany are available to the pregnant woman's husband, civil partner or partner (including same-sex partners), the father or parent of the pregnant woman's child, and intended parents in a surrogacy arrangement who meet specified conditions.

An employee or agency worker who is denied one of the rights to time off considered in this chapter may bring a claim of unreasonable refusal of time off – see 'Remedies – complaints under Part V1 ERA'. Additionally, there may be scope for a claim of unlawful detriment and, where the worker is an employee, automatically unfair dismissal. Furthermore, there is also the possibility of a discrimination claim under the Equality Act 2010. These remedies are considered briefly at the end of this chapter but for more detailed analyses, see Chapter 12, 'Detriment and unfair dismissal', and Chapter 13, 'Discrimination and equal pay'.

Note that employees and agency workers who are going through the process of **1.2** adopting a child enjoy similar rights to time off to attend adoption meetings. These rights are considered in Chapter 6, 'Adoption leave and pay', under 'Time off for adoption appointments'.

Note that statutory references in this chapter are to the Employment Rights Act 1996 (ERA), unless otherwise stated.

1.3   Right to time off for ante-natal care

The right of pregnant female employees to paid time off during working hours for ante-natal care is set out in Ss.55–57 ERA and has two elements:

- the right not to be unreasonably refused time off to attend ante-natal care appointments during working hours – Ss.55(1) and 57(1)(a); and

- the right to be paid for this period of absence – S.56(1).

An equivalent right for agency workers to take paid time off during working hours is set out in Ss.57ZA–ZD.

European law also provides a right to time off for ante-natal care. Article 9 of the EU Pregnant Workers Directive (No.92/85) stipulates that Member States must take the necessary measures to ensure that pregnant workers are entitled, in accordance with national legislation and/or practice, to time off without loss of pay in order to attend ante-natal examinations, if such examinations have to take place during working hours. Article 2 defines a 'pregnant worker' as one 'who informs her employer of her condition, in accordance with national legislation and/or national practice'. In practice, Article 9 adds nothing to the rights already contained in the ERA as outlined above.

1.4   Who has the right?
The right to paid time off for ante-natal care applies to pregnant employees and agency workers. However, there are some categories of employees and workers who are specifically excluded from the scope of the provisions – see 'Excluded employees and workers' below.

1.5 Employees. Section 55(1) ERA provides that 'an employee, who is pregnant, and has, on the advice of a registered medical practitioner, registered midwife or registered nurse, made an appointment to attend at any place for the purpose of receiving ante-natal care, is entitled to be permitted by her employer to take time off during the employee's working hours in order to enable her to keep the appointment'.

An 'employee' is an individual who works under a contract of service, as opposed to a contract for services – S.230 ERA (see IDS Employment Law Handbook, 'Contracts of Employment' (2014), Chapter 2, 'Employment status'). No minimum period of qualifying service is necessary. A female employee has the right to time off for ante-natal care from the day she starts her job, whether she is full time or part time and whether she is engaged on a permanent or temporary basis.

1.6 Agency workers. The right for agency workers to be permitted to take paid time off for ante-natal care was introduced into the ERA with effect from 1 October 2011 by the Agency Workers Regulations 2010 SI 2010/93 (AWR).

S.57ZA(1) provides that 'an agency worker who is pregnant, and has, on the advice of a registered medical practitioner, registered midwife or registered nurse, made an appointment to attend at any place for the purpose of receiving ante-natal care, is entitled to be permitted, by the temporary work agency and the hirer, to take time off during the agency worker's working hours in order to enable her to keep the appointment'.

The terms 'agency worker', 'temporary work agency' and 'hirer' are defined in the AWR. An agency worker is a worker who has either a contract of employment with the temporary work agency, or any other contract to perform work and services personally for the agency (Reg 3), while a 'temporary work agency' is an employment business that supplies individuals to work temporarily for and under the supervision and direction of a hirer (Reg 4). A 'hirer' is the person to whom individuals are supplied temporarily (Reg 2). (For a more detailed discussion of these definitions, see IDS Employment Law Handbook, 'Atypical and Flexible Working' (2014), Chapter 1, 'Agency workers', under 'Rights under the Agency Workers Regulations – who is covered by the AWR?').

In contrast to the position in respect of employees, agency workers will only **1.7** become eligible for the right to ante-natal care where they have completed a 'qualifying period' –S.57ZD(1)(a). This period is set out in Reg 7(2) AWR, which provides that an 'agency worker must work in the same role with the same hirer for 12 continuous calendar weeks, during one or more assignments' to be eligible – see further IDS Employment Law Handbook, 'Atypical and Flexible Working', Chapter 1, 'Agency workers', under 'Rights under the Agency Workers Regulations – equal treatment: the qualifying period'.

Seafarers and Crown employees. Seafarers employed on ships registered under **1.8** S.8 of the Merchant Shipping Act 1995 are covered provided that the ship is registered as belonging to a port in Great Britain, that under her contract of employment the employee does not work wholly outside Great Britain, and that she is ordinarily resident in Great Britain – S.199(7) and (8) ERA. Crown employees and parliamentary staff are also covered – Ss.191, 194 and 195.

Excluded employees and workers. Employees excluded from the right to paid **1.9** time off under S.55 are:

- those employed in the armed forces – S.192
- those employed in share fishing – S.199(2)
- those employed in the police service – S.200.

Under S.126 of the Criminal Justice and Public Order Act 1994 prison officers are covered by the employment protection legislation and so will qualify for the right to time off for ante-natal care.

Apart from agency workers (as discussed above), all other workers who are not 'employees' within the meaning of S.230 ERA are not entitled to paid time off for ante-natal care. So, for example, casual workers, homeworkers and labour-only subcontractors – unless they are employees or otherwise satisfy the definition of 'agency worker' in Reg 3 AWR – will not qualify for ante-natal rights.

1.10 Conditions

There are a number of prerequisites for the right to time off for ante-natal care:

- the employee or agency worker must be pregnant – Ss.55(1)(a) and 57ZA(1)(a) ERA

- she must have made an appointment to receive ante-natal care on the advice of a registered medical practitioner, registered midwife or registered nurse – Ss.55(1)(b) and 57ZA(1)(b), and

- for the second and subsequent appointments she must, if the employer (or, in the case of an agency worker, hirer or temporary work agency) requests her to do so, produce a certificate from a registered medical practitioner, midwife or nurse stating that she is pregnant and an appointment card or other document showing that the appointment has been made – Ss.55(2)–(3) and 57ZA(2)–(3).

For these purposes, a registered nurse is a person who is included in the Specialist Community Public Health Nurses part of the register maintained under the Nursing and Midwifery Order 2001; and the definition of such a person extends to anyone whose entry in that part of the register shows them to hold a qualification in health visiting – S.55(5) ERA.

1.11 It is made clear by S.55(3) (in the case of employees) and S.57ZA(3) (in the case of agency workers) that the third condition set out above does not apply where the ante-natal care appointment in question is the first such appointment during the employee's/worker's pregnancy. Accordingly, an employee or agency worker attending her first appointment is not required to produce a certificate stating that she is pregnant or an appointment card or other similar document should the employer (or, as the case may be, hirer or temporary work agency) ask for this.

1.12 Scope of 'ante-natal care'

Although the term 'ante-natal care' is not defined in the ERA, it clearly covers appointments with midwives or other specialists to check that all is well with mother and baby. However, there is ongoing debate as to whether classes that are not directly connected with the health of the woman and her unborn child, such as ante-natal relaxation or parentcraft classes, are included.

Relaxation and parentcraft classes. As early as 1982 a tribunal upheld an **1.13** employee's claim for paid time off to attend ante-natal appointments and relaxation classes – Gregory v Tudsbury Ltd 1982 IRLR 267, ET. Furthermore, in the debates on the Trade Union Reform and Employment Rights Act 1993 the Government accepted that ante-natal care could cover parentcraft classes – see Hansard Standing Committee F, 12 January 1993, cols 291–292; Hansard (HL), 25 March 1993, cols 531–532. In addition, various incarnations of official Government guidance on the maternity provisions (including the guidance currently available online) state that ante-natal care may include relaxation and parentcraft classes where they are recommended by a registered medical practitioner, midwife or nurse.

However, in Bateman v Flexible Lamps Ltd ET Case No.3204707/97 an employment tribunal refused to accept that the definition of 'ante-natal care' in S.55 covered parentcraft classes. The tribunal noted that such classes were 'optional' and were concerned with education concerning the birth itself and care of the newborn infant. This, said the tribunal, was quite distinct from the medical matters dealt with at the ante-natal clinic. The employee referred the tribunal to an earlier version of the Government guidance published by the then Department of Trade and Industry, which, as stated above, stipulated that ante-natal care extended to parentcraft classes, but the tribunal decided that, although there may be some cases in which such classes fall within the ambit of ante-natal care, this was not one of them.

Given that the Government guidance has maintained its position regarding **1.14** parentcraft and relaxation classes notwithstanding the decision in Bateman, and in light of the fact that neither the guidance nor the Bateman decision is binding on other tribunals, the true legal position remains uncertain. A decision from the EAT on the issue would therefore be welcome.

Pregnancy testing. Although it is clear that a pregnant woman who turns up **1.15** for her first ante-natal appointment will be entitled to time off, the question arises whether the right to time off would cover an appointment made by an employee to see her doctor in order to ascertain whether she is pregnant in the first place. Assuming it turns out that she is, the answer would seem to depend on whose advice it was upon which she made the initial appointment. As explained above, to qualify for the right to time off in respect of a first appointment, a female employee must satisfy the two conditions set out in S.55(1)(a) and (b): namely, that she is pregnant and has made an appointment to receive ante-natal care on the advice of a registered medical practitioner, midwife or nurse. An agency worker must satisfy identical conditions in S.57ZA(1)(a) and (b). Thus, provided the employee/agency worker has made the appointment on the advice of one of these registered persons, she qualifies. This may be the case, for example, if she has acted on the advice of someone from NHS Direct or a family health visitor. If, however, she makes the appointment after having done a home pregnancy test or on the advice of, say, a pharmacist, then it is difficult to see how she satisfies the condition in S.55(1)(b)/S.57ZA(1)(b). In these circumstances, it is likely that she would be excluded from the right to time off or to be paid for any time off permitted by the employer.

1.16 IVF treatment. Questions also arise over medical care received for the purposes of IVF (in vitro fertilization) treatment. IVF treatment can involve frequent medical appointments necessitating time away from work. Moreover, many patients undergo several attempts at conception, as the treatment is often unsuccessful. If the meaning of 'ante-natal care' under Ss.55 and 57A covers every appointment associated with IVF treatment, then employees and agency workers may end up taking a considerable amount of time off work under those provisions. If, however, pregnancy – and, by extension, the need for ante-natal care – is not considered to have begun until IVF treatment is successful, then employees and agency workers undergoing such treatment will have no right to any time off at all during the course of the treatment (unless, of course, they have a contractual right to such time off). As far as we are aware, no domestic courts have considered the position under S.55 or S.57A, but the ECJ has held that a woman is not pregnant, and therefore not covered by the EU Pregnant Workers Directive (No.92/85), until the fertilized ova has been implanted in the uterus – Mayr v Bäckerei und Konditorei Gerhard Flöckner OHG 2008 IRLR 387, ECJ. That decision would seem to indicate that the right to time off for ante-natal care would not arise until this stage in IVF treatment is reached.

Note, however, that while a woman who is undergoing the early stages of IVF may not enjoy any rights under the ERA to time off for ante-natal care, the less favourable treatment of a woman because she is undergoing IVF treatment might nevertheless be considered sex discrimination – see Chapter 13, 'Discrimination and equal pay', in the section 'Direct discrimination', under 'Pregnancy and maternity discrimination – protected period'.

1.17 When is a refusal reasonable?
Since the statutory right is not to be *unreasonably* refused time off (see Ss.57(1)(a) and 57ZC(1)(a) ERA), it follows that there may be circumstances in which a refusal to allow time off will be reasonable. The ERA does not give any guidance on how to determine reasonableness, although, generally speaking, tribunals are reluctant to find a refusal reasonable when appointments have been made on proper medical advice. However, in Gregory v Tudsbury Ltd 1982 IRLR 267, ET, the tribunal thought that it might be reasonable for an employer to refuse time off work if it was reasonable in the circumstances for the employee to make arrangements outside normal working hours. The tribunal did not specify which situations would justify a reasonable refusal but simply stated that each case must be judged on its merits. It may be that a

woman who only works two days a week should attend a non-urgent ante-natal appointment/class on a non-working day. However, this assumes that the employee has some control over the timing of the appointment, which is not usually the case.

Employers should bear in mind that the right to paid time off is a right to be permitted time off during 'working hours' – see below. The number and frequency of ante-natal appointments is usually dictated by medical advice and, apart from the first appointment, employers are entitled to see medical evidence in advance in order to confirm that an appointment has been made and is therefore presumably necessary – see 'Conditions' above. So unless the frequency gets completely out of hand, it is probably best to assume that it would be unreasonable to refuse paid time off if, on request, the employee is able to adduce evidence that an appointment has been scheduled.

Time off during working hours

1.18

The term 'working hours' for the purposes of the right to take time off during working hours to attend ante-natal appointments is defined in S.55(4) ERA as 'any time when, in accordance with her contract of employment, the employee is required to be at work'. An equivalent provision applies in the case of agency workers: in that case, such hours are defined in S.57ZA(4) as 'any time when, in accordance with the terms under which the agency worker works temporarily or under the supervision and direction of the hirer, [he or she] is required to be at work'.

In Pollard v Greater Manchester Passenger Transport Executive ET Case No.2402582/96 the employer claimed that P was a casual worker and that when she took time off work to attend ante-natal appointments, she was not required to be 'at work' in accordance with her contract of employment. An employment tribunal held that P would have attended work on the days in question had it not been for the appointments. It was the expectation of the parties that P would invariably attend work and would be provided with work unless the employer contacted her in advance to say that there was no work available. Accordingly, the employer was ordered to pay P for the time she had taken off work to attend the appointments in question.

As mentioned above, the right is to time off during the employee's (or agency **1.19** worker's) working hours and it will not be reasonable for the employer (or, as the case may be, temporary work agency or hirer) to avoid this by rearranging the individual's working schedule or requiring her to make up lost time. The following four cases illustrate this:

- **Edgar v Giorgione Inns Ltd** ET Case No.20961/86: E's employer tried to justify a refusal to pay for time off by saying that she should have organised her appointments outside working hours or come into work on Sundays in lieu of her time off. But, as the employment tribunal pointed out, an employee's right is to time off during her working hours and nothing in the ERA requires her to make up for lost time

- **Sajil v Carraro t/a Foubert's Bar** ET Case No.04824/87: S reached an arrangement with her employer that she would have Wednesdays off whenever she needed to attend ante-natal appointments and would work Saturdays instead in those weeks. Later she became aware of her statutory right to paid time off. Her claim to be paid for the time she had taken on Wednesdays to attend the appointments succeeded because Saturday was not one of her normal working days and she had been attending appointments during her normal working hours. In this case there had been a mutually beneficial arrangement, but the employment tribunal remarked that it is important not to allow unscrupulous employers any scope for requiring or persuading a pregnant woman to reorganise her working hours or to make up for lost time

- **Riley v British Telecommunications plc** ET Case No.43125/95: after informing the employer of her pregnancy, R, a part-time worker, came under pressure from her shop manager to arrange hospital appointments outside her working hours or make up the time on another occasion. R was able to arrange appointments with her GP outside her working hours, but was not able to do so in respect of hospital appointments. After consulting with her union about her rights, R refused to make up the time she took off for two hospital appointments. She did, however, come in early one day to make up the time for another hospital appointment after being threatened with dismissal. An employment tribunal found that by requiring R to make up the time for this appointment unpaid, the employer was in effect not paying her for the time spent attending the hospital appointment. The employer was therefore ordered to pay R for the make-up time she worked

- **Holmwood v Smith and Gardener Ltd** ET Case No.6001899/98: when H sought time off for ante-natal care on two days, her employer insisted that she take her weekly day off on the days on which she had the appointments. An employment tribunal upheld H's claim that this was a failure to allow time off and awarded her two days' pay.

1.20 Similar considerations apply in respect of pregnancy and maternity discrimination. In Frances v Parklife Ltd ET Case No.3200563/05, for example, F agreed under pressure to work extra hours to make up for the time taken to attend private ante-natal care classes in return for which she would be entitled to take paid 'time off in lieu' (TOIL). However, the employer reneged on this agreement by failing to pay the claimant in respect of her accrued TOIL. A tribunal upheld her claim of discrimination on the ground that the employer's actions constituted less favourable treatment by reason of the claimant's pregnancy. Taken together with two other incidents of less favourable treatment, the tribunal awarded the claimant a global figure of £2,000 for injury to feelings.

Amount of time off

1.21

The right for employees under S.55(1) ERA and agency workers under S.57ZA(1) ERA is to time off 'to enable [the woman] to keep the appointment'. This does not simply cover the time taken up by the appointment but also travelling and waiting time.

In Dhamrait v United Biscuits Ltd ET Case No.10128/83 D was allowed time off for an appointment, which lasted longer than expected. As a result she missed the works bus (the only available means of transport) and instead of missing only the first hour of her shift, as was expected, she missed the whole of it. An employment tribunal decided that she was entitled to be paid for the entire shift.

The timing of the appointment and the employee's or agency worker's working hours will affect the amount of work an employee or agency worker can reasonably be expected to perform on the day of the appointment. In Edgar v Giorgione Inns Ltd (see 'Time off during working hours' above) E worked from 9 am – 3 pm six days a week. She attended five ante-natal appointments at 3 pm, 11 am, 9 am, 10.30 am and 11.15 am respectively. The employment tribunal ruled that in order to attend the 3 pm appointment she only needed to leave work at 2 pm, and for the 9.05 am appointment she was able to work from 12–3 pm. In respect of the other appointments, however, the tribunal found that 'the timing was such that it was impracticable for her to put in a significant period either before or after' her appointment. Accordingly, E was entitled to be paid for taking the whole shift off in order to attend those appointments.

1.22

Abusing time off for ante-natal care

1.23

It should be noted that the right under Ss.55(1) and 57ZA(1) ERA is to be 'permitted' to take time off. Thus, the employee or agency worker must seek prior permission before taking time off work to attend an ante-natal appointment. If a woman who is refused permission goes ahead and attends an appointment she may face disciplinary action, and possibly even dismissal for misconduct. Were a tribunal subsequently to find that the request for time off was unreasonably refused, it would be likely to view any dismissal as one connected with the woman's pregnancy and therefore automatically unfair (see Chapter 12, 'Detriment and unfair dismissal', under 'Automatically unfair dismissal – pregnancy, childbirth and maternity'), as well as pregnancy and maternity discrimination. However, if the tribunal considered the refusal to be reasonable, or if the woman did not seek permission in the first place, then it might view the dismissal as both fair and non-discriminatory.

In Gough v Country Sport (Wales) Ltd ET Case No.01075/89, for example, the employer became concerned that G was taking more time off than was necessary. Matters came to a head when G had an afternoon appointment and the employer refused to allow her to take the morning off as well to go to the hairdresser. G nevertheless took the full day off for ante-natal care and was dismissed when she returned to work. Although she established before the tribunal that she had been entitled to the time off for travel and to attend her appointment, the tribunal found that she had acted with flagrant disobedience in taking the whole day off. She did not have the two years' qualifying service necessary at that time to pursue a claim for unfair dismissal. Regarding her discrimination claim, the tribunal held that G had not been dismissed on the ground of pregnancy but on the ground of disobedience and 'irresponsible conduct'.

1.24 A different conclusion was reached in Dealy and anor v Scarlett EAT 81/97, however. Like the claimant in Gough (above), S had a poor attendance record. Over the course of her employment, she had received two informal warnings concerning her absences from work and the alleged poor quality of her work. On or around 4 December 1995 S informed her employer that she was pregnant and subsequently the employer granted her permission to attend ante-natal appointments in December 1995 and February 1996. On 14 March S was due to attend the hospital for an ultrasound scan and an ante-natal appointment and she was given permission to attend, but warned that she must return to work afterwards. S left the hospital at 3.10 pm but did not return to work, as the bus schedule indicated that she would not have got back to the office until 15 minutes before her shift ended. The next morning she was dismissed. An employment tribunal found that, while it was possible for S to have returned to work on 14 March, the practical consequences of her failure to do so were slight. It went on to find that S's dismissal was by reason of her pregnancy and therefore amounted to sex discrimination and unfair dismissal. Nevertheless, the tribunal found that S's failure to return to work on 14 March was deliberate and could have been avoided. As such, S's actions contributed to her dismissal, and a deduction of 20 per cent was made from her award. The employer's appeal on the question of liability and the employee's cross-appeal on the finding of 20 per cent contribution were dismissed by the EAT.

1.25 ## Right to payment for time off for ante-natal care

Once an employee or agency worker is permitted to take time off, she is entitled to be paid for it at the appropriate hourly rate – S.56(1)/S.57ZB(1) ERA. In Gregory v Tudsbury Ltd 1982 IRLR 267, ET, the employer allowed time off but refused to pay for it on the ground that the leave could reasonably have been refused. The employment tribunal pointed out that once an employer allows time off it is bound to pay for it. Had G's employer refused time off, that would have been a different matter: it would then be for the tribunal to decide whether the refusal was reasonable.

The right to paid time off only applies when an employee is allowed time off 'under S.55' or, in the case of agency workers, 'under S.57ZA'. This means that the employee/agency worker must comply with any request from the employer/hirer/temporary work agency to produce a certificate of pregnancy and an appointment card (on the second and subsequent appointments). If she fails to do so, the employer/hirer/temporary work agency will not be obliged to pay her for any time off she is allowed. However, the employee/agency worker need only produce the certificate and appointment card if the employer/hirer/temporary work agency asks to see them. In Edgar v Giorgione Inns Ltd ET Case No.20961/86 the employer asserted that E had never produced her appointment cards, but as the employer had never asked to see them this was irrelevant.

Calculation of pay   1.26

Pay is for the period of absence at the appropriate hourly rate – S.56(1)/S.57ZB(1). In the context of employment, where the employee is paid a fixed annual salary, she should simply be paid as normal. In other cases, the appropriate hourly rate is found by dividing a week's pay by the number or average number of normal working hours in a week – S.56(2) and (3). Equivalent calculation rules apply to agency workers – see S.57ZB(2) and (3). The rules governing the calculation of a week's pay are set out in Chapter II of Part XIV of the ERA – see IDS Employment Law Handbook, 'Wages' (2011), Chapter 10, 'A week's pay'. There is no ceiling on the amount of a week's pay for the purposes of calculating paid time off for ante-natal care as there is, for example, in the case of calculating redundancy payments.

Employees. There are three ways of ascertaining an employee's 'normal 1.27 working hours':

- if the number of normal working hours does not vary from week to week, that is the number to be used – S.56(2)

- if the number of normal working hours varies from week to week, take the total number of hours worked during the 12 weeks ending with the last complete week before the day of the appointment for ante-natal care and divide by 12 – S.56(3)(a)

- if the number of normal working hours varies from week to week, but the employee has worked for less than 12 weeks, take a number that fairly represents her normal working hours in a week – S.56(3)(b). Regard may be had, as appropriate, to the average number of hours she could expect to work under her contract and to the average hours worked by employees in comparable jobs – S.56(4).

The calculation date for establishing the rate of payment is the day of the appointment concerned – S.225(3).

1.28 **Agency workers.** So far as agency workers are concerned, the appropriate hourly rate where normal working hours do not vary is calculated by taking the amount of one week's pay and dividing it by the number of normal working hours in a week in accordance with the terms under which the worker works temporarily for and under the supervision and direction of the hirer in force on the date when the time off is taken – S.57ZB(2). However, where the working hours during the temporary assignment vary from week to week, the same calculation as set out in S.56(3)(a) above is applied – see S.57ZB(3).

Note that there is no provision equivalent to S.56(4) with regard to calculating remuneration for agency workers with fewer than 12 weeks' service, as such workers will not have met the 12-week qualifying period on which the entitlement to paid time off for ante-natal classes depends.

1.29 In one slightly unusual case, Vadivelu v Industrial Temporaries ET Case No.2200568/96, the employee was employed by an employment agency on a short-term contract. Under the contract she was entitled to a bonus of £180 based on timekeeping and attendance. The agency reduced her bonus by £70 solely because of her attendance at ante-natal appointments. An employment tribunal held that this was an unlawful deduction from the employee's wages under Part II of the ERA and ordered that the agency pay her the sum of £70.

1.30 **Rate of pay and set off.** Where an employee or agency worker has a contractual right to be paid for the time off, she is entitled to claim her contractual or statutory rate, whichever is the greater, but no more – S.56(5)/S.57ZB(4). Payment under one head also discharges liability under the other – S.56(6)/S.57ZB(5).

1.31 Right to time off to accompany pregnant woman

As discussed under 'Right to time off for ante-natal care – who has the right?' above, the right of employees to time off to attend ante-natal appointments under S.55 ERA, and the right to remuneration for that time off under S.56, are only available to pregnant women. The same is also true of the equivalent rights for agency workers in Ss.57ZA and 57ZB. Given the clear terms in which they are drafted, it is not possible to interpret these provisions as affording any right for the other parent, or the mother's partner, to also attend ante-natal appointments. However, new rights to this effect were inserted into the ERA by the Children and Families Act 2014 and came into effect on 1 October 2014.

Section 57ZE(1) ERA states: 'An employee who has a qualifying relationship with a pregnant woman or her expected child is entitled to be permitted by his or her employer to take time off during the employee's working hours in order that he or she may accompany the woman when she attends by appointment at any place for the purpose of receiving ante-natal care.' This right can only be exercised twice in respect of a given pregnancy – S.57ZE(2).

In very similar terms, S.57ZG(1) states: 'An agency worker who has a qualifying **1.32** relationship with a pregnant woman or her expected child is entitled to be permitted, by the temporary work agency and the hirer, to take time off during the agency worker's working hours in order that he or she may accompany the woman when she attends by appointment at any place for the purpose of receiving ante-natal care.' This right can also only be exercised twice in respect of a given pregnancy – S.57ZG(2).

Time off is unpaid. It should be noted that there is no statutory obligation on **1.33** the employer/temporary work agency/hirer to pay for any time off taken under S.57ZE(1) or S.57ZG(1). However, that does not prevent a right to payment being granted under the contract.

Qualifying relationships **1.34**
An employee or agency worker will only have the right to time off to accompany a pregnant woman to an ante-natal appointment if he or she has a 'qualifying relationship' with the woman or the expected child. The same definition of 'qualifying relationship' is found in both Ss.57ZE(7) and 57ZG(7). It covers:

- the husband or civil partner of the pregnant woman

- a person who lives with the pregnant woman in an enduring family relationship but is not a relative of that woman

- the father of the expected child

- a woman who is deemed to be the parent of the expected child under S.42 or S.43 of the Human Fertilisation and Embryology Act 2008

- a person who is a potential applicant for a parental order under S.54 of the Human Fertilisation and Embryology Act 2008 in respect of the expected child.

Spouse or civil partner. Although Ss.57ZE(7)(a) and 57ZG(7)(a) both state **1.35** that a person is in a qualifying relationship with a pregnant woman if he or she is the *husband or civil partner* of that woman, it is presumably the case that this category would also extend to the wife of the pregnant woman. Para 1(1)(c) of Schedule 3 to the Marriage (Same Sex Couples) Act 2013 provides that any reference in legislation to a person who is married is to be read as including a reference to a person who is married to a person of the same sex.

Enduring family relationship. An employee or agency worker will enjoy the **1.36** right to time off to accompany a pregnant woman to ante-natal appointments if he or she lives with that woman in an enduring family relationship, and is not a relative – S.57ZE(7)(b)/S.57ZG(7)(b). No further definition of 'enduring family relationship' is provided in the legislation.

The term 'relative' for these purposes means the pregnant woman's parent, grandparent, sister, brother, aunt or uncle – S.57ZE(8)/S.57ZG(8). The definition covers relationships of full blood or half blood. In the case of an adopted person, it covers such of those relationships as would exist but for the adoption, and also includes the relationship of a child with the child's adoptive, or former adoptive, parents, but does not include any other adoptive relationships – S.57ZE(9)/S.57ZG(9).

1.37 **Surrogacy.** Section 54 of the Human Fertilisation and Embryology Act 2008 sets out a procedure by which the commissioning parents in a surrogacy arrangement can apply for a parental order in respect of the expected child. A 'potential applicant' under this procedure is entitled to the right to time off to accompany the pregnant woman to ante-natal appointments under S.57ZE (if an employee) or S.57ZG (if an agency worker).

A person (A) is a potential applicant for a parental order under S.54 in respect of an expected child only if:

- A intends to apply, jointly with another person (B), for such an order in respect of the expected child within six months of the birth

- the expected child is being carried by the pregnant woman, who is not A or B, as a result of the placing in her of an embryo or sperm and eggs or her artificial insemination

- the gametes of A or B (or both) were used to bring about the creation of the embryo

- at the time A seeks to exercise the right to time off, A and B are married, in a civil partnership, or are two persons who are living as partners in an enduring family relationship and are not within prohibited degrees of relationship in relation to each other, and

- when the application under S.54 of the 2008 Act is considered, A expects that A and B will satisfy the conditions in S.54(2), (4), (5) and (8) as to the family relationship, the place at which the applicants and child live, the age of the applicants, and the absence of any unauthorised payments to the surrogate mother.

1.38 There is nothing in S.57ZE or S.57ZG which indicates that the right to accompany a pregnant woman to ante-natal appointments is restricted to one companion per pregnant woman. Accordingly, it appears that both intended parents in a surrogacy arrangement could exercise the right, provided they meet the above conditions.

Conditions

The rights to time off under Ss.57ZE and 57ZG are restricted to:

- two ante-natal appointments in relation to a particular pregnancy

- a maximum amount of time off during working hours of six and a half hours on each occasion. (For the meaning of 'working hours' in this context, see 'Right to time off for ante-natal care – time off during working hours' above.)

As with the right to time off for ante-natal care, the rights under Ss.57ZE and 57ZG are to be 'permitted' to take time off by the employer, temporary work agency or hirer, as the case may be. Thus, the employee or agency worker must *request* the time off and cannot simply rely on these provisions as an after-the-fact justification for the absence from work.

Employers/temporary work agencies/hirers do not have to obtain signed declarations from applicants for time off. However, if they choose to make this a requirement, the employee/agency worker must sign the declaration in order for the right to time off to be engaged – S.57ZE(5)/S.57ZG(5). A declaration can be in print or electronic format, and the employee/agency worker must state:

- that he or she has a qualifying relationship with the pregnant woman (see 'Qualifying relationships' above)

- that his or her purpose in taking time off is to accompany the pregnant woman when she attends an appointment for the purpose of receiving ante-natal care

- that the appointment in question is made on the advice of a registered medical practitioner, registered midwife or registered nurse, and

- the date and time of the appointment.

The term 'ante-natal care' is not given any further definition in S.57ZE or S.57ZG. Presumably, however, it will be interpreted consistently with Ss.55 and 57ZA – see 'Right to time off for ante-natal care – scope of "ante-natal care"' above.

When is a refusal reasonable?

As with the right to time off for ante-natal care, the right to time off to accompany a pregnant woman to ante-natal appointments is actually a right not to be *unreasonably refused* such time off – see S.57ZF(1)/S.57ZH(1). Thus, the statute leaves open the possibility that there are circumstances where it would be reasonable to refuse a request for time off under S.57ZE or S.57ZG. However, as the provisions only came into force on 1 October 2014, no case law has arisen to consider this point.

1.39

1.40

1.41

It is worth reiterating, however, that time off under these provisions can only be taken if the appointment has been made on the advice of a medical practitioner and is limited to two appointments of no more than six and a half hours each. Furthermore, the employee or agency worker has no right to be paid for the time off. Thus, it is perhaps safest to assume that it will generally be unreasonable to refuse time off if the statutory conditions (see 'Conditions' above) have been satisfied.

1.42 Remedies

An employee or agency worker who is unreasonably denied time off for ante-natal care, or time off to accompany a pregnant woman to ante-natal appointments, can bring a complaint under the provisions in Part VI of the ERA. However, that is not the only means by which aggrieved individuals can seek redress. If they have been victimised as a result of exercising the right to time off, they may be able to claim sex discrimination or unlawful detriment or, in the case of employees, automatically unfair dismissal. We consider these remedies below.

1.43 Complaints under Part VI ERA

If an employer unreasonably refuses time off for ante-natal care or allows time off but refuses to pay for it (either in whole or in part), the employee may complain to an employment tribunal – S.57(1) ERA. Similar provisions apply to agency workers, save that whereas a complaint can be brought against a temporary work agency both in respect of a failure to permit time off and a failure to pay the worker for any time off taken, a complaint can only be brought against a hirer in respect of a failure to permit time off – S.57ZC(1) and (2). In other words, a complaint by an agency worker solely concerned with a failure to *pay* for time off taken can only be brought against the temporary work agency.

Where an employer unreasonably refuses to allow an employee to take time off to accompany a pregnant woman to an ante-natal appointment, the employee may bring a complaint to an employment tribunal – S.57ZF(1). Similarly, an agency worker unreasonably refused such time off by a temporary work agency or hirer may bring a complaint to an employment tribunal under S.57ZH(1) or S.57ZH(2).

1.44 If the tribunal finds that the complaint is justified, it must make a declaration to that effect – S.57(3)/S.57ZC(4)/S.57ZF(4)(a)/S.57ZH(5)(a). It must also award compensation, although the approach taken in this regard will differ depending on whether the claim is in respect of time off for ante-natal care or time off to accompany a pregnant woman to ante-natal appointments.

1.45 **Compensation – time off for ante-natal care.** If the complaint is of unreasonable refusal to allow time off, the tribunal must order the employer

16

to pay the employee an amount equal to the remuneration she would have received for the period of time off requested – S.57(4). If the equivalent complaint is brought by an agency worker, then the tribunal must require the temporary work agency or, if appropriate, the hirer to pay such an amount – S.57ZC(5). S.57ZC(6) confers on a tribunal the power to apportion this payment between the temporary work agency and hirer in such a manner as is 'just and equitable having regard to the extent of each respondent's responsibility for the infringement'.

If the complaint is that the employer or temporary work agency allowed time off but refused to pay for it, either in whole or in part, the tribunal must order the employer or agency to pay the amount due – S.57(5)/S.57ZC(7). Anything that the employer/agency has already paid for the time off may be offset against the amount due – S.56(6)/S.57ZB(5).

Compensation – time off to accompany. If a complaint under S.57ZF(1) or S.57ZH(1) or (2) is upheld, the tribunal must award compensation according to the formula set out in Ss.57ZF(5) and 57ZH(6). This provides that the amount payable to the employee or agency worker is calculated by multiplying the appropriate hourly rate of pay for the employee by the number of working hours for which the employee would have been entitled to be absent if the time off had not been refused, and then doubling the result. For example, if an employee paid £12 per hour were to be denied six hours off work to accompany a pregnant woman to an ante-natal appointment, the compensation under S.57ZF(5) would amount to £144 (12 x 6 x 2). **1.46**

Time limits. Complaints under Ss.57, 57ZC, 57ZF and 57ZH should be presented within a period of three months beginning with the date of the ante-natal appointment concerned. So, for example, if the appointment was on 10 June, time runs out on 9 September and not, as the unwary often think, on 10 September. However, if it was not reasonably practicable to present the complaint within the three-month time limit, the tribunal may extend the time limit by such further period as it considers reasonable. The time limit may also be extended to facilitate early conciliation or cross-border mediation. The law on time limits is explained in IDS Employment Law Handbook, 'Employment Tribunal Practice and Procedure' (2014), Chapter 5, 'Time limits'. **1.47**

Conciliation and settlements. The services of an Acas conciliator are available to try to settle a complaint relating to time off work without the need for tribunal proceedings – S.18(1)(d) Employment Tribunals Act 1996. Alternatively, provided the employee or agency worker has received independent legal advice from a qualified lawyer or other relevant independent adviser, the parties may settle their dispute by means of a 'settlement agreement' – see S.203 ERA and Reg 15 AWR. For further details, see IDS Employment Law Handbook, 'Employment Tribunal Practice and Procedure' (2014), Chapter 3, 'Conciliation, settlements and ADR'. **1.48**

1.49 ## Unlawful detriment

Section 47C(1) ERA stipulates that an employee 'has the right not to be subjected to any detriment by any act, or any deliberate failure to act, by his employer done for a prescribed reason'. Subsection (2) goes on to state that 'a prescribed reason' must be one that is prescribed by regulations and which relates, inter alia, to pregnancy, childbirth or maternity. Reg 19 of the Maternity and Parental Leave etc Regulations 1999 SI 1999/3312 ('the MPL Regulations') provides that an employee has the right not to be subjected to any detriment by any act, or any deliberate failure to act, by her employer done for a reason which relates, inter alia, 'to the fact that she is pregnant'.

It should be noted that no specific mention is made in the list set out in Reg 19 of a reason relating to time off work for the purpose of attending ante-natal appointments. On a very strict interpretation of the relevant provisions this might lead to the conclusion that a pregnant employee who is subjected to detriment by her employer for seeking to enforce her rights under Ss.55–57 ERA in respect of paid time off would not be protected by S.47C. However, we think the better view is that such a woman would be protected. This is because, arguably, the need for ante-natal care is so inextricably bound up with the fact that an employee is pregnant – which is one of the specific reasons set out in Reg 19 and therefore a reason that has been 'prescribed by regulations' for the purposes of S.47C(2) ERA – that the refusal of paid time off for ante-natal care, or any other detrimental treatment related to the fact that the employee took or requested paid time off for ante-natal care, seems sensibly to be caught by these provisions.

1.50 There does, however, appear to be a lacuna in the protection afforded to employees who take time off under S.57ZE to accompany a woman to an ante-natal appointment. S.47C(2) was amended with effect from 1 October 2014 so that a prescribed reason *can* be one which relates to 'time off under S.57ZE'. However, this amendment has only done half the job: it simply provides the statutory authority for regulations prescribing reasons for unlawful detriment that relate to time off under S.57ZE. For detriment relating to S.57ZE to be covered by S.47C, it would either need to be directly prescribed in new regulations – which have not yet been forthcoming – or it would need to be construed as falling within one of the existing prescribed reasons for detriment found in Reg 19 MPL Regulations, Reg 28 of the Paternity and Adoption Leave Regulations 2002 SI 2002/2788 or Reg 42 of the Shared Parental Leave Regulations 2014 SI 2014/3050 (for details of these prescribed reasons, see Chapter 12, 'Detriment and unfair dismissal', under 'Right not to suffer detriment'). Crucially, however, none of the reasons prescribed in these Regulations have any clear association with the right to time off to accompany a pregnant woman to ante-natal appointments. It follows that an employee exercising this right under S.57ZE, and suffering a detriment as a result, does not currently have a remedy under S.47C ERA.

The Government's apparent oversight in failing to enact any detriment protection for employees exercising the right under S.57ZA does not come as a huge surprise, given its past record with similar provisions. When the AWR introduced a new right to time off for ante-natal care for agency workers in 2010, no corresponding detriment provisions were included in S.47C or in the Regulations themselves. It was not until 2014 that the ERA was amended to provide agency workers with more explicit protection in relation to time off to attend ante-natal appointments.

This protection is now provided by S.47C(5), which was inserted into the ERA **1.51** on 1 October 2014. It provides that agency workers have a right not to suffer a detriment in relation to having exercised, or proposed to exercise, the right to take time off to attend ante-natal appointments under S.57ZA, or the right to accompany a pregnant woman to such an appointment under S.57ZG. As agency workers cannot benefit from the right not to be unfairly dismissed (unless they are also employees of the temporary work agency, which is unusual), these detriment rights provide the means of redress should the detriment take the form of the termination of the agency worker's contract with the temporary work agency or working assignment with the hirer.

Automatically unfair dismissal   1.52

As explained in Chapter 12, 'Detriment and unfair dismissal', under 'Automatically unfair dismissal', it is automatically unfair to dismiss a female employee (or select her for redundancy), for a reason connected with her pregnancy – S.99 ERA and Reg 20 MPL Regulations. A dismissal connected with the right to take time off for ante-natal care would fall within the scope of this provision. So, for example, in Bland v Laws (Confectioners) Ltd ET Case No.31081/84 B was dismissed when she refused to rearrange her working hours to enable her to attend ante-natal appointments without missing work. An employment tribunal found that B's dismissal was clearly connected with her pregnancy and was therefore automatically unfair.

In Wainwright v Haltom t/a Hair Talk ET Case No.11642/96 the relationship between the employee and the employer deteriorated once W informed her employer of her pregnancy. The employer refused to allow W time off work for ante-natal care and generally treated her very badly because of her pregnancy. Eventually W resigned and claimed automatically unfair constructive dismissal. An employment tribunal upheld her claim. In its view, the employer had never intended to be bound by one or more of the fundamental terms of the employment contract – namely, the right to time off work for ante-natal care and the right to continue working during pregnancy – and was in breach of the implied duty of mutual trust and confidence. As a result the employee was entitled to resign and claim unfair constructive dismissal for a reason connected with her pregnancy.

1.53 The fact that a woman requires time off work to attend ante-natal care appointments cannot be used as a basis for selecting her for redundancy. In Dobson v Heskin t/a CACHE ET Case No.1100004/06 the employer was initially uncooperative about allowing D to attend ante-natal classes but relented following the intervention of D's midwife. Shortly afterwards, however, D was informed that she was being made redundant. An employment tribunal concluded that the dismissal was pregnancy-related and that, although there was a genuine redundancy situation, the employer had taken the opportunity of D's pregnancy to select her for redundancy. D's dismissal was therefore both unfair and discriminatory on the ground of sex.

Section 99(3)(aa) ERA provides an enabling power allowing for regulations prescribing reasons for dismissal that relate to time off under S.57ZE as automatically unfair. However, no regulations have yet been made under this power, so dismissing an employee because he or she has exercised the right to time off work to accompany a pregnant woman to an ante-natal appointment will not infringe S.99 ERA. However, this does not present the same lacuna in protection that arises under the detriment provisions (see 'Unlawful detriment' above) because an employee dismissed in such circumstances would be able to pursue a claim under S.104 ERA – see 'Asserting a statutory right' below.

1.54 Section 99 ERA and Reg 20 MPL only apply to employees. As a result, agency workers are only covered if they are employees employed under a contract of employment, which is generally not the case. The employment status of agency workers is discussed in detail in IDS Employment Law Handbook, 'Atypical and Flexible Working' (2014), Chapter 1, 'Agency workers', under 'Employment status'.

1.55 Discrimination
The law governing discrimination because of the protected characteristics of sex and of pregnancy and maternity is considered in depth in Chapter 13, 'Discrimination and equal pay'. It is sufficient to note here that any unfavourable treatment of an employee or agency worker because of her pregnancy will amount to pregnancy and maternity discrimination under S.18 EqA. This includes a refusal to allow a woman to exercise her statutory right to paid time off for ante-natal care. Indeed, in many tribunal cases concerning a refusal of the right to time off, the claimant will include a separate claim of pregnancy discrimination. This allows her to claim for injury to feelings – a head of damages not available in a straightforward claim under S.57 or S.57ZA ERA. Three examples:

- **Sanders v Hesketh and anor t/a The Phoenix Club** ET Case No.2401441/98: S began work as a barmaid and then a cleaner in May 1997. In September she discovered she was pregnant. She took time off work to attend ante-natal appointments but H consistently refused to pay her for the time. In

March she approached H again to ask about payment for the time off. He told her that he was fed up with the situation and that she was more trouble than she was worth. He asked her how much money she was owed, gave her the money from his pocket and dismissed her. An employment tribunal held that S was dismissed because H had discovered that she was entitled to paid ante-natal care and because he believed that she would not return to work when her baby was born. This constituted an automatically unfair dismissal under S.99 ERA and also amounted to sex discrimination. Her dismissal was aggravated by the fact that she was pregnant and was already a single mother. That said, the tribunal felt that S had reacted fairly stoically and in those circumstances made an award of £375 for injury to feelings, which was 'at the very lowest end of the scale'

- **Brown v Stonehenge Linen Services Ltd** ET Case No. 3103059/07: on being informed that B was pregnant, the employer joked that he would not let her leave the workplace until the birth. There was no mention of maternity leave, no risk assessment was carried out, and B was not paid when she had to be absent to attend ante-natal appointments. An employment tribunal determined that B suffered discrimination meriting an award of £4,000: she had been treated very badly by the employer but was a naturally cheerful and resilient person who had the full and active support of her partner

- **Day v T Pickles Farms Ltd** ET Case No.2404031/97: the tribunal awarded the employee £1,000 for injury to feelings in respect of a failure to allow time off for ante-natal care. The tribunal took into account the fact that the employer's approach was unsympathetic, even though the employer knew that the employee was feeling unwell and had recently suffered a miscarriage. The tribunal found that the employee's feelings were hurt and she was distressed by the employer's insistence that she either make up her hours or lose pay for time off taken for ante-natal care. (Note that this case was subsequently appealed to the EAT on other grounds – Day v T Pickles Farms Ltd 1999 IRLR 217, EAT).

Discrimination and the right to time off to accompany. The provisions of 1.56 the EqA are unlikely to be engaged in circumstances where an employer/ temporary work agency/hirer refuses to allow time off to accompany a pregnant woman to an ante-natal appointment. Such a refusal, although unfavourable treatment, would not amount to pregnancy and maternity discrimination under S.18 EqA, because the employee or agency worker denied time off in such a scenario is not pregnant or on maternity leave.

If the person refused time off is male, and can point to women being allowed time off for ante-natal care by the same employer, then he might be able to argue that the failure to allow time off to accompany amounts to direct sex discrimination under S.13 EqA. However, such a comparison would appear to be ruled out by S.13(6)(b) EqA, which provides that, if the protected characteristic is sex, in a case where the complainant is a man, 'no account is to be taken of special treatment afforded to a woman in connection with pregnancy or childbirth'.

1.57 Asserting a statutory right

If an employee is dismissed as a result of trying to exercise either the right to take time off for ante-natal care or the right to accompany a pregnant woman to ante-natal appointments, then one avenue of complaint would be a claim under S.104 ERA. This provides that an employee's dismissal will be automatically unfair if the reason or principal reason for the dismissal was that:

• the employee brought proceedings against the employer to enforce a relevant statutory right, or

• the employee alleged that the employer had infringed a relevant statutory right.

For these purposes, a 'relevant statutory right' includes any right under the ERA for which the remedy for its infringement is by way of a complaint or reference to an employment tribunal – S.104(4)(a).

1.58 It is immaterial whether the employee actually has the statutory right in question or whether it has been infringed, but the employee's claim to the right must be made in good faith – S.104(2) ERA. Furthermore, it is sufficient that the employee made it reasonably clear to the employer what the right claimed to have been infringed was; it is not necessary actually to specify the right – S.104(3).

In Sanders v Hesketh and anor t/a The Phoenix Club ET Case No.2401441/98 (discussed under 'Discrimination' above) the employment tribunal mentioned the fact that the claimant could have argued that her dismissal was automatically unfair as it was brought about by the assertion of the statutory right to paid ante-natal care. However, the tribunal proceeded to decide the case on other grounds and we are not aware of any other decisions where the claimant has successfully claimed under S.104.

Dismissals for asserting a statutory right are dealt with in detail in IDS Employment Law Handbook, 'Unfair Dismissal' (2010), Chapter 12, 'Dismissal for asserting a statutory right'.

2 Health and safety protection

Scope of Regulations

Risk assessments

Risk avoidance measures

Suspension on maternity grounds

Night-time work

Remedies

In addition to the legislative provisions allowing pregnant mothers time off **2.1** work for ante-natal care, there exists a legislative regime providing substantial protection for pregnant women and new mothers as regards their health and safety in the workplace. The EU Pregnant Workers Directive (No.92/85) ('the Pregnant Workers Directive') makes provision for the health and safety of pregnant workers, workers who have recently given birth and workers who are breastfeeding. It requires employers to assess the health and safety risks posed to these three groups of workers by certain physical, biological and chemical agents, industrial processes and working conditions, and to avoid exposing the workers to such risks by temporarily adjusting their working conditions or hours. If this is not feasible, workers should be moved to another job or, as a last resort, granted paid leave.

The Pregnant Workers Directive is implemented into UK law by the Management of Health and Safety at Work Regulations 1999 SI 1999/3242 ('the 1999 Regulations'), the Employment Rights Act 1996 (ERA) and the Equality Act 2010.

Scope of Regulations   2.2

The 1999 Regulations are widely drawn and cover most workers, employers and self-employed persons who employ others. They do not, however, apply to the master or crew of a seagoing ship or to the employers of such persons in respect of the normal shipboard activities of a ship's crew under the direction of the master – Reg 2(1). Note, however, that provisions for offering alternative employment or suspension from work on maternity grounds in respect of women working on merchant shipping and fishing vessels are contained in a separate Order (see 'Risk avoidance measures – suitable alternative work' below). There are no other exemptions and the Regulations apply across all sectors of the working population, including temporary and casual workers and female workers in private households.

2.3 Work outside Great Britain

Subject to Reg 2, the 1999 Regulations apply in relation to specified activities and premises outside Great Britain – see Reg 23. The activities and premises covered are those to which the Health and Safety at Work etc Act 1974 applies by virtue of the Health and Safety at Work etc Act 1974 (Application outside Great Britain) Order 2001 SI 2001/2127. The position with regard to those rights contained in the ERA that are brought into play by the 1999 Regulations – for example, the right to remuneration while suspended from work on health and safety grounds (see under 'Suspension on maternity grounds' below) – is not set out in legislation. However, case law has established that those who ordinarily work abroad, but have a sufficiently close connection with Great Britain, can enjoy rights under the ERA. This is explored in IDS Employment Law Handbook, 'Employment Tribunal Practice and Procedure' (2014), Chapter 2, 'Tribunals' jurisdiction', in the section 'Territorial limitations', under 'Territorial reach – unfair dismissal and other ERA rights'.

2.4 HSE Guidance

Until recently, the 1999 Regulations were accompanied by the Health and Safety Executive (HSE)'s 'Approved Code of Practice and Guidance on the Management of Health and Safety at Work Regulations'. The provisions of this Code of Practice could be taken into account in prosecution proceedings brought in respect of any breach of the Regulations. However, the Code was withdrawn with effect from 31 July 2013 and in its place there is non-statutory guidance, set out on the HSE's website. This includes a specific section covering new and expectant mothers, but overall is considerably less extensive than the withdrawn Code.

2.5 Risk assessments

This section looks at the statutory provisions and case law concerned with the employer's obligation to carry out risk assessments associated with pregnancy and pregnant workers.

2.6 Duties of employers

Regulation 3(1) 1999 Regulations sets out the general duty of employers to safeguard the health and safety of their employees and any other persons who may be affected by the employer's work or business. It states that an employer must make a suitable and sufficient assessment of:

- the risks to the health and safety of its employees to which they are exposed while they are at work, and

- the risks to the health and safety of persons not in its employment arising out of or in connection with the conduct by it of its undertaking

2 Health and safety protection

for the purpose of identifying the measures it needs to take to comply with the requirements imposed upon it by the relevant statutory provisions.

By virtue of Reg 16(1) the employer must include in the assessment under Reg 3(1) an assessment of particular risks to new or expectant mothers and their babies where:

- the persons working in an undertaking include women of childbearing age – Reg 16(1)(a), and

- the work is of a kind which could involve risk, by reason of her condition, to the health and safety of a new or expectant mother, or to that of her baby, from any processes or working conditions, or physical, biological or chemical agents, including those specified in Annexes I and II to the EU Pregnant Workers Directive (No.92/85) (see 'Types of risk – Annexes I and II to the Pregnant Workers Directive' below) – Reg 16(1)(b).

A 'new or expectant mother' is defined as a woman who is pregnant; who has **2.7** given birth within the previous six months; or who is breastfeeding – Reg 1(2). 'Given birth' means having delivered a living child or, after 24 weeks of pregnancy, a stillborn child – Reg 1(2). Protection does not extend beyond the six months after childbirth unless an employee continues to breastfeed after that period, in which case protection will carry on until she ceases to do so.

Two types of risk assessment: 'general' and 'individual'. In Page v Gala **2.8** Leisure and ors EAT 1398/99 the EAT pointed out that there are two types of risk assessment or consideration that may be material when an undertaking employs women of childbearing age. The first is the general duty to assess risk under Reg 3(1), taken together with (what is now) Reg 16(1). The need for this general type of assessment arises not by reason of any particular pregnancy being notified to the employer, but simply because the employer employs one or more women of childbearing age in the undertaking and an employer should not wait until an employee is pregnant before making such an assessment – see Home Farm Trust Ltd v Nnachi EAT 0400/07.

The second type of assessment identified by the EAT in Page arises when an employee gives notice under Reg 18 to the employer in writing of being pregnant, of having given birth within the last six months or of breastfeeding (see 'Risk avoidance measures – when duty under Reg 16 arises' below). This second kind of assessment requires the employer to consider, *in relation to the particular individual* who has given the notice, whether, even if the relevant statutory provisions were complied with, risk of the kind described in Reg 16(1)(b) would not be avoided. If such risks cannot be avoided, the employer must then comply with the other duties under Reg 16 (see 'Risk avoidance measures' below). The guidance on risk assessments on the HSE website stresses that there is no freestanding legal requirement to carry out a specific risk assessment when a worker gives notice that she is pregnant.

IDS Handbook • Maternity and Parental Rights

25

The HSE explains that the need to undertake a specific risk assessment may arise as part of the employer's general requirement under Reg 3(1) and 16(1) to assess risks in the workplace. The accompanying HSE flowchart suggests that, if no risk to a specific pregnant worker is identified, the employer need do nothing more than continue to monitor the situation.

2.9 It is arguable that the Pregnant Workers Directive only requires an employer to carry out an assessment of risks to new and expectant mothers if there is at the time a pregnant worker, or a worker who has recently given birth or who is breastfeeding, at the particular establishment. If this is the case, then Reg 16 improves on the protection afforded by the Directive by requiring a risk assessment to be carried out wherever the employees include women of childbearing age.

The EAT considered an employer's general obligations towards women of childbearing age in Day v T Pickles Farms Ltd 1999 IRLR 217, EAT – i.e. with regard to the general – pre-emptive – type of risk-assessment identified in Page v Gala Leisure and ors (above). In that case D, an assistant in a sandwich shop where food was cooked on the premises, left work when she became pregnant. She suffered from severe morning sickness and the smell and handling of food in the shop made her feel so nauseated that her doctor certified her unfit for work. The EAT ruled that the employment tribunal had erred in holding that the requirement to carry out an assessment under Reg 16 does not arise until an employer has a pregnant employee in employment. The employer should have carried out a general assessment and a Reg 16 assessment at the start of D's employment at the very latest. The EAT stated that there is no triggering event to bring these duties into play: they simply arise out of the fact of employment and the fact that women of childbearing age are employed in the undertaking. This interpretation accords with common sense and is in line with the EAT's decision in the Page case. A woman is not normally aware that she is pregnant to begin with. If the start of the pregnancy is unknown, the only way to ensure that risks are avoided is to have anticipated the matter by carrying out a risk assessment before an employee discovers that she is pregnant.

2.10 General principles of prevention. Where an employer implements any preventive or protective measures in order to comply with the 1999 Regulations or any other relevant legislation, it must do so on the basis of the general principles of prevention set out in Schedule 1 to the Regulations – Reg 4. These principles mirror those set out in Article 6(2) of EU Directive No.89/391 on the introduction of measures to encourage improvements in the safety and health of workers at work. They include:

- avoiding risks
- evaluating risks that cannot be avoided
- combating risks at the source

- adapting the design of workplaces and the choice of equipment to suit the individual

- developing an overall prevention policy covering technology, organisation of work, working conditions, social relationships and the influence of factors relating to the working environment.

Employers must make arrangements for the effective planning, organisation, control, monitoring and review of the preventive and protective measures taken in order to comply with the 1999 Regulations. Where an employer employs five or more employees, a record must be kept of the arrangements made – Reg 5(1) and (2).

Duties in respect of temporary and agency workers 2.11
It is important to note that all of the duties under Regs 3(1) and 16 1999 Regulations outlined under 'Duties of employers' above apply in respect of both employees and workers, and that employers engaging temporary workers must undertake both general and pregnancy-specific assessments in the normal way with regard to both their employees and agency staff. Similarly, where an employment agency directly employs the workers it supplies, it will be under the same duty of risk assessment as any other employer.

In addition, by virtue of the fact that all employers are required to make 'an assessment of the risks to the health and safety of persons *not* in [their] employment arising out of or in connection with the conduct by [the employer] of [the employer's] undertaking' under Reg 3(1)(b) (our stress), the duty to make risk assessments also applies in respect of individuals whose services are provided through the agency, but who are not actually working for it. In Brocklebank v Silveira EAT 0571/05, for example, S had entered into an agreement with an employment agency to find work and had informed the agency that she was pregnant. A potential end-user of her services requested that the agency undertake a risk assessment, which it failed to do. An employment tribunal found that this failure to carry out an initial risk assessment, as it was required to do, amounted to an act of sex discrimination and the EAT dismissed the appeal (see 'Remedies – discrimination' below).

Note that employment agencies and those engaging their services are under 2.12 specific notification requirements contained in Reg 15 (see 'Information for workers' below). Furthermore, Reg 16A imposes certain additional duties on any 'hirer' who uses a temporary work agency to engage agency workers. For details of these provisions, see under 'Risk avoidance measures – agency workers' below.

Types of risk 2.13
In R v Chargot Ltd (trading as Contract Services) and ors 2009 ICR 263, HL, Lord Hope observed (with general reference to the Health and Safety at Work

etc Act 1974) that 'when the legislation refers to risks it is not contemplating risks that are trivial or fanciful… The law does not aim to create an environment that is entirely risk free. It concerns itself with risks that are material. That, in effect, is what the word "risk" which the statute uses means. It is directed at situations where there is a material risk to health and safety, which any reasonable person would appreciate and take steps to guard against.'

Self-evidently, the general type of risk assessment identified in Page v Gala Leisure and ors (see under 'Duties of employers' above) requires an employer to identify the workplace hazards and risks to new and expectant mothers in terms that are not specific to an individual worker. It does not require an employer to consider more remote risks that may be suffered by a few individuals. As noted by the EAT in Day v T Pickles Farm Ltd (above), employers conducting a general risk assessment 'cannot be expected to have in mind the most particular kind of conditions or objections or disabilities that some women might suffer from, for example, being nauseous at handling fish or hard-boiled eggs or something really very much applicable only to the particular individual'.

2.14 In Furbear v Heddmara Ltd ET Case No. 2340258/09 an employment tribunal held that the employer, H Ltd, which ran a care home for the elderly, had carried out a suitable and sufficient general assessment of the risks to new and expectant mothers, notwithstanding the fact that the assessment did not specifically assess the risks to them and their babies arising out of contact with bodily fluid. H Ltd had assessed the risk of such contact for the whole workforce. The tribunal considered that the risk of infection arising from contact with bodily fluid is not peculiar to a pregnant employee and it was reasonable for H Ltd to believe that its existing procedures (for example, the provision of gloves for all employees to minimise the risk of infection) were adequate and sufficient.

Regulation 16(1)(b) appears to leave open the possibility that a risk assessment need not be carried out for new and expectant mothers if the work is not 'of a kind which could involve risk' to them or their babies. Nevertheless, Mr Justice Lindsay in Day v T Pickles Farms (above) thought it 'debatable whether [that wording] adds anything of substance'. We suggest that it would be rare indeed for a work environment to be risk-free for new and expectant mothers. There may be occasional instances where the risks are only minor and therefore no action need be taken. However, apart from perhaps the most straightforward cases involving small employers, a risk assessment would still be needed in order to establish whether or not that was the case.

2.15 **EU Commission Guidelines on risk assessments for new or expectant mothers.** The following (non-exhaustive) lists of potential risks are taken from the 'EU Communication from the Commission' (COM/2000/0466), which provides guidance to the assessment of risk as required by the Pregnant Workers Directive.

Examples of potential hazards for new or expectant mothers include:

- long working hours or early shift work
- working at heights
- working alone
- lack of rest and other welfare facilities or inadequate hygiene facilities
- vibration or noise
- radiation
- extremes of cold or heat or poor ventilation
- manual handling of loads
- travelling
- work equipment
- exposure to substances such as lead, organic solvents and pesticides or to strong or nauseating smells; and
- prolonged standing or sitting.

Examples of potential harm to new or expectant mothers include:

- fatigue
- infection
- varicose veins
- morning sickness
- stress
- backache
- contamination of breast milk.

Annexes I and II to the Pregnant Workers Directive. As we have seen, **2.16** Reg 16(1)(b) expressly states that an employer must have regard to the risks set out in the Annexes to the Pregnant Workers Directive when carrying out a risk assessment – see 'Duties of employers' above. Annex I to the Directive sets out a non-exhaustive list of agents, processes and working conditions that are regarded as posing a risk and which therefore have to be assessed in compliance with the obligations imposed by Reg 16(1)(b). The list specifies the following:

- physical agents regarded as causing foetal lesions and/or likely to disrupt placental attachment; in particular: shocks, vibration or movement; handling of loads entailing risks; noise; ionising and non-ionising radiation; extremes

29

of cold or heat; movements and postures; travelling (either inside or outside the establishment); mental and physical fatigue

- biological agents set out in the EU Biological Agents Directive (No.2000/54) in so far as it is known that these agents, or the therapeutic measures necessitated by these agents, endanger the health of pregnant women or the unborn child

- substances and mixtures which are classified as presenting a hazard in respect of germ cell mutagenicity, carcinogenicity, reproductive toxicity or specific target organ toxicity after single exposure

- chemical agents, including agents listed in Annex I to the EU Carcinogens at Work Directive (No.2004/37), mercury and mercury derivatives, antimitotic drugs, carbon monoxide and chemical agents of known and dangerous percutaneous absorption, in so far as it is known that they endanger the health of pregnant women or the unborn child

- industrial processes listed in Annex I to the Carcinogens at Work Directive

- underground mining work.

2.17 Annex II, together with Article 6, prohibits exposure to certain agents and working conditions in the case of pregnant and breastfeeding workers. It provides that:

- pregnant workers may not be exposed to work in hyperbaric atmosphere, e.g. pressurised enclosures and underwater diving; to toxoplasma or rubella virus, unless they are proved to be adequately protected against such agents by immunisation; to lead and lead derivatives which are capable of being absorbed by the human organism; or to underground mining work; where the assessment carried out by the employer has revealed a risk of exposure to such agents or conditions and where exposure would jeopardise health or safety – Article 6(1) and Annex II, Section A

- workers who are breastfeeding may not be exposed to lead and lead derivatives that are capable of being absorbed by the human organism or to underground mining work, where the assessment carried out by the employer has revealed a risk of exposure to such agents or conditions and where exposure would jeopardise health or safety – Article 6(2) and Annex II, Section B.

Online guidance on the assessment of the chemical, physical and biological agents and industrial processes considered hazardous for the health or safety of pregnant and breastfeeding mothers at work – i.e. those specified in Annexes I and II – is given by the HSE on its website in the section on 'New and expectant mothers' under 'FAQs – risk assessments'.

Infectious and contagious diseases. Regulation 16(4) 1999 Regulations states **2.18** that, in relation to risk from any infectious or contagious disease, the references to risk in Reg 16(1) and (3) are 'references to a level of risk at work which is in addition to the level to which a new or expectant mother may be expected to be exposed outside the workplace'. This is rather cumbersome statutory drafting, but it would seem that, with regard to risk of contraction of infectious and contagious diseases, an employer's obligation to evaluate risk surrounding infectious or contagious disease as part of a general or individual risk assessment, or to suspend an employee from work on maternity grounds if an identified risk cannot be avoided, applies only if the nature of the workplace or the circumstances of the individual specifically increase the level of risk beyond that which would apply outside the workplace. In other words, risks must be assessed where, in view of the workplace or nature of the work in question, workers are exposed to particular diseases or to an increased risk of contracting common diseases that may be injurious to new or expectant mothers – e.g. rubella. An example of the latter might be schools or hospitals, where the likelihood of exposure is heightened.

Conducting a risk assessment
2.19

The 1999 Regulations do not contain a specific definition of what amounts to a 'risk assessment', but, as His Honour Judge McMullen explained in Stevenson v JM Skinner and Co EAT 0584/07, it is generally understood that 'risk' refers to the exposure of some sort of harm or danger, and an 'assessment' is an evaluation of when that risk is likely to occur and what its consequences will be for the pregnant employee (or an employee of childbearing age).

There is no requirement under the Regulations that this assessment be in writing. According to HHJ McMullen, 'it is a thought process', which is – when the assessment is in relation to a particular individual – best conducted with the pregnant employee herself so that any difficulties which she may encounter can be addressed specifically. With this in mind, he held that the tribunal had been entitled to dismiss the claimant's claims of unfair constructive dismissal and sex discrimination on the ground that the employer had failed to conduct a risk assessment after being notified of her pregnancy. The employer had met with the claimant on four separate occasions and had adapted its written general risk assessment by oral communications during the meetings to deal with the claimant's specific needs – in particular, her concerns regarding walking up and down three flights of stairs and lifting heavy boxes.

'Suitable and sufficient' risk assessment. As previously noted, by virtue of **2.20** Regs 3(1) and 16 1999 Regulations, employers must carry out 'a suitable and sufficient' risk assessment in respect of pregnant and breastfeeding employees. However, the Regulations do not define what constitutes a suitable and sufficient risk assessment for these purposes.

2.21 In practice, employment tribunals – which most often deal with the question of risk assessments in the context of pregnancy discrimination claims (see 'Remedies – discrimination' below) – have had to apply common sense when interpreting the relevant statutory provisions. Not surprisingly, most cases have concerned individual risk assessments in relation to particular pregnant employees. Some examples:

- **Mather v Secretary of State for Justice** ET Case No. 3500223/09: during her pregnancy, M suffered from hyperemesis gravidarum, a condition which causes excessive nausea and vomiting. Her employer carried out a risk assessment, but did not seek out a report from a suitably qualified occupational health expert. Had this been done, it is likely that the expert would have recommended that M not work at all. An employment tribunal held that the employer had failed to carry out a suitable and sufficient risk assessment: M's condition necessitated the obtaining of expert advice, but the employer had shied away from doing this for financial reasons

- **Bruce and anor v Saffronland Homes** ET Case Nos.3101493–4/98: the employer, which ran nursing and residential care facilities, carried out a risk assessment when two of the support workers gave notice of their pregnancies. The employer concluded that the Special Needs Unit, which housed clients classified as having challenging behaviour that was unpredictable and occasionally violent, was not a safe place for the pregnant employees to work, as such violence could have serious consequences for an unborn child. However, in the employer's opinion, the regular care unit for physically disabled persons was a suitable and safe working environment for a pregnant woman. Although the physical needs of the clients meant that a large proportion of the work undertaken by support workers involved physical activity, the employer was satisfied that the premises were adequately equipped with lifting hoists and that, in accordance with the standing instructions to all support staff, whenever a client needed lifting, a hoist would be used. The employer also felt that there was adequate staffing to ensure that the pregnant employees would not have to undertake too much physical work. The employment tribunal found this analysis to constitute a careful and fair risk assessment in compliance with the relevant regulations

- **Bates v Booker Cash and Carry Ltd** ET Case No.2601799/04: the employer carried out a risk assessment on being notified that B was pregnant. As a result of the assessment, B's manual handling duties were replaced by a lighter regime that involved checking goods leaving the employer's store. After two days, B claimed that the lighter duties were causing pain in her legs and back, and requested that a chair be provided. The employer, unconvinced that the checking could be done from a seated position, refused the request, but stated that it would be reconsidered if and when medical evidence was provided that a chair was necessary. B was then off sick for four days, after which she self-certified her absence as being due to pregnancy-related pains in her back and legs. An employment tribunal found that the initial assessment was suitable and sufficient, and that the self-certificate was insufficient to trigger the need for a new risk assessment

- **Taylor v Thomas Bee Ltd** ET Case No.63877/95: T was a car valet who worked with various cleaning agents in a garage where there were carbon monoxide emissions from vehicles being serviced. At her request, she was transferred to office work after she notified TB Ltd of her pregnancy. TB Ltd wanted T to return to her original duties, however, and decided to carry out a risk assessment. One of the company's directors tested carbon monoxide levels and consulted with his wife, an obstetrician, as to whether there were any risks in the workplace. She concluded that there were none. The tribunal found serious shortcomings in the way TB Ltd carried out the risk assessment. The assessment was limited and done in an informal way. The results were not put in writing, which would have allowed T to get a second opinion. In fact, T was never informed in detail of the assessment, other than to be told that valeting work involved no risk

- **Cox v Bernard Matthews Ltd** ET Case No.1500554/05: C was employed on the production line in a turkey factory. When she became pregnant, she was sent to see BM Ltd's nurse, who assessed standing all day as low risk; and slippery floors, foot dips, palletising and lifting as high risk. The nurse did not, however, inspect C's job area or witness her performing any tasks, and nor was a further risk assessment undertaken when C suffered a suspected miscarriage. An employment tribunal held that this was insufficient to meet BM Ltd's obligations under Reg 16.

As previously noted, His Honour Judge McMullen in Stevenson v JM Skinner **2.22** and Co (above) considered that individual risk assessments are best conducted with the employee herself so that any particular difficulties that she may encounter can be addressed specifically. Lack of proper consultation with the employee can be costly, as the following cases demonstrate:

- **Barlow v John Michael Hair Design Group Ltd** ET Case No.3203366/07: B, a senior hair stylist, informed her employer that she was pregnant. An employment tribunal found that the employer's risk assessment for B had been carried out in a 'somewhat casual or slapdash manner', largely without consulting B. The assessment was not a 'serious or genuine evaluation' of the risks or harm that might occur or to which B might be exposed. The tribunal concluded that this failure to conduct a 'suitable and sufficient' risk assessment amounted to sex discrimination

- **Gandam v Coseley Systems Ltd (t/a Meadow Lodge Care Home)** ET Case No.1303446/08: G was employed by CS Ltd as deputy manager of a care home for the elderly. Upon discovering she was pregnant, her GP advised her to avoid any heavy lifting and provided her with a letter to hand to her employer confirming the position. There was no generic risk assessment in place for new or expectant mothers. After being informed of G's pregnancy, CS Ltd completed a risk assessment, but, in the employment tribunal's view, it was neither suitable nor sufficient: there were no meetings or discussions with G regarding the risks and the results of the risk assessment were not communicated to the remaining staff. In the light of G's duties, which included lifting clients, this failure to carry out an adequate assessment amounted to an act of sex discrimination on the ground of G's pregnancy

- **Plottke v Swallowfield plc** ET Case No.1701402/08: P, a Polish immigrant with (in the employment tribunal's words) 'virtually no command of English', was employed by S plc to work in its packages factory filling aerosols and making toiletries. She gave her employer written notification of her pregnancy, in the form of a medical certificate for a pregnancy-related illness. S plc had no generic risk assessment for pregnant women, but carried out ad hoc assessments as and when required. P's risk assessment took the form of a 15-minute meeting between her and a manager, M. M identified in his own mind certain risks, such as heavy lifting, which he claimed to have discussed with P. However, in the tribunal's view, this assessment was a 'total failure'. It would have taken a great deal longer than 15 minutes to have had a full meaningful session with P, given her poor grasp of English. Indeed, it was doubtful whether any meeting with her without an interpreter present could have resulted in successful communication. P's sex discrimination claim was upheld.

2.23 However, as the EAT pointed out in O'Neill v Buckinghamshire County Council 2010 IRLR 384, EAT, there is nothing in the Pregnant Workers Directive or the 1999 Regulations that legally requires the employer to meet with the employee when carrying out a risk assessment so the necessity of holding such a meeting will depend very much on the circumstances of the case. In that case, the EAT agreed with the tribunal that a risk assessment had been carried out notwithstanding that a meeting had not taken place.

2.24 **Delay.** Undue delay in carrying out a risk assessment will mean that an employer is in breach of its obligations under Regs 3(1)(a) and 16. In Home Farm Trust Ltd v Nnachi EAT 0400/07 N worked in a role which exposed her to aggression, lifting, carrying and stressful situations. She informed her employer that she was pregnant on 9 May 2005, but due to staff absences a risk assessment was not undertaken until 22 May. The employment tribunal, with which the EAT agreed, held that this delay meant that there was a failure to carry out a risk assessment under Reg 16(1), even though it held that the assessment eventually carried out on 22 May was suitable and sufficient.

However, in Marshall and anor v Woolstone Community Centre ET Case No.1201459/08 an employment tribunal made the point that the 1999

Regulations cannot require a risk assessment to be carried out instantaneously and it must be the case that the employer has reasonable time to deal with the matter. In that case, M informed her employer that she was pregnant on 9 September 2008. On 25 September WCC held a meeting to discuss, among other things, M's pregnancy. WCC then wrote to M in order to arrange a meeting with her. At about the same time, M delivered a letter of resignation containing a number of complaints, including that WCC had not yet carried out a risk assessment. The tribunal concluded that the employer had acted within a reasonable period of time and that, accordingly, it could not be said to be in breach of the Regulations. In reaching this decision, the tribunal considered that it was important to note that M was not alleging that she was carrying out any activities between 9 and 25 September that were inherently unsafe for her and her unborn child. Since the employer was not in breach of the Regulations, it followed that M's claim for sex discrimination based upon a failure to carry out a risk assessment could not succeed.

2.25 The Nnachi and Marshall cases involved very similar periods of delay. The distinguishing factor appears to be that in the former case the tribunal found the work involved an inherent risk to the employee and her baby during the relevant period, whereas in the latter case there was found to be no such risk.

2.26 **Recording and notifying the findings.** Following a general or specific risk assessment, Reg 3(6) requires the employer to keep a record of its findings where it employs five or more employees. Employees should also be provided with 'comprehensible and relevant' information on the risks to their health and safety identified by the assessment, and with details of the preventive and protective measures which the employer needs to take to comply with the relevant statutory provisions – Reg 10(1)(a) and (b). However, the Regulations do not require the employer to hand over the results of the assessment to employees in writing. Although, according to HHJ McMullen in Stevenson v JM Skinner and Co (above), this may seem 'odd', the correct interpretation of the Regulations is that the information under Reg 10(1) can be given orally. So, in that case, the employer had complied with the Regulations when it recorded the significant findings of the risk assessment in relation to the pregnant employee and, as mentioned above, it discussed with her at the meetings the risks she was exposed to and the steps it was taking to avoid them.

In Arnold v Clippers Hull Ltd ET Case No.1802222/00 the employer carried out an appropriate risk assessment on being informed of A's pregnancy. As a result, the employer ascertained that A should have extra breaks, refrain from lifting, and spend more of her work time in a less physically demanding position at reception. However, the employer failed to inform the employee that the risk assessment had been undertaken or of its results. The employment tribunal found that this failure amounted to a breach of Reg 10.

35

2.27 **Temporary and agency workers.** There are specific duties of notification in respect of temporary and agency workers. Reg 15(1) 1999 Regulations states that an employer must provide a temporary worker employed under a fixed-term contract with comprehensible information on:

- any special occupational qualifications or skill required to be held by that worker if she is to carry out her work safely, and

- health surveillance required to be provided to that worker by or under any of the relevant statutory provisions

before the worker commences her duties.

Similar information must be provided by employers to workers employed by an employment agency who are to carry out work in their undertaking – Reg 15(2). Employers must also ensure that the employment agency supplying the workers is provided with comprehensible information on:

- any special occupational qualifications or skills required to be held by those workers if they are to carry out their work safely, and

- the specific features of the jobs to be filled by those workers (in so far as those features are likely to affect their health and safety) – Reg 15(3).

It is the duty of the employment agency to ensure that the information provided is then given to the employees in question.

2.28 **Reviewing the risk assessment**

Regulation 3(3) 1999 Regulations provides that a risk assessment must be reviewed by the employer if:

- there is reason to suspect that it is no longer valid, or

- there has been a significant change in the matters to which it relates. The provision goes on to stipulate that where, as a result of any such review, changes to an assessment are required, the employer must make them.

As noted by an employment tribunal in Fernandez v Secretary of State for Justice ET Case No.2328732/08, 'the nature of the whole risk assessment process is necessarily an ongoing exercise and it is unwise for employers and employees simply to treat the formula "risk assessment" as being a one-off exercise which has either been "completed" or "not completed"'.

2.29 In its online guidance for new and expectant mothers, the HSE recommends that the risk assessment in relation to the individual pregnant employee should be regularly monitored and reviewed, as different stages in the pregnancy may pose different risks – see the HSE's website in the section on 'New and expectant mothers' under 'FAQs – risk assessments'. It is worth emphasising, however, that the employer only has a duty to avoid any health and safety risk caused by the working environment or the job requirements. Where the pregnancy itself causes the risk – for instance, morning sickness affecting a pregnant worker's ability to drive – the employer is not legally required to act. However, it is advisable for both parties to find a solution that would enable her to continue working wherever possible.

Failure to carry out a risk assessment
2.30

Failing to carry out a risk assessment in respect of pregnant workers can have a number of legal repercussions. The 1999 Regulations themselves provide for two means of enforcement: civil and criminal. If an employer fails to carry out a risk assessment under Reg 16, and this results in damage to a new or expectant mother, it will entitle her to claim damages for breach of statutory duty – Reg 22 (see 'Remedies – breach of statutory duty' below). However, Reg 22 is limited to cases where the claimant has suffered damage, which means that a mere technical failure to undertake a risk assessment cannot be litigated as a breach of statutory duty (it may, however, be actionable as a discrimination claim – see further below).

In terms of criminal liability, S.33(1)(c) of the Health and Safety at Work etc Act 1974 states that: 'It is an offence... to contravene any health and safety regulations or any requirement or prohibition imposed under any such regulations.' In this context the employer has to take complete and sole responsibility for ensuring compliance with the 1999 Regulations, since Reg 21 stipulates that: 'Nothing in the relevant statutory provisions shall operate so as to afford an employer a defence in any criminal proceedings for a contravention of those provisions by reason of any act or default of (a) an employee of his, or (b) a person appointed by him.'

It is also well established by case law that a failure to carry out a risk assessment **2.31** in accordance with the Regulations can amount to sex or pregnancy discrimination – see, for example, Hardman v Mallon t/a Orchard Lodge Nursing Home 2002 IRLR 516, EAT (discussed in detail under 'Remedies – discrimination' below). Furthermore, a dismissal in these circumstances will almost certainly be automatically unfair under S.99 ERA, read with Reg 20 of the Maternity and Parental Leave etc Regulations 1999 SI 1999/3312, provided that the reason or principal reason for the dismissal is related to pregnancy – see 'Remedies – automatically unfair dismissal' below.

It should be noted that an employer cannot excuse its failure to carry out a risk assessment by claiming that the employee is fully aware of all relevant risks and is coping with them. This is demonstrated by Thomas v English Churches Housing Group ET Case No.1900317/09, where the employer had had general discussions with the claimant from time to time about her well-being upon being notified that she was pregnant but no formal risk assessment was ever carried out. The atmosphere within the office was relaxed and, although there

37

were no prescribed breaks (apart from 30 minutes for lunch), there were no prohibitions whatsoever about employees taking breaks as and when they wished, within reason. Although the claimant took advantage of this flexibility – she would take breaks as she wished and would regularly take longer than the allocated time – an employment tribunal upheld her claim that the employer had failed to carry out a risk assessment and that this amounted to sex discrimination. Within the relaxed atmosphere no specific attention was ever paid to the provision of rest breaks for a pregnant woman. There was no system in place to ensure that breaks were taken regularly or that appropriate rest facilities were provided. By leaving it entirely to the discretion of the individual employee, it left open the possibility that appropriate breaks would not always be taken. The tribunal awarded what it considered to be the 'conventional minimum sum' of £750 for injury to feelings.

2.32 Risk avoidance measures

Once a 'suitable and sufficient' risk assessment has been carried out, the employer must – in accordance with its statutory health and safety obligations – take measures to reduce or remove any risks identified. The fact that, at least so far as the employer is aware, there are no pregnant employees or workers in the workplace does not mean that no action need be taken. In particular, if significant risks have been highlighted by the risk assessment, the employer should take action to reduce or eliminate those risks, so far as they can be eliminated generally in the workplace.

When an employer learns that an individual worker is pregnant or is breastfeeding or has given birth within the previous six months, it should put in place any measures originally identified in the course of a general assessment that have been 'on standby'. Such measures are not dependent on the employer receiving written notification, given that they stem from the general risk assessment. In addition, the employer should check that no significant changes in the risk level to new and expectant mothers have occurred since the last assessment was carried out, requiring it to review the general risk assessment and make any necessary changes – Reg 3(3) 1999 Regulations.

2.33 With regard to individual risk assessments carried out in response to written notification from a particular worker, if the results of this reveal a risk to the health or safety of the new or expectant mother, or to that of her baby, the employer must follow a series of steps to ensure that she is not exposed to the risk or damaged by it. The first step is to take any reasonable measures to avoid the risk. In so doing, the employer must ensure that it complies with any relevant health and safety legislation in respect of the substances or agents in question.

Where the risk to any individual would not be avoided by the employer taking any reasonable action that is required under the relevant statutory provisions, the employer must alter the employee's working conditions or hours of work if it is reasonable to do so and if such measures would 'avoid the risk' – Reg 16(2) (see 'Altering working conditions or hours of work' below). If it is not reasonable to alter the employee's working conditions or hours of work, or if doing so would not avoid the relevant risk, the employer must suspend the employee from work for as long as it is necessary to avoid the risk – Reg 16(3) (see 'Suspension on maternity grounds' below). This is subject, however, to S.67 ERA, which provides that, where there is suitable alternative work available, the employee has a right to be offered that work before being suspended on maternity grounds (see 'Suitable alternative work' below).

In New Southern Railway Ltd v Quinn 2006 ICR 761, EAT, the Appeal **2.34** Tribunal confirmed that the word 'avoid' in Reg 16 does not place an unqualified obligation on the employer to eliminate the risk entirely, but rather to reduce it to its lowest acceptable level. Since the implementation of Reg 16(2) involves a restriction on the right of a woman to carry out her ordinary job, a balancing exercise is required. The employer must show that it is necessary for health and safety reasons in effect to discriminate. The principle of proportionality requires that the greater the discriminatory act, the greater the necessity must be.

Agency workers   2.35
Similar responsibilities to take risk avoidance measures as apply to employers under Reg 16 (see 'Risk avoidance measures' above) also apply to hirers who engage agency workers via a temporary work agency. These are set out in Reg 16A 1999 Regulations, which was inserted by the Agency Workers Regulations 2010 SI 2010/93 (AWR). For these purposes, an 'agency worker' is a person who is 'supplied by a temporary work agency to work temporarily for and under the supervision and direction of a hirer' in circumstances where the person has a contract of employment or some other contract with the temporary work agency to perform services personally – Reg 3(1) AWR. A 'hirer' means 'a person… to whom individuals are supplied to work temporarily for and under the supervision and direction of that person' – Reg 2 AWR.

Regulation 16A(1) 1999 Regulations provides that where the requisite actions by the hirer would not avoid the risk to the agency worker, then the hirer is under a duty to alter the agency worker's working conditions or hours if it would be reasonable to do so. However, if this is not reasonable, the hirer must inform the temporary work agency of that fact and the agency must then end the supply of the agency worker to the hirer – Reg 16A(2). In this scenario the temporary work agency comes under a duty to offer suitable alternative work with another hirer, if available – S.68B ERA. This duty – which is analogous to that which applies to an employer who is forced to suspend an employee on maternity grounds – is discussed in more detail under 'Suitable alternative work' below. If no alternative work is available, the agency worker has a limited right to be paid remuneration during the remaining period of the engagement that has been brought to an end by virtue of the operation of Reg 16A(2) – see 'Suspension on maternity grounds – ending supply of agency worker on maternity grounds' below for further details.

2.36 Where any risk to an agency worker who is a new or expectant mother relates to infectious or contagious disease, Reg 16A(3) suggests that a hirer does not have to take specific avoidance measures provided that the level of risk within the workplace is no greater than that which the worker may encounter outside it. This provision, which is not particularly well drafted, is identical to that which is applicable to employers by virtue of Reg 16(4) – see the section 'Risk assessments' above, under 'Types of risk – infectious and contagious diseases'.

Note that the provisions of Reg 16A only apply where the agency worker has completed the necessary 12-week qualifying period required by the AWR – Reg 18AB 1999 Regulations (see IDS Employment Law Handbook, 'Atypical and Flexible Working' (2014), Chapter 1, 'Agency workers', under 'Rights under the Agency Workers Regulations – equal treatment: the qualifying period'.

2.37 ## Notification requirements

As previously stated, no specific notification of pregnancy – written or otherwise – is required to trigger an employer's duty to conduct a general risk assessment under Reg 16(1) 1999 Regulations for the purposes of identifying general risks with regard to new and expectant mothers. Such a duty arises simply on account of an employer employing women of childbearing age.

However, the position is different in respect of risk assessments for particular individuals who are pregnant. In that case an employer is not obliged to take any action under Reg 16(2) or (3) until the employee has notified it in writing that she is pregnant, has given birth within the previous six months, or is breastfeeding – Reg 18(1). Furthermore, the employer is not required to maintain action taken in relation to an employee in any of the following circumstances:

- the employee has notified the employer that she is pregnant but has failed, within a reasonable time of being asked to do so in writing by the employer, to produce a certificate from a registered medical practitioner or registered midwife stating that she is pregnant – Reg 18(2)(a)

- the employer knows that she is no longer a new or expectant mother – Reg 18(2)(b), or

- the employer cannot establish whether she remains a new or expectant mother – Reg 18(2)(c).

2.38 Although Reg 18 states that an employer is not required to take any action in relation to a pregnant worker until she has notified him in writing that she is pregnant, the EAT has taken a purposive approach to the construction of this requirement. In Day v T Pickles Farms Ltd 1999 IRLR 217, EAT, D told her employer that she was pregnant and provided medical certificates from her doctor saying that she suffered from morning sickness. Some of the certificates stated that she was suffering from 'hyperemesis gravidarum', which is severe vomiting associated with pregnancy. Her employer also knew that she was going to an ante-natal clinic. Nonetheless, an employment tribunal held that the employer had been under no obligation under Reg 16(2) or (3) as D had failed to give written notice that she was pregnant in accordance with Reg 18. The EAT disagreed. It said that common sense suggested that D was either pregnant or suffering from a condition that was more probably than not an indication of pregnancy. If the tribunal had asked itself whether the medical certificates amounted to notice in writing that D was pregnant, it was hard to see how it could have concluded otherwise than that they did.

The EAT pointed out that there were a number of cases in which tribunals have been told not to take a technical view of the burden of proof and in which that burden switches from one side to the other. The tribunal had approached the case by asking whether D had discharged the burden of proving that she had notified the employer in writing of the fact that she had become pregnant. If, technically, that were the right approach, then in all the circumstances of the case the burden of proof would have shifted to the employer. The employer was in receipt of the medical certificates; it was for the employer to show that the certificates did not in the circumstances amount to an indication of pregnancy. If, therefore, it had simply been a matter of burden of proof, it was hard for the EAT to see how the tribunal could have concluded that written notification of pregnancy had not been given. The case was remitted to the same tribunal to reconsider.

An employee who has not provided any form of written notice at all cannot **2.39** complain about the lack of an individual risk assessment. In Kilmarnock Football Club Ltd v Ross EATS 0031/13 the employer had carried out a general risk assessment, with the results displayed on a notice board. In January 2012, R discovered she was pregnant, and shared this information verbally with a number of colleagues, including her supervisor. However, she did not give the employer written notice of her pregnancy. She subsequently complained to an employment tribunal that she had suffered pregnancy discrimination by, among other things, her employer's failure to carry out a risk assessment. Her claim was successful before the tribunal, but on appeal the EAT held that the employer had satisfied the requirements of the 1999 Regulations with its general risk assessment. R had not given the notice required by Reg 18(1), so the employer was not obliged to carry out a specific risk assessment.

Agency workers. The Agency Workers Regulations 2010 SI 2010/93 (AWR), **2.40** which came into force on 1 October 2011, added Reg 18A into the 1999 Regulations, requiring similar notification provisions by agency workers in relation to the hirer. Furthermore, Reg 18A(2) provides that the agency will not be required to end the supply of the agency worker under Reg 16A(2) (where it is not reasonable for the hirer to alter working conditions, or such alterations would not avoid the risk) unless the agency worker notifies the agency in writing that she is pregnant, has given birth within the last six months, or is breastfeeding. As previously noted, these provisions only apply to agency workers who have met the requisite 12-week qualifying period under the AWR – Reg 18AB 1999 Regulations.

2.41 Altering working conditions or hours of work

An employer's duty to take action under Reg 16(2) 1999 Regulations following an individual risk assessment can extend to changing the pregnant or breastfeeding employee's working conditions or hours of work. In this context, 'working conditions' extend beyond the physical conditions in which the employee works and can encompass targets and goals set by the employer. In Evans v Lloyds TSB Asset Finance Division Ltd ET Case No.1602666/06, for example, E was employed on a probationary basis in a call centre where employees were given monthly sales targets. She became pregnant during her probationary period and had a number of pregnancy-related absences. This led to her missing her targets for two consecutive months. Her employer extended the probationary period by a further month, during which she had fewer absences and only narrowly missed her targets. Following this, E was dismissed. She brought a claim of sex discrimination, arguing that her targets should have been revised in light of her pregnancy and the associated absences. Upholding her claim, the tribunal held that the employer had failed to undertake a risk assessment. If an assessment had been undertaken, the tribunal concluded, the likely result would have been a reduction in E's targets.

The fact that an employer has carried out a risk assessment, and identified changes that could be made to the employee's working conditions, is unlikely to be sufficient to defeat a claim of pregnancy discrimination if the employer fails to ensure that those changes are effectively implemented. In Plottke v Swallowfield plc ET Case No.1701402/08 the claimant, P, was a Polish national employed by S plc to work in its packages factory filling aerosols and making toiletries. When P notified the employer of her pregnancy, an individual risk assessment was carried out and certain particular risks were identified. P had a very poor grasp of English and therefore understood little of what was communicated to her regarding the risk assessment. Although the health and safety officer who conducted the assessment drew up a series of risk-avoidance steps, certain of P's managers failed to put these fully into effect. An employment tribunal upheld P's claims of sex and pregnancy discrimination on the basis that her working conditions had not been adjusted in compliance with Reg 16(2). In doing so, it rejected the employer's contention that where a risk assessment is carried out, there can be no discrimination. The tribunal reasoned that, if that were the case, an employer who had carried out a risk assessment which found that a pregnant woman should not do heavy lifting would not be answerable if supervisors expressly instructed the pregnant woman to do lifting. The tribunal went on to conclude that, even if it were assumed that P fully understood the employer's instructions regarding risk-avoidance measures but nonetheless continued to work normally, the employer had a responsibility for supervision. The information given to the supervisors did not appear to have contained a full instruction that they were simply not to permit P to do work other than that which the health and safety officer had considered appropriate.

The fact that an employer may have legitimate business concerns about altering **2.42** an employee's working conditions is no excuse for a failure to do so. In Olubanjoko v Yamaha Music (UK) Ltd and anor ET Case No.3300231/10, for example, the employer decided to terminate its working from home policy in April 2009 because of concerns that it was being abused by certain employees, including O. At around the same time O became pregnant. A risk assessment was carried out, as a result of which certain ergonomic alterations were made to the office environment to deal with risks to O. She subsequently sought permission to work from home, supporting her application with a GP's letter stating that she was suffering bouts of morning sickness and pregnancy-related fatigue, and that her five-hour daily commute was an aggravating factor. From early May O was allowed to work from home for two days a week, but that arrangement was terminated in July when she acknowledged that her morning sickness had settled down. O raised a grievance and requested that the working-from-home arrangement be reinstated for the remainder of her pregnancy. The employer refused, noting that all reasonable adjustments had been made to O's work environment following ergonomic and occupational health advice. Furthermore, the employer mentioned its concerns about O's lack of productivity and quality of work while working at home. In September 2009, O's hospital consultant wrote to YM Ltd to 'strongly recommend' that she be allowed to work from home, as she was 'under constant surveillance by the hospital' due to 'several medical difficulties' associated with her pregnancy. Thereafter, O simply started working at home without authorisation and, as a result, was dismissed.

An employment tribunal found that the termination of the home working arrangement in July was not pregnancy-related as it was instigated because of concerns over O's performance and suspicion that she was carrying on her own business activities on the employer's time. The company's genuine belief that morning sickness was no longer a factor (and that all workplace issues had been satisfactorily resolved) provided the opportunity to take this action on those other grounds. However, the position materially changed following the consultant's letter in September. The tribunal considered that the employer's concerns about O's performance, productivity, and suspected other activities when working from home, although legitimate, were no longer sufficient to maintain its stance following receipt of this letter. Although the employer did partially relax its position – when it indicated that once consent to access to medical records was provided, the two-day working-from-home arrangement could resume, pending receipt of a medical report – the tribunal considered that the contents of the consultant's letter made it incumbent upon the employer to do more. In its view, the minimum proportionate response at this point would have been to revert to the two-day working-from-home arrangement, without making this conditional on consent. Accordingly, the tribunal upheld O's claim for sex and pregnancy discrimination, and also found that her dismissal was automatically unfair contrary to Reg 20 of the Maternity and Parental Leave etc Regulations 1999 SI 1999/3312.

2.43 **Rest breaks, rest areas and breastfeeding.** The health and safety of pregnant workers may be put at particular risk where they are required to work for long periods without a break, particularly where the employee's job involves standing. A key measure of risk avoidance, therefore, is the provision of additional rest breaks. In Cox v Bernard Matthews Ltd ET Case No.1500554/05 C was told that she could have two additional rest breaks of 20 minutes each day since her factory job involved long periods of standing. However, her manager's attitude was that these breaks could only be taken if C felt tired; that she would have to ask to take a break rather than be allowed to take one as of right; and that they would have to be taken at a time that was convenient for the production line. Moreover, C was still expected to perform tasks while she was on a break. An employment tribunal found that these were gross and blatant breaches of the spirit of an individual risk assessment.

An employer's obligations in respect of rest areas are set out in Reg 25(4) of the Workplace (Health, Safety and Welfare) Regulations 1992 SI 1992/3004. Employers are required to provide suitable and sufficient rest facilities for all employees and workers at readily accessible places – Reg 25(1). In addition, Reg 25(4) provides that 'suitable facilities shall be provided for any person at work who is a pregnant woman or nursing mother to rest'. The 1992 Regulations do not specify what amounts to 'suitable and sufficient' rest areas, but guidance on the HSE website states that the facilities should be suitably located near to toilets. This implies that the toilets themselves would not be adequate rest areas. The HSE guidance also states that, where necessary, the rest area should provide appropriate facilities for the new or expectant mother to lie down.

2.44 At present, there is no statutory right to time off work – or for specific rest periods – for breastfeeding. Nor is there any legislation requiring the provision of facilities specifically for breastfeeding. However, the HSE recommends that employers should provide a private, healthy and safe environment for nursing mothers to express and store milk, which should not be the toilets. Where the employee has given written notice to the employer that she is breastfeeding, the employer should carry out a risk assessment and take action to avoid any identified risks, which may include altering her working hours or working conditions (or suspending her from work – see 'Suspension on maternity grounds' below). Less favourable treatment because of breastfeeding may also amount to direct sex discrimination, although the specific provisions in Ss.13(6) and 17 of the Equality Act 2010 (EqA) that refer to breastfeeding do not apply in an employment or work context – see Ss.13(7) and 17. Employers may also be liable for indirect discrimination if they refuse to make adjustments to working time or conditions for breastfeeding mothers and cannot show that the refusal was justifiable as a proportionate means of achieving a legitimate aim – see Chapter 13, 'Discrimination and equal pay', under 'Direct discrimination – breastfeeding'.

Imposing changes unilaterally. Although it is clear that Reg 16(2) 1999 **2.45** Regulations requires an employer to make reasonable changes to hours of work as a means of avoiding identified risks to a worker who is pregnant, breastfeeding or who has recently given birth, it is important that such changes are made consensually – if not, the employer risks liability for pregnancy-related discrimination and unfair constructive dismissal. This is particularly so if the unilaterally imposed measures take the form of altering working hours that have a consequential knock-on effect on the employee's pay packet. Two examples:

- **Ahir v The Good Food Company of Harefield Ltd** ET Case No.3300822/10: A, a kitchen assistant, told her employer that she was pregnant and asked that she be allowed to opt out of working more than 48 hours a week because she was finding it difficult to work ten or more hours a day. P, the consulting managing director, agreed to her request and – due to a belief that all pregnant women suffer from morning sickness – stipulated that she should only work between the hours of 10 am and 7 pm. A was not happy with these hours as she preferred an earlier start because she suffered from pregnancy-related sickness in the evenings. Furthermore, starting at 10 am would mean that she would not be able to work 40 hours per week, as some days production finished early. An employment tribunal recognised that P's motives were benign, but the consequence was that A could earn less money. The tribunal failed to see why P imposed a 10 am start when A was suffering from sickness in the evenings, not the mornings. The tribunal considered this to be less favourable treatment on the ground of A's pregnancy and awarded her £2,000 for injury to feelings

- **Woods v Foster and anor** ET Case No.3101075/10: W was employed as a waitress from November 2008. She took the job on condition that her hours of work would be between 10 am and 6 pm so that her parents could drive her to and from work, as her inability to drive and inadequate public transport meant that she would not otherwise be able to take the job. W suffered a miscarriage in May 2009 and was subsequently signed off work with depression. In July she discovered that she was pregnant again and verbally informed her employer in August. She then gave written notification in December. In January 2010 the owner of the business, F, prepared a risk assessment in W's absence that suggested that W should not lift baggage and on her return to work in February 2010, W's hours were reduced due to the employer's 'duties under health and safety legislation'. Because the new hours would make it almost impossible for W to work, due to her transport difficulties, she resigned and claimed that the employer was in breach of contract. An employment tribunal upheld W's claims for sex discrimination and unfair constructive dismissal: the employer had put forward a proposal that made W's work impossible for her to perform and which would result in a material reduction of her income at a time when her doctor had certified her fit for full contractual duties. F had taken it upon herself to base a risk assessment not on conversations with W, but on her own experience of pregnancy.

2.46 Faced with a worker who refuses to consent to measures that in the employer's view – based on sound health and safety advice – are absolutely essential to avoid specific risks, the only legitimate options would be to offer the worker suitable alternative work if available – see 'Suitable alternative work' below – or, if such alternative work is not available, to suspend the worker on maternity grounds – see 'Suspension on maternity grounds' below.

2.47 Suitable alternative work

As noted previously – see 'Risk avoidance measures' above – an employer will be obliged to suspend a pregnant employee on maternity grounds in accordance with Reg 16(3) of the 1999 Regulations if it is impossible to alter her working conditions or hours in order to avoid identified risks *unless* there is suitable alternative employment available for the employee. If suitable alternative work is available, the employee has a right to be offered that work before being suspended – S.67(1) ERA. (Similar but not identical provisions apply to temporary work agencies vis-à-vis non-avoidable risks to agency workers – Reg 16A(2) and S.68B ERA – see 'Risk avoidance measures – agency workers' above.)

The definition of 'suitable alternative work' is substantially the same as that which applies where an employee is made redundant during her maternity leave – see Chapter 4, 'Returning to work after maternity leave', under 'Redundancy during maternity leave'. Briefly, an offer of alternative work will be suitable for the purposes of the health and safety provisions if:

- it is of a kind which is both suitable in relation to the employee and appropriate for her to do in the circumstances – S.67(2)(a), and

- the terms and conditions applicable, if they differ from the corresponding terms and conditions applicable to the employee for performing the work that she normally performs under her contract of employment, are not substantially less favourable than those corresponding terms and conditions – S.67(2)(b).

If an employee unreasonably refuses an offer of alternative work, she will lose her right to be paid remuneration during the period of suspension from her normal duties – S.68(2)(b) (see 'Suspension from work – right to be paid' below).

Agency workers. Analogous provisions apply in the case of agency workers. **2.48** As previously noted, if a hirer cannot reasonably alter an agency worker's working conditions or hours to avoid identified risks, it has no option but to inform the temporary work agency. The agency is then obliged to end the supply of the worker to the hirer on maternity grounds – see 'Risk avoidance measures – agency workers' above. In these circumstances, the agency comes under a duty to offer to propose the worker to another hirer if suitable alternative work is available – S.68B(1) ERA. For this purpose, 'suitable alternative work' is defined as:

- work of a kind that is both suitable in relation to the agency worker and appropriate for her to do in the circumstances, and

- in respect of which the terms and conditions applicable, if they differ from the corresponding terms and conditions that would have applied had the supply of the agency worker to the original hirer not been ended on maternity grounds, are not substantially less favourable – S.68B(2).

The duty to offer alternative work does not apply if the agency worker has confirmed in writing that she no longer requires the work-finding services of the temporary work agency – S.68B(3)(a). Nor does it apply beyond the original intended duration, or likely duration (if longer), of the assignment that was terminated when the supply of the agency worker to the hirer was ended on maternity grounds – S.68B(3)(b).

If the agency worker has been offered alternative work by the temporary work **2.49** agency but refuses it, she will lose her right to be paid remuneration by the agency – S.68C(2) (see 'Suspension on maternity grounds – ending supply of agency worker on maternity grounds' below).

Sea-going workers. Note that the Suspension from Work on Maternity **2.50** Grounds (Merchant Shipping and Fishing Vessels) Order 1998 SI 1998/587, made under the Merchant Shipping and Fishing Vessels (Health and Safety at Work) Regulations 1997 SI 1997/2962, extends protection to new and expectant mothers at sea. The Order gives women at sea the right to be offered suitable alternative work on maternity grounds before being suspended from work. If there is no suitable alternative work, they must be given paid leave.

Suspension on maternity grounds   2.51

As previously outlined, the scheme of the 1999 Regulations is such that, where a new or expectant mother would be exposed to risk if she continued to perform her normal contractual duties, the employer is obliged to alter her working conditions or working hours if it is reasonable do so and if it would avoid the risk. If it is not reasonable to make such alterations, or if doing so would not avoid all of the identified risks, the employer must offer the employee suitable alternative work or, failing that, suspend the employee from work for so long as is necessary to avoid the risk – Reg 16(2) and (3) 1999 Regulations/Ss.66 and 67 ERA.

As with the requirement to alter working hours or conditions, the duty to suspend an employee from work does not arise unless and until the employee has given the employer written notice that she is pregnant, has given birth within the previous six months (including the birth of a stillborn child after 24 weeks of pregnancy) or is breastfeeding – Reg 18(1). Furthermore, the employer is not required to maintain action taken in relation to an employee in any of the following circumstances:

- the employee has notified the employer that she is pregnant but has failed, within a reasonable time of being asked to do so in writing by the employer, to produce a certificate from a registered medical practitioner or registered midwife stating that she is pregnant – Reg 18(2)(a)

- the employer knows that she is no longer a new or expectant mother – Reg 18(2)(b), or

- the employer cannot establish whether she remains a new or expectant mother – Reg 18(2)(c).

2.52 In Day v T Pickles Farms Ltd 1999 IRLR 217, EAT, the Appeal Tribunal held that an employee was likely to have satisfied the requirement to give written notice of her pregnancy to the employer when she told the employer that she was pregnant and provided medical certificates stating that she was suffering from morning sickness – a condition associated with pregnancy. Thus, it seems that the EAT encourages a purposive approach being taken to the interpretation of the requirement of written notice (see 'Risk avoidance measures – when duty under Reg 16 arises' above) rather than strict adherence to the letter of the law.

If a woman is suspended from work on health and safety grounds before her baby is born, the question arises as to when her maternity leave period begins. A woman may normally choose to begin her maternity leave at any time from the beginning of the 11th week before the expected week of childbirth (EWC) until the birth of her child, provided she complies with the notice requirements discussed in Chapter 3, 'Maternity leave', under 'Entitlement to maternity leave – notice provisions'. If the period of suspension is likely to last up to the birth, a woman would be well advised to give notice that she intends to commence her leave at the EWC, otherwise she may be required to start her maternity leave at the beginning of the fourth week before her EWC – see Chapter 3, 'Maternity leave', under 'Commencement of ordinary maternity leave'.

Right to payment during suspension   2.53

An employee who has been suspended from work on maternity grounds under the 1999 Regulations is entitled to be paid remuneration during the period of suspension (unless she has unreasonably refused an offer of suitable alternative work – see 'Unreasonable refusal of suitable alternative work' below) – S.68(1) ERA. The employee will be regarded as suspended from work only if, and for so long as, she continues to be employed by her employer but is not provided with work or (disregarding alternative work under S.67 – see 'Risk avoidance measures – suitable alternative work' above) does not perform the work she normally performed before the suspension – S.66(3). An employee is suspended on 'maternity grounds' for these purposes where she is suspended from work by her employer on the ground that she is pregnant, has recently given birth or is breastfeeding, and the suspension is in consequence of either:

• a requirement imposed by or under any specified provision of a statute or statutory instrument, or

• a recommendation in any specified provision of a Code of Practice issued or approved under S.16 of the Health and Safety at Work etc Act 1974 – S.66(1) and (2).

A 'specified provision' is one for the time being specified in an order made by the Secretary of State. The Suspension from Work (on Maternity Grounds) Order 1994 SI 1994/2930 specifies the following two provisions of (what are now) the 1999 Regulations:

• Reg 16(3) on the suspension from work of new or expectant mothers to avoid risk from any processes or working conditions, or physical, biological or chemical agents

• Reg 17 on the suspension from work of new or expectant mothers working at night.

In other words, if the reason for the employee's suspension is that it is required   2.54
by one of the two provisions above, her suspension will be on maternity grounds within the meaning of S.66. (See also the Suspension from Work on Maternity Grounds (Merchant Shipping and Fishing Vessels) Order 1998 SI 1998/587, which specifies Regs 8(3) and 9(2) of the Merchant Shipping and Fishing Vessels (Health and Safety at Work) Regulations 1997 SI 1997/2962 for the purposes of S.66.)

In Hickey v Lucas Service UK Ltd ET Case No.1400979/96 H was a van driver who was disciplined in June 1996 following customer complaints. H was pregnant at the time, the baby being due in December, and her duties were changed to those of store assistant. H was concerned that as the new duties would involve lifting heavy objects, they would damage her health and put her baby at risk. She did not report for the new job but expressed her concerns to her doctor, who signed her off sick. The employer had not carried out any risk assessment and gave H sick pay for a month, after which she was given statutory sick pay. H returned to work in October when her employer gave her a different clerical job. An employment tribunal upheld H's claim that she had been suspended from work on health and safety grounds within the meaning of S.66 ERA from June to October and had been entitled to her normal pay for the whole period. H continued to be employed by her employer and was no longer provided with the work she performed before the suspension (as a van driver). H was also suspended from work on maternity grounds in consequence of a relevant requirement – i.e. Reg 16 1999 Regulations.

2.55 Employees suspended within the meaning of S.66 ERA are entitled to receive a week's pay in respect of each week of the period of suspension (or proportionately for part of a week) – S.69(1). A 'week's pay' is calculated in accordance with Ss.220–29 ERA – see IDS Employment Law Handbook, 'Wages' (2011), Chapter 10, 'A week's pay'. The calculation date for the purposes of working out a week's pay is the day before the suspension begins. There is an exception where the day prior to the beginning of a maternity suspension falls within the employee's maternity leave period, in which case the calculation date is the day before the beginning of the maternity leave period – S.225(5).

Section 69(2) ERA provides that an employee's right to suspension pay does not affect any right she may have to remuneration under her contract of employment. However, any contractual remuneration paid by the employer in respect of a period of suspension goes towards discharging liability to pay remuneration during suspension and vice versa – S.69(3).

An employee on maternity suspension continues to be employed during the suspension period, which therefore counts towards her period of continuous employment for the purposes of assessing seniority, pension rights and other personal length-of-service requirements. Contractual benefits are also likely to continue as normal during the maternity suspension unless employer and employee have mutually agreed to vary them.

2.56 Members of the armed forces, share fisherwomen and the police are excluded from the right to claim remuneration under S.68 ERA – Ss.192 (read with para 16, Sch 2), 199(2) and 200. Seafarers employed on ships registered under S.8 of the Merchant Shipping Act 1995 are covered by S.68 provided that the ship is registered as belonging to a port in Great Britain; that under her contract of employment the employee does not work wholly outside Great Britain; and that she is ordinarily resident in Great Britain – S.199(7) and (8). Crown employees and parliamentary staff are also covered – Ss.191, 194 and 195.

2.57 **Unreasonable refusal to perform suitable alternative work.** Under S.68(2) ERA an employee loses her statutory right to be paid during periods of suspension if she has unreasonably refused to perform suitable alternative work which was offered under S.67 (see 'Risk avoidance measures – suitable alternative work' above). Thus, in Bruce and anor v Saffronland Homes ET Case Nos.3101493–4/98 two pregnant employees who refused the suitable alternative work offered by their employer and took long-term sick leave were not entitled to full remuneration for suspension on maternity grounds. The employer offered the employees, who worked as support workers in nursing and residential care facilities, similar jobs in a facility the employer – based on a properly carried out risk assessment – deemed to be safe. Both employees were assured that their terms and conditions of employment, including pay, would remain the same but both expressed the desire to remain in their current posts. Soon thereafter both employees, having obtained medical notes from their doctors, commenced periods of sick leave. The employer accepted that their sickness was genuine and paid them statutory sick pay. The employment tribunal held that as a result there was no suspension on maternity grounds and the employees were not entitled to be paid under S.68. It went on to find that even if their absences had been due to a maternity suspension, the employees would not have been entitled to remuneration during the suspensions because they had been offered suitable alternative work which they had unreasonably refused to perform.

Ending supply of agency worker on maternity grounds 2.58
The Agency Workers Regulations 2010 SI 2010/93 (AWR) introduced similar (though not identical) provisions for agency workers to those that apply to employees (discussed above) (see Ss.68A–D and 69A ERA). The key difference is that a hirer who is unable to alter working conditions or hours to avoid identified risks to an agency worker who is pregnant, breastfeeding or has given birth within six months must inform the temporary work agency of that fact without delay, and the latter must then end the supply of that worker to the hirer. This contrasts with the position of an employee in similar circumstances, in that her employer must suspend her from work on maternity grounds. However, as with an employee, an agency worker has the right to be offered any suitable alternative work by the agency, at least for the period of the original assignment that has had to be ended – S.68B; and if no suitable work is available, the agency is then obliged to remunerate the worker for the remaining period of the original assignment – S.68C(1). The right to remuneration is lost, however, if the agency worker unreasonably refuses an offer by the agency to propose her to another hirer where suitable alternative work is available or unreasonably refuses to perform such work – S.68C(2) ERA.

Where the right to be remunerated by the agency does apply, calculation of the remuneration is based on a week's pay in respect of each week for which remuneration is payable, with a proportionate reduction in respect of any part-week – S.69A(1). Any contractual remuneration paid by the temporary work agency to the agency worker in respect of any period goes towards discharging the temporary work agency's liability under S.68C in respect of the same period – S.69A(3). For these purposes, a week's pay comprises the weekly amount that would have been payable to the worker for performing the work according to the terms of the contract with the temporary work agency – S.69A(4).

2.59 Two preconditions must be satisfied by an agency worker to secure any of the above rights. These are that she must have:

- completed the 12-week qualifying period with the hirer upon which the rights deriving from the AWR depend – Reg 18AB 1999 Regulations, and

- complied with the written notification requirements set out in Reg 18A 1999 Regulations. (These are similar to the notification requirements applicable to employees under Reg 18 – see 'Suspension on maternity grounds' above – save for the fact that the notification of the worker's pregnancy or the fact that she has given birth or is breastfeeding must have been given to the hirer and, in a case where the worker's assignment is required to be brought to an end on maternity grounds, also to the temporary work agency.

2.60 Right to equal pay

The question arises whether the right to be paid during medical suspension on maternity grounds implies a right to be paid the same amount as a male comparator who remains working. In British Airways (European Operations at Gatwick) Ltd v Moore and anor 2000 ICR 678, EAT, the two applicants were female cabin crew who were removed from flying duties, under the terms of a relevant collective agreement, after their 16th week of pregnancy. Both women continued to work on other duties but lost a proportion of their pay because, as grounded crew, they were no longer entitled to 'flying allowances'. The EAT upheld the tribunal's decision that British Airways had breached the applicants' right to remuneration on suspension under S.68 ERA as the alternative work they were given was on substantially less favourable terms and conditions than their normal work.

However, the EAT accepted the employer's argument that the applicants had no right to make an equal pay claim in respect of the flying allowances. It took the view that a woman suspended from her normal work on maternity grounds is, like a woman on maternity leave, in a special position that requires her to be afforded special protection, but which is not comparable either with that of a man or with that of a woman engaged on normal duties. Just as a woman will have no equal pay claim in respect of a period of maternity leave where 'adequate allowance' is made under national legislation, so she can have no claim during a period of suspension from normal work on maternity grounds where she is entitled to 'adequate allowance' in the form of remuneration under S.68 ERA.

In Parviainen v Finnair Oyj 2011 ICR 99, ECJ, a Finnish stewardess was **2.61** transferred to ground duties during her pregnancy. As a result, she lost various supplementary allowances, amounting to around 40 per cent of her pay. The ECJ ruled that this did not amount to a breach of the EU Pregnant Workers Directive (No.92/85) ('the Pregnant Workers Directive'): a pregnant woman who is transferred to alternative duties is not entitled to receive the same pay that she received before the transfer, where some of that pay depends on the performance of specific functions. Where a pregnant worker is temporarily transferred to another job, she remains entitled to the pay components or supplementary allowances that relate to her professional status, such as seniority, length of service, and professional qualifications, but the Directive does not require maintenance of supplementary allowances, which are dependent on the performance of specific functions.

Similarly, in Gassmayr v Bundesminster für Wissenschaft und Forschung 2011 1 CMLR 7, ECJ, the European Court held that a pregnant doctor who was suspended on health grounds was not entitled to continue to receive an on-call allowance during her suspension. The payment of the on-call allowance was paid in accordance with the length of time the worker was on call. As the worker was prohibited from working, she could not perform the duties entitling her to payment of that allowance.

The ECJ noted that the Directive only provided for minimum protection with **2.62** regard to pay, and that there was nothing to prevent Member States from introducing legislation providing for the maintenance of all pay components during transfer or suspension on pregnancy grounds. In a UK context, the EAT's decision in British Airways (European Operations at Gatwick) Ltd v Moore (above) suggests that while claimants would not have claims under the Equality Act 2010 in the circumstances that pertained in the two ECJ decisions, they might be entitled to medical suspension payments equivalent to the pay received for the work from which they were suspended under S.68 ERA. In this sense, the position under domestic law may indeed be more generous than that required by EU law.

Night-time work

2.63

A worker covered by the 1999 Regulations is not obliged to perform night-time work if to do so would pose a risk to her health and safety. Reg 17 provides that, where a new or expectant mother performs night-work and a certificate from a registered medical practitioner or registered midwife shows that it is necessary for her health and safety that she should not do so for any period, the employer must suspend her from work for as long as is necessary. This is subject to S.67 ERA, which gives the employee the right to be offered suitable alternative work before being suspended on maternity grounds – see 'Risk avoidance measures – suitable alternative work' above. Suitable alternative work would, in this context, presumably be day-time work. The employer is not obliged to maintain the suspension once it knows that the employee is no longer a new or expectant mother or if it cannot establish whether she remains a new or expectant mother – Reg 18(2)(b) and (c) 1999 Regulations.

The Agency Workers Regulations 2010 SI 2010/93 introduced a similar provision in respect of agency workers. Reg 17A 1999 Regulations provides that where an agency worker, who is also a night worker, presents a certificate from a registered medical practitioner or registered midwife which shows that it is necessary for her health and safety that she should not work at night for any period, then the hirer must 'without delay' inform the temporary work agency, which must then end the supply of the worker to the hirer.

2.64 The ECJ considered night-time work in Habermann-Beltermann v Arbeiterwohlfahrt, Bezirksverband Ndb/Opf eV 1994 IRLR 364, ECJ. H's contract of employment stipulated that she was to be assigned night-time work only. Shortly after she was recruited, it emerged that she was pregnant. Neither party had been aware of this at the time the contract was entered into. The employer sought to terminate the employment contract by relying on a German law prohibiting women who are pregnant or breastfeeding from doing overtime or night-time work between 8 pm and 6 am. In Germany, as a rule, a contravention of a prohibition on night-time work renders a contract void. The employer also relied on a German law allowing an employer to treat a contract as void on account of a mistake concerning an essential characteristic of the other party to the contract. The ECJ, however, held that the relevant domestic law was in contravention of the EU Equal Treatment Directive (No.76/207) – now consolidated into the recast EU Equal Treatment Directive (No.2006/54). For further details, see Chapter 13, 'Discrimination and equal pay', under 'Direct discrimination – statutory prohibition and pregnancy'.

2.65 Remedies

An employee who considers that her employer has failed to comply with the health and safety provisions relating to expectant, new and breastfeeding mothers has a number of possible avenues of redress. By virtue of S.70 ERA an employee may present a complaint to an employment tribunal where her employer has failed:

- to pay the whole or any part of remuneration to which she is entitled during a period of suspension on maternity grounds – S.70(1), or

- to offer her suitable alternative work before suspending her from work on maternity grounds – S.70(4).

Where the employee's complaint is that her employer has failed to pay her remuneration in respect of any day during a period of suspension, that complaint must be presented before the end of the three-month period beginning with the day in respect of which the claim is made or, where that is not reasonably practicable, within such further period as the tribunal considers reasonable – S.70(2). The time limit may also be extended to allow for early conciliation or cross-border mediation. Where the tribunal finds the complaint well founded, it must order the employer to pay the amount of remuneration due to the employee – S.70(3).

A complaint about failure to offer suitable alternative work must be presented **2.66** before the end of the period of three months beginning with the first day of the suspension or, where that is not reasonably practicable, within such further period as the tribunal considers reasonable – S.70(5). The time limit may also be extended to allow for early conciliation or cross-border mediation. Where the tribunal finds the complaint well founded, it may award the employee compensation – S.70(6). The amount of the compensation will be such as the tribunal considers just and equitable in all the circumstances, having regard to the infringement of the employee's right and to any loss sustained by her which is attributable to the failure to provide her with alternative work – S.70(7). Time limits for tribunal claims are dealt with in IDS Employment Law Handbook, 'Employment Tribunal Practice and Procedure' (2014), Chapter 5, 'Time limits'.

Agency workers. A very similar enforcement regime applies to agency workers. **2.67** Such workers are entitled to bring a tribunal complaint on the basis that the temporary work agency has failed to pay the whole or any part of remuneration to which she is entitled as a result of her assignment with a hirer being ended on maternity grounds – S.70A(1) ERA. Such a complaint has to be presented within three months beginning with the day on which the supply of the agency worker to a hirer was ended or, where that is not reasonably practicable, within such further period as the tribunal considers reasonable – S.70A(2). The time limit may also be extended to allow for early conciliation or cross-border mediation. Where a complaint is upheld, the tribunal must order the temporary work agency to pay the agency worker the amount of remuneration that is due – S.70A(3).

In addition, an agency worker may present a complaint that, in contravention of S.68B ERA, the temporary work agency has failed to propose the worker to any hirer that has suitable alternative work available – S.70A(4). If that complaint is successful, the tribunal must order the agency to pay the worker such compensation as the tribunal considers just and equitable in all the circumstances having regard to (a) the infringement of the worker's right, and (b) any loss sustained by her that is attributable to the failure of the agency – S.70A(6) and (7). Again, a three-month time limit applies – subject to an extension where it is not reasonably practicable to comply with that limit – beginning on the day on which the supply of the worker to the hirer was ended on maternity grounds – S.70A(5). The time limit may also be extended to allow for early conciliation or cross-border mediation.

2.68 Breach of statutory duty

In addition to these specific remedies under the ERA, it is open to an employee to present a complaint to the HSE or to pursue a civil action for damages against her employer. The 1999 Regulations were made under powers conferred by the Health and Safety at Work etc Act 1974 (HSWA). S.47 of that Act used to impose civil liability on employers in health and safety cases if breach of a statutory duty caused damage, even where the employer had taken all reasonable steps to prevent the injury. However, S.69 of the Enterprise and Regulatory Reform Act 2013, which came into force on 1 October 2013, amended S.47 to remove this strict liability provision, meaning that claims will only succeed if it can be shown that the employer was negligent. However, an exception has been made for pregnant workers. The Health and Safety at Work etc Act 1974 (Civil Liability) (Exceptions) Regulations 2013 SI 2013/1667 amended Reg 22 of the 1999 Regulations so as to provide that breach of a duty imposed by Reg 16, 16A, 17 or 17A will, so far as it causes damage, be actionable by the new or expectant mother. This exception for pregnant workers is required to ensure compatibility with the EU Pregnant Workers Directive (No.92/85).

In a civil action for breach of statutory duty under Reg 22, a claimant will be required to prove that she has suffered damage – such as personal injury or economic loss – as a result of the employer's breach of the relevant duty. However, in so far as a claim concerns a failure by an employer to undertake a risk assessment, the claimant may be better served pursuing the matter as a claim of pregnancy discrimination in an employment tribunal (see 'Discrimination – failure to conduct a risk assessment' below) since this will enable her to recover compensation for injury to feelings. A further disadvantage of actions for breach of statutory duty in the High Court and county courts is the risk of having to pay the other side's costs, but such action may be particularly attractive in circumstances where the deadline for bringing a claim in an employment tribunal has expired – the time limit for a personal injury claim in the civil courts is three years, as opposed to the standard three months in employment tribunals.

2.69 Unlawful detriment

Section 47C ERA and Reg 19 of the Maternity and Parental Leave etc Regulations 1999 SI 1999/3312 ('the MPL Regulations') provide that an employee has a right not to be subjected to any detriment short of dismissal by any act, or deliberate failure to act, by her employer for a reason that relates to (among other things) the fact that the employee is the subject of a relevant requirement or recommendation as defined in S.66(2) ERA – see Reg 19(2)(c).

Thus, where it would be contrary to a statutory requirement or a recommendation in a Code of Practice for an expectant, new or breastfeeding mother to continue in her normal job and, as a result, the employer is required to offer her alternative employment or suspend her on full pay, the employee has the right not to suffer a detriment as a result. An employee who has suffered a detriment in contravention of S.47C and Reg 19(2)(c) may make a complaint to an employment tribunal – S.48(1). Unlawful detriment is discussed in detail in Chapter 12, 'Detriment and unfair dismissal'.

Automatically unfair dismissal 2.70

It is automatically unfair to dismiss an employee (or select her for redundancy), regardless of her length of continuous employment, for a reason connected with the application of a relevant requirement or recommendation as defined in S.66(2) ERA – S.99 ERA and Reg 20(3)(c) MPL Regulations. Thus, where it would be contrary to a statutory requirement or a recommendation in a Code of Practice for an expectant, new or breastfeeding mother to continue in her normal job and, as a result, the employer dismisses her instead of offering her alternative employment or suspending her on full pay, the employee will be able to claim that she has been automatically unfairly dismissed. In these circumstances there will be no scope for the employer to argue that the decision to dismiss was a reasonable one to have taken in all the circumstances. Unfair dismissal is discussed in detail in Chapter 12, 'Detriment and unfair dismissal'.

Even where a relevant requirement or recommendation does not apply, a dismissal for a reason connected with the fact that the employee is genuinely concerned about her health and safety at work may still be automatically unfair as it is a reason connected with her pregnancy – S.99 ERA and Reg 20(3)(a) MPL Regulations. Much will depend on whether the employer's risk assessment was suitable and sufficient and on whether the employee's concern was reasonable.

Two examples: 2.71

• **Taylor v Thomas Bee Ltd** ET Case No.63877/95: an employment tribunal found that a pregnant employee's dismissal for refusing to do work that she believed was harmful to her unborn child was unfair. T was a car valet who worked with various cleaning agents in a garage where there were carbon monoxide emissions from vehicles being serviced. At her request, she was transferred to office work after she notified TB Ltd of her pregnancy. TB Ltd wanted T to return to her original duties, however, and after conducting a risk assessment – which the tribunal found to be insufficient – concluded that there were no risks to T in resuming her previous duties. When T refused to return to valeting work, she was dismissed. The tribunal found that the dismissal resulted from T's refusal to work in the valeting area. As this refusal was connected to her pregnancy, her dismissal was automatically unfair

- **Palmer v WH Hill and Son (Holloware) Ltd** ET Case No.1304127/98: P was a holloware assembler/press worker. When she informed her employer of her pregnancy, she requested that she not be required to work at its Seymour Road premises, as she was concerned about fumes resulting from the galvanising, painting, de-greasing and finishing work done there. The employer nevertheless required P to work at these premises on more than one occasion and declined her request for a face mask. When she refused to attend for work there, she was told to get her bag and go home. The tribunal found that P was unfairly dismissed by reason of her pregnancy. The fact that she refused to work at the Seymour Road plant was directly related to her genuine concerns about risks to her unborn child. She had also been subjected to unlawful sex discrimination (see 'Discrimination' below).

A pregnant employee who is dismissed for raising concerns about her health and safety at work may also be able to claim automatically unfair dismissal under S.100 ERA (health and safety dismissals). S.100 is discussed in detail in IDS Employment Law Handbook, 'Unfair Dismissal' (2010), Chapter 11, 'Health and safety dismissals'.

2.72 Constructive dismissal. In the absence of an express dismissal, an employee may nevertheless be able to bring an unfair dismissal claim against her employer on the basis that its failure to conduct a proper risk assessment constituted a repudiatory breach of contract entitling her to treat herself as constructively dismissed – see Bunning v GT Bunning and Sons Ltd (No.2) 2005 EWCA Civ 104, CA.

2.73 Discrimination

Any unfavourable treatment of a woman because of her pregnancy will amount to pregnancy discrimination under S.18 of the Equality Act 2010 (EqA) – see Chapter 13, 'Discrimination and equal pay', under 'Direct discrimination – pregnancy and maternity discrimination'. This would extend to any unfavourable treatment of a pregnant employee based on any health and safety concerns of the employee for herself or her unborn child.

2.74 Employer's failure to carry out a risk assessment. It is now well established that an employer's failure to carry out a risk assessment under the 1999 Regulations can, in the case of a pregnant worker, entitle her to bring a complaint of pregnancy and maternity discrimination under S.18 EqA. The first indications to this effect came from the EAT in Day v T Pickles Farms Ltd 1999 IRLR 217, EAT, where it held that a failure to carry out a risk assessment could amount to a detriment under the Sex Discrimination Act 1975 (SDA) (now repealed and replaced by the EqA), entitling the worker to bring a sex discrimination claim. The employer, who ran a sandwich shop where food was cooked on the premises, argued that D's position had not been prejudiced by the company's failure to carry out a risk assessment. As it was the smell and handling of food that brought on or aggravated D's severe morning sickness, D was not prevented from working by anything that a risk assessment would have disclosed. The EAT thought that that depended on the facts, and it could only speculate as to the kind of issues that the assessment might have brought to light. If the risk assessment had found, for example, that the ovens gave off too much heat and this could have been resolved by better ventilation, who was to say that the smell of food and the risk of nausea might not have been reduced? As there was no evidence as to what such an assessment would have disclosed, the EAT remitted the case to the tribunal for it to hear evidence as to whether D had suffered a detriment.

The EAT went further in Hardman v Mallon t/a Orchard Lodge Nursing Home 2002 IRLR 516, EAT, where it definitively held that a failure to carry out a risk assessment resulted in a detriment to a pregnant employee and constituted sex discrimination. In July 1999 H was employed as a care assistant by M, who ran a nursing home. Four months later H told M that she was pregnant. In March 2000 H and M discussed the need for a risk assessment and M offered H the job of cleaner. H refused the offer because the job was less favourable than her existing one. The care of elderly patients involved heavy lifting, and at a subsequent meeting H produced a medical certificate stating that she should refrain from such lifting. She then told M that she had the right to be suspended on full pay but M merely repeated the offer of a cleaning job. H complained to an employment tribunal that, as a woman suspended on maternity grounds, she had not been offered suitable alternative employment, contrary to the ERA; that there had been a failure to carry out a risk assessment; and that she had been discriminated against on the ground of sex. The tribunal found in H's favour with regard to the claim under the ERA, but dismissed her claim of sex discrimination. It considered the Day case but was not satisfied that, on the wording of S.6(2)(b) SDA (now S.39(2)(d) EqA), a failure to carry out a risk assessment, resulting in a detriment, amounted to sex discrimination.

On appeal, the EAT stated that the tribunal had been bound by the decision **2.75** in the Day case in which Mr Justice Lindsay had indicated that a failure to carry out a risk assessment could be a detriment. In the EAT's view, the proper approach was to construe the SDA by reference to the Equal Treatment Directive and the EU Pregnant Workers Directive (No.92/85). Consequently, it was not necessary to compare the employer's treatment of the pregnant employee with that of either a comparable male employee or a non-pregnant employee, as the tribunal had. Where the basis of an employer's treatment is pregnancy, it is unlawful irrespective of the employer's treatment of comparable men or non-pregnant women. The EAT stated that, although an employer is obliged to carry out a risk assessment in respect of all workers, a failure to do so has a disparate impact on pregnant workers. Thus, the employer's failure to carry out a risk assessment in respect of a pregnant worker constituted sex discrimination.

The Hardman case was decided prior to amendments made to the SDA by the Employment Equality (Sex Discrimination) Regulations 2005 SI 2005/2467, which introduced new provisions explicitly prohibiting discrimination on grounds of pregnancy and maternity leave – see Chapter 13, 'Discrimination and equal pay', under 'Direct discrimination – pregnancy and maternity discrimination'. However, the EAT confirmed in Stevenson v JM Skinner and Co EAT 0584/07 that the principle in Hardman – that a failure to carry out a risk assessment under Regs 3(1)(a) and 16 1999 Regulations amounted to discrimination – remained good law in light of the amendments.

2.76 The position remains unchanged under the EqA. The relevant provisions are now contained in S.18 EqA, which – like S.3A SDA before it – makes specific provision prohibiting discrimination on the grounds of pregnancy or maternity leave. As under the SDA, a failure to carry out a risk assessment for a pregnant employee will amount to discrimination for these purposes. An example:

- **Clayton v Retail Merchant Services Ltd** ET Case No.1200965/12: RMS Ltd failed to carry out a risk assessment on being informed by C that she was pregnant, despite knowing that she suffered high blood pressure and her work involved driving alone for several hours each day. At a time when she was heavily pregnant, C was informed that she would have to personally return her company car to head office in Milton Keynes the next day. Her husband interceded and expressed concerns for C's health and that of the unborn child, and alternative arrangements were eventually made for the car. An employment tribunal found that C had suffered pregnancy discrimination when RMS Ltd failed to undertake the risk assessment. Had it done so, it would have been apparent that an instruction to drive the vehicle to Milton Keynes could lead to substantial harm. She was awarded £7,000 for injury to feelings: although the instruction to return the car was subsequently withdrawn, it had caused her distress, high blood pressure and a stay in hospital.

2.77 However, while it has been accepted as binding by tribunals, there are difficulties with the EAT's analysis in both Hardman v Mallon t/a Orchard Lodge Nursing Home (above) and Stevenson v JM Skinner and Co (above). A claim of pregnancy discrimination does not require the claimant to identify a comparator who has been treated less favourably, but it does require her to establish that she has experienced unfavourable treatment 'because of' her pregnancy or an illness related to it – S.18(2) EqA. It is not sufficient that pregnancy merely be the 'background' to the unfavourable treatment; it must be the 'reason why' she was treated in that way. In circumstances where there has not been a risk assessment for *any* employee, then it is arguable that the unfavourable treatment has arisen 'because of' the employer's general disregard for its obligations under the 1999 Regulations, rather than because of the pregnancy. However, the EAT's analysis effectively shuts down any consideration of the employer's reason for the omission – the mere fact that it has failed to carry out the risk assessment will give rise to liability.

As explored under 'Breach of statutory duty' above, Reg 22 provides that a breach of the 1999 Regulations in respect of a pregnant employee can only give rise to an action for breach of statutory duty if she has suffered damage – such as personal injury or economic loss – as a result of the breach. There is no such requirement in respect of claims under the EqA. By making a failure to carry out a risk assessment as required by Reg 16 an act of pregnancy discrimination, Hardman v Mallon t/a Orchard Lodge Nursing Home (above) and Stevenson v JM Skinner and Co (above) offer claimants the means to recover greater compensation than they would be able to obtain in the civil courts: a successful discrimination claim in an employment tribunal will invariably be accompanied by an award for injury to feelings, even if the claimant has suffered no other loss. Thus, it is no surprise that the majority of cases considering the duty to undertake risk assessments in respect of pregnant employees are discrimination claims rather than actions for breach of statutory duty.

2.78 There is, however, one way in which an employer who has not carried out a specific risk assessment for a pregnant worker may seek to evade a finding of pregnancy discrimination – by challenging the existence of a risk in the first place:

*   **Madarassy v Nomura International plc** 2007 ICR 867, CA: M brought various claims of sex discrimination to an employment tribunal, one of which was that NI plc, on being notified that she was pregnant, had failed to carry out a risk assessment under Reg 16(1) 1999 Regulations. All of her other claims failed, but the tribunal found that NI plc had discriminated against M when it failed to undertake the assessment. On appeal, however, NI plc successfully argued that there had not been sufficient evidence from which the tribunal could base a finding that M's work 'could involve risk' to a pregnant mother (as required by Reg 16(1)(b)). The Court of Appeal upheld this finding, and in so doing drew a distinction between the circumstances in Hardman v Mallon t/a Orchard Lodge Nursing Home (above) and the instant case. In Hardman, the Court explained, there had been 'direct medical evidence that the employee's work, as a care assistant in a nursing home for the elderly, could involve heavy lifting, which posed a risk to her or her baby's health and safety'. In M's case, however, no such evidence had been adduced. Instead, the tribunal had based its finding on M's testimony that she found sitting at a computer workstation for long periods to be uncomfortable, and on the uncorroborated claim that radiation might emanate from a computer. If the tribunal were to find that NI plc was in breach of Reg 16(1), it first had to find that the work involved a risk to health and safety; thus the EAT had been correct to remit the matter to the tribunal.

2.79 The Madarassy case was followed by the EAT in O'Neill v Buckinghamshire County Council 2010 IRLR 384, EAT. There, the Appeal Tribunal ruled that,

61

in the absence of evidence that the work of a pregnant teacher would involve a risk to her health and safety, there had been no obligation on the employer to carry out a risk assessment under Reg 16 1999 Regulations. The EAT also affirmed the absence of any automatic right to a specific risk assessment for pregnant workers. The obligation to carry out a risk assessment of a pregnant worker arose only where (a) the employee notified the employer in writing that she was pregnant, (b) the work was of a kind that could involve a risk of harm or danger to the health and safety of a new or expectant mother or her baby, and (c) the risk arose from any processes or working conditions, or physical, biological or chemical agents, including those specified in Annexes I and II of the Pregnant Workers Directive. In the instant case there had been no material before the tribunal from which it could have concluded that the kind of work carried out by the claimant involved a risk of harm or danger to her as a pregnant worker as defined by the Directive and the 1999 Regulations.

2.80 **Liability of employment agencies.** As mentioned under 'Risk assessments – duties of employment agencies' above, employment businesses are required to carry out a general risk assessment for workers they supply to an end-user – Reg 3(1)(b). When considering a possible discrimination claim, this requirement falls to be read with S.55(1)(c) EqA, which makes it unlawful for an employment agency to discriminate against a woman by not offering to provide any of its services. In Brocklebank v Silveira EAT 0571/05 S had entered into an agreement with SP Ltd that she would come to the UK and that it would find her work. She subsequently informed SP Ltd that she was pregnant and SP Ltd passed this information on to P, a potential client. P indicated that it could not employ S until SP Ltd had completed a risk assessment. SP Ltd did not complete the assessment, with the result that S did not go to work for P. In upholding her claim of sex discrimination, an employment tribunal held that the undertaking of a risk assessment was one of the services to be provided by SP Ltd and that, in failing to carry one out, SP Ltd had deliberately omitted to provide that service to P. In dismissing SP Ltd's appeal, the EAT confirmed that a risk assessment was one of the 'services' to be provided by the employment agency for the purposes of S.15(1)(b).

2.81 **Employee's concerns.** Even in the absence of a failure to carry out a risk assessment, tribunals have held that the dismissal of a pregnant employee who refuses to carry out certain duties because of concerns about risks to herself or her unborn child can constitute sex discrimination. In Porter v Flowertouch Ltd ET Case No.10643/96, for example, P worked as a care assistant at a nursing home. When she became pregnant she refused to lift any patients because of difficulties she had experienced in previous pregnancies. She was subsequently dismissed. Before the tribunal, the employer conceded that the principal reason for P's dismissal was her refusal to lift patients. The tribunal found that this reason was connected with P's pregnancy and that her dismissal therefore constituted sex discrimination.

Non-payment of sick pay. In P and O European Ferries (Dover) Ltd and anor v **2.82** Iverson 1999 ICR 1088, EAT, the EAT found that an employer discriminated against a pregnant employee when she was not paid during a period of medical suspension due to pregnancy, while employees on medical suspension on account of other conditions were entitled to full pay. In order to comply with health and safety orders relating to employees on UK ships, I should have started her maternity leave on 12 April 1997. However, she refused to sign the maternity leave form prepared for her because she wanted to work until 1 June. She also refused offers of alternative shore-based jobs because the salaries were roughly half what she earned on board ship. I's employer put her on authorised unpaid leave and she brought tribunal proceedings claiming that she was entitled to be paid during the leave period. The tribunal found that I was not entitled to sick pay under the terms of her contract. However, if she had been suspended on any of the medical grounds listed in the UK shipping regulations other than pregnancy, she would have been entitled to full sick pay. The tribunal concluded that the employer had directly discriminated against I on the ground of her sex. The employer appealed. The EAT acknowledged that it was a well-established principle that pregnant women are in a class of their own and that it is not appropriate to compare them with a sick man for the purposes of establishing or negating sex discrimination. Parliament has decreed that those with a wide range of medical conditions, of which pregnancy is but one, are precluded from working at sea. Under the employer's contractual provisions for determining entitlement to sick pay, all those conditions were treated as sickness, except pregnancy. The EAT could not see any possible explanation for the detriment suffered by pregnant women other than sex discrimination. Thus, I's pregnancy was the causative factor of her not receiving sick pay and the tribunal was correct to find that the employer had discriminated against her on the ground of her sex.

Finally, in Mahlburg v Land Mecklenburg-Vorpommern 2001 ICR 1032, ECJ, the European Court held that it is unlawful under EU law to refuse to appoint a pregnant woman on the ground that a prohibition on employment because of the pregnancy would prevent her from being employed from the outset and for the duration of her pregnancy – see further Chapter 13, 'Discrimination and equal pay', under 'Direct discrimination – statutory prohibition and pregnancy'.

Asserting a statutory right   2.83
If an employee is dismissed because she has tried to exercise her right to be offered alternative employment under S.67 ERA or to be paid while suspended on maternity grounds under S.68, she may be able to claim that she has been dismissed for asserting a statutory right. Under S.104(1) ERA an employee's dismissal will be automatically unfair if the reason or principal reason for the dismissal was that:

- the employee brought proceedings against the employer to enforce a relevant statutory right, or

- the employee alleged that the employer had infringed a relevant statutory right.

2.84 It is immaterial whether the employee actually has the statutory right in question or whether it has been infringed, but the employee's claim to the right must be made in good faith – S.104(2). Furthermore, it is sufficient that the employee made it reasonably clear to the employer what the right claimed to have been infringed was; it is not necessary actually to specify the right – S.104(3).

Dismissals for asserting a statutory right are dealt with in detail in IDS Employment Law Handbook, 'Unfair Dismissal' (2010), Chapter 12, 'Dismissal for asserting a statutory right'.

3 Maternity leave

The maternity leave scheme is set out in Chapter 1 of Part 8 (Ss.71–75) of the **3.1** Employment Rights Act 1996 (ERA) and in the Maternity and Parental Leave etc Regulations 1999 SI 1999/3312 ('the MPL Regulations'), which provide details of how the scheme operates in practice. All statutory references in this chapter are to the ERA (as amended) and all references to regulations are to the MPL Regulations (as amended), unless otherwise stated. The equivalent Regulations in Northern Ireland are the Maternity and Parental Leave etc Regulations (Northern Ireland) 1999 SR 1999/471.

General considerations   3.2

Several important amendments have been made to the current scheme since it was first introduced in December 1999 by the Employment Relations Act 1999, but the overall structure remains the same. The major changes were introduced by the Work and Families Act 2006 and the Maternity and Parental Leave etc and the Paternity and Adoption Leave (Amendment) Regulations 2006 SI 2006/2014 issued under it, and by the Sex Discrimination Act 1975 (Amendment) Regulations 2008 SI 2008/656 and the Maternity and Parental Leave etc and the Paternity and Adoption Leave (Amendment) Regulations 2008 SI 2008/1966. These changes:

- abolished the 26-week qualifying service requirement for additional maternity leave. The assumption now is that a woman will take both ordinary and additional maternity leave unless she gives her employer

---

notice of her intention to return to work earlier (see 'Entitlement to maternity leave' below)

- increased to eight weeks the amount of notice an employee must give if she wishes to return to work early (see 'Entitlement to maternity leave – employer's notice of end date' below, and Chapter 4, 'Returning to work after maternity leave', under 'Date of return to work')

- introduced 'keeping-in-touch' days, giving employees the chance to work for up to ten days during the maternity leave period without bringing it to an end. The amendments also made it clear that 'reasonable contact' could be made between the employee and her employer during the maternity leave period to discuss relevant matters (see '"Reasonable contact" during maternity leave' and 'Work during maternity leave' below).

In 2008, ordinary and additional maternity leave periods were harmonised yet further with the removal of the distinction between them in respect of the terms and conditions of employment that apply – see 'Terms and conditions during maternity leave' below.

3.3 Note that on 1 December 2014 a new statutory system of shared parental leave and pay came into force under powers established by the Children and Families Act 2014, allowing a woman who satisfies certain eligibility criteria to curtail the amount of statutory maternity leave she intends to take and to share the balance of her entitlement to leave with the father of her child (or her spouse, civil partner or partner). This scheme, which is entirely distinct from the unpaid parental leave scheme already in existence, is available in respect of children due on or after 5 April 2015. For more information about the new scheme, see 'New scheme for parents to *share* leave' below, and Chapter 8, 'Shared parental leave and pay'.

3.4 Maternity leave periods

There are three periods of statutory maternity leave:

- *ordinary maternity leave* – all pregnant employees are entitled to take 26 weeks' ordinary maternity leave, regardless of their length of service, provided they satisfy the conditions laid down in Reg 4 (see 'Entitlement to maternity leave' below)

- *compulsory maternity leave* – no employee may work for her employer for a period of two weeks starting with the day on which childbirth occurs. This period of compulsory leave forms part of the ordinary maternity leave period

- *additional maternity leave* – all pregnant employees are entitled to take a further 26 weeks' additional maternity leave at the end of their ordinary maternity leave period, regardless of their length of service, provided they satisfy the conditions laid down in Reg 4 (see 'Entitlement to maternity leave' below).

Women who are employed by more than one employer are entitled to exercise their maternity leave rights separately in relation to each. So a woman who has two employers may, for example, decide to return to work for one employer before her leave entitlement has run out, while continuing to enjoy her full leave entitlement in respect of the other employer.

Note, however, that if the employee intends to share any remaining balance of **3.5** her maternity leave entitlement under the new shared parental leave scheme (see 'New scheme for parents to *share* leave' below and Chapter 8, 'Shared parental leave and pay'), she must bring forward the date on which her maternity leave ends with each employer. She can do this by either returning to work for that employer or giving a 'leave curtailment notice' to each employer (at the same time) to end her maternity leave on a specific date. An employee cannot take shared parental leave if she has only brought forward the date on which her maternity leave period ends with one of her employers, as she cannot be on maternity leave in one job and on shared parental leave in another.

New scheme for parents to *share* leave **3.6**

The Work and Families Act 2006 introduced a statutory right for employed fathers or partners of a mother or an adopter following the birth or adoption of a child to take additional paternity leave (APL) of up to 26 weeks. That right, which was brought into force in April 2010 for babies due (and children placed for adoption) on or after 3 April 2011, gave rise to the concept of 'transferable' maternity leave, although the right to leave was in fact a freestanding right. However, it was only available where the mother or adopter had returned to work. And the right to additional statutory paternity pay (ASPP) was only available if the mother or adopter had not used up his or her entitlement to statutory maternity pay, Maternity Allowance or statutory adoption pay at the time of his or her return to work. According to the DTI consultation document, 'Work and Families: Choice and Flexibility – Additional Paternity Leave and Pay' (March 2006), this scheme was intended to provide 'an opportunity for equal division of paid leave for mothers and fathers and provide an opportunity for them to have equal caring responsibilities for their child during the first year of its life' – although strictly speaking it was only the pay, not the leave itself, which was 'transferable'.

However, the additional paternity leave and pay scheme was abolished on 5 April 2015 by S.125 of the Children and Families Act 2014 and in its place the Government has introduced the right, for parents whose baby is expected on or after 5 April 2015, to take shared parental leave and pay. This new scheme allows a woman who is eligible for statutory maternity leave and statutory maternity pay to choose to curtail her entitlement to maternity leave and pay and to share the balance with the father of her child (or her spouse, civil partner or partner). Unlike APL, where the mother 'transferred' her unused leave to the father, the shared parental leave and pay scheme allows parents to share the remaining pot of leave. They can decide to be off work at the same time and/or take it in turns to take periods of leave to look after the child. Similar rights apply to employees who adopt (for children who are placed for adoption on or after 5 April 2015) and to parents of a child born through a surrogacy arrangement if they have a parental order (or have applied or intend to apply for such an order) and are eligible for adoption leave. For full details of this new shared parental leave and pay scheme, see Chapter 8, 'Shared parental leave and pay'.

3.7 European law reform

In October 2008 the European Commission published proposals to amend the EU Pregnant Workers Directive (No.92/85) ('the Pregnant Workers Directive') to increase the rights and protections of new and expectant mothers. The proposals included:

- extending the minimum length of maternity leave under the Directive from 14 to 18 weeks

- a recommendation that women be paid their full salary for the 18-week minimum maternity leave period, but with the opportunity for Member States to set a ceiling on the level of maternity pay in the 18-week period of 'at least the level of sick pay'

- increasing compulsory maternity leave from two to six weeks, to be taken after childbirth

- that, where childbirth occurs after the due date, the pre-natal portion of leave should be extended to the actual date of birth, without any reduction in the post-natal portion of the leave

- that Member States should decide on the length of additional leave to be granted in the event of premature birth, children hospitalised at birth, newborn children with disabilities, and multiple births

- that any period of pregnancy-related sick leave, up to four weeks before confinement, should not shorten the period of maternity leave.

3.8 However, in October 2010 the European Parliament voted in favour of more controversial amendments. Among other things, the proposed changes provided for 20 weeks' maternity leave on full pay (with some opaque exceptions) and a right to time off for breastfeeding. Other measures agreed by the European Parliament included:

- two separate one-hour periods of time off for breastfeeding, unless another arrangement is agreed with the employer, with an increase of 30 minutes for each individual child in the case of multiple births

- a prohibition on workers being obliged to perform night work or overtime during the ten weeks prior to childbirth, during the remainder of the pregnancy where the mother or unborn child have health problems, and during the entire period of breastfeeding

- a compulsory period of fully paid maternity leave for at least six weeks after childbirth, regardless of the number of days worked prior to confinement.

The text of the Pregnant Workers Directive (as agreed by the European Parliament) needed to be approved by a qualified majority of the Council of the European Union to become law. However, in December 2010, at a meeting of the EU Employment Council, a large majority of ministers rejected the proposal for 20 weeks of maternity leave on full pay. They expressed concerns regarding the cost implications of extending paid maternity leave and plans to include paternity leave in a draft Directive on maternity leave. In their view, the main purpose of the Directive was to improve the health and safety at work of pregnant women, not to reconcile work, family and private life.

The Council considered the proposals again on 17 June 2011 but the length of **3.9** and payment for maternity leave were left out of the working party discussions as these were considered the most sensitive topics on which reaching an agreement was likely to take some time. At this meeting, majority support could not be established for most of the European Parliament's amendments and, in general, the national delegations considered that the Directive should cover only maternity leave. The issue was discussed again at a Council meeting in December 2011 which considered a Polish Presidency report that concluded that 20 weeks of maternity leave on full pay, or even a shorter period, was unacceptable to the Council. The report considered that the financial implications of introducing such proposals during the financial crisis could have counterproductive effects – presumably, that employers would be less likely to hire women. However, the report also noted that the Commission did not intend to withdraw its proposal and called for 'further constructive dialogue between the co-legislators' to reach a compromise.

There were no further developments on the proposals for amendment following that meeting and, in June 2014, the European Commission indicated that the proposals were to be withdrawn. In a press release issued on 18 June 2014, the Commission stated that, following close scrutiny of all proposals before the legislator, it had identified some that were either 'outdated or without support' and which should therefore be withdrawn. These included the proposals relating to pregnant workers. The Commission noted that the withdrawal would allow for 'a fresh start or for alternative ways to achieve the intended legislative purpose'. However, the European Commission has not made any further proposals to amend the Pregnant Workers Directive.

3.10 Detriment and unfair dismissal rights

Note that an employee who is subjected to a detriment or dismissed by her employer as a result of exercising her right to take maternity leave can bring a claim for unlawful detriment or automatically unfair dismissal under the ERA and the MPL Regulations. Detriment and unfair dismissal are considered in detail in Chapter 12, 'Detriment and unfair dismissal'.

3.11 Entitlement to maternity leave

The right to take statutory maternity leave (SML) is governed by Ss.71 and 73 ERA and Part II of the MPL Regulations. There is no minimum period of qualifying service for the right to SML – it is available to all employees, regardless of length of service, hours of work, the number of people employed by the employer, or whether employment is temporary or permanent. However, in order to qualify for statutory maternity pay (SMP), a woman must have completed 26 weeks' continuous service by the beginning of the 14th week before the expected week of childbirth – see Chapter 5, 'Statutory maternity pay'.

Note that since 'childbirth' is defined in Reg 2 as 'the birth of a living child or the birth of a child whether living or dead after 24 weeks of pregnancy', an employee would still be entitled to SML in the event of her child surviving for only a short time after birth, or in the event of a stillbirth 24 weeks or more into the pregnancy.

3.12 **Multiple births.** Maternity leave is the same for multiple as for single births. In its proposals to amend the Pregnant Workers Directive (see under 'General considerations – European law reform' above) the European Parliament proposed that the compulsory period of maternity leave should be increased for each additional child, in accordance with national law. However, this proposal was ultimately withdrawn.

3.13 **Surrogacy.** For the purpose of taking maternity leave, it is the birth mother who is regarded as the child's mother. Surrogate mothers are therefore entitled to take full maternity leave, regardless of whether or not they continue to have contact with the child following the birth – as are mothers who give their child up for adoption following the birth. But what legal rights does the intended mother in a surrogacy arrangement have?

In C-D v S-T ET Case No.2505033/11 the Newcastle employment tribunal made a reference to the European Court of Justice (ECJ) for a preliminary ruling as to whether, under the Pregnant Workers Directive and/or the recast

EU Equal Treatment Directive (No.2006/54) ('the recast Equal Treatment Directive'), a woman who becomes a mother through a surrogacy arrangement is entitled to maternity leave in order to bond with her baby, establish breastfeeding and maintain and develop her family life. Advocate General Kokott delivered her opinion in the case on 26 September 2013 (Case C-167/12). In her view, an intended mother who begins to care for an infant directly after it is born, as planned pursuant to an agreement concluded in advance with the surrogate mother, takes the place of its biological mother and, from that point onwards, must have the same rights as would otherwise be conferred on the surrogate mother. She concluded that, where surrogacy is permitted in the Member State concerned and the national requirements regarding surrogacy have been satisfied, the intended mother must be given the right to take maternity leave following the birth of the child if she takes the child into her care. The AG considered that both the intended mother and the surrogate must take the two weeks' compulsory leave required under the Directive, but that any further leave taken by the surrogate mother must be deducted from that available to the intended mother, and vice versa.

However, on the same day that AG Kokott delivered her opinion, a different **3.14** Advocate General came to the opposite conclusion in Z v A Government Department and the Board of Management of a Community School (Case C-363/12), a reference from the Equality Tribunal in Ireland. In that case, AG Wahl considered that the purpose of the Directive is to help women recover from the physical and mental constraints of enduring pregnancy and the aftermath of childbirth. This being so, he felt unable to read the Directive as according a right to paid leave equivalent to maternity leave in the case of a mother who has had her genetic child through a surrogacy arrangement. He pointed out that to extend the Directive in this way would be inconsistent, since no such right would be extended to adoptive mothers, who are not currently entitled to paid leave under EU law (although they may be entitled to take adoption leave under domestic UK law).

The ECJ handed down judgment in CD v ST 2014 ICR D26, ECJ, on 18 March 2014. It held that a commissioning mother who has had a baby through a surrogacy arrangement is not entitled to the maternity leave provided for in Article 8 of the Directive. The Court noted that pregnant workers and workers who have recently given birth or who are breastfeeding are in an especially vulnerable situation which makes it necessary for them to be granted the right to maternity leave. While the Court had previously held that maternity leave is also intended to ensure that the special relationship between a woman and her child is protected, that objective concerns only the period after 'pregnancy and childbirth'. Thus, the granting of maternity leave pursuant to Article 8 presupposes that the worker has been pregnant and has given birth to a child. This was confirmed by the ECJ's decision in Mayr v Bäckerei und Konditorei Gerhard Flöckner OHG 2008 IRLR 387, ECJ. There, the Court stated that it is apparent, both from the wording of Article 10 of the Directive, which protects against dismissal, and from the Directive's primary objective, that to benefit from the protection in Article 10 the pregnancy in question must have started. Consequently, Member States are not required to grant a commissioning mother who has had a baby through a surrogacy arrangement a right to maternity leave under Article 8, even if she may or does breastfeed the baby following the birth. However, the Directive does not preclude Member States from introducing provisions more favourable to commissioning mothers who have babies through surrogacy arrangements.

3.15 And this is exactly what has happened in the UK. Attempts to grant intended parents in a surrogacy arrangement rights to leave and pay equal to those available to birth parents were initially made through a Private Member's Bill – the Surrogate Parents (Leave, Pay and Allowance Arrangements) Bill – which was presented to Parliament on 17 April 2012. However, the Bill failed to complete its passage through Parliament before the end of the session. Nevertheless, the Government confirmed in July 2012 that it was considering the possibility of granting paid leave to mothers of children born by surrogates. Subsequently, S.122 of the Children and Families Act 2014 (CFA), which received Royal Assent on 13 March 2014, extended the right to take paternity leave and pay and adoption leave and pay to intended parents in a surrogacy arrangement who are eligible for, and intend to apply for, a parental order. Details of the new scheme are contained in the Paternity, Adoption and Shared Parental Leave (Parental Order Cases) Regulations 2014 SI 2014/3096, which came into force on 1 December 2014. In addition, 'parental order parents' who are eligible for adoption leave may be entitled to shared parental leave. Adoption leave is discussed in Chapter 6, 'Adoption leave and pay', while shared parental leave is considered in Chapter 8, 'Shared parental leave and pay'.

Note that individuals who become parents through a surrogacy arrangement may have an entirely separate right to adoption or paternity leave and pay, depending on the circumstances – see further Chapter 6, 'Adoption leave and pay', and Chapter 7, 'Paternity leave and pay'.

3.16 Employees only

SML can only be taken by employees and not by other types of 'worker' or the self-employed. 'Employee' means an individual who has entered into or works under a contract of employment, which is defined as a contract of service or apprenticeship, whether express or implied, and (if express) whether oral or in writing – Reg 2(1) MPL Regulations. These definitions are identical to those that apply for the purposes of unfair dismissal and redundancy under the ERA and reference should be had to IDS Employment Law Handbook, 'Contracts of Employment' (2014), Chapter 2, 'Employment status', for discussion of the law in this area.

Share fisherwomen and the police are specifically excluded from the statutory right to take SML – Ss.199(2) and 200 ERA. However, seafarers employed on ships registered under S.8 of the Merchant Shipping Act 1995 are covered provided that the ship is registered as belonging to a port in Great Britain, that under her contract of employment the employee does not work wholly outside Great Britain, and that she is ordinarily resident in Great Britain – S.199(7) and (8). Crown employees and parliamentary staff are also covered – Ss.191, 194 and 195, but members of the armed forces are not – S.192 ERA (read with para 16, Sch 2). (Note, however, that provision for maternity leave equating to the statutory arrangements is made by the Armed Forces Occupational Maternity Scheme.)

Employee shareholders. Section 31 of the Growth and Infrastructure Act **3.17** 2013, which came into force on 1 September 2013, added a new S.205A to the ERA that introduced a new type of employment contract: an 'employee shareholder' contract. Under this type of contract, an individual agrees to waive certain employment rights, including the right to claim ordinary unfair dismissal, in return for at least £2,000 worth of free shares in the employer's company. These shares are subject to a number of favourable tax concessions. The right to take SML is not one of the rights that an individual must waive in order to become an employee shareholder and such an employee is therefore entitled to take SML in the normal way. However, an employee shareholder is required to give 16 weeks' notice of her intention to return to work during a period of maternity leave (as opposed to the eight weeks' notice that would usually be required) – S.205A(3)(a). For more information about the employee shareholder scheme, see IDS Employment Law Handbook, 'Atypical and Flexible Working' (2014), Chapter 7, 'Employee shareholders'.

Workers and the self-employed. It is worth noting here that an employer's **3.18** obligations to safeguard the health and safety of new and expectant mothers apply in respect of risks to the health and safety of persons not in its employment arising out of or in connection with the conduct by it of the undertaking – see Chapter 2, 'Health and safety protection'. This could entail those workers or self-employed people who are not employees (including agency workers) being granted a period of time off following childbirth akin, at least, to the compulsory maternity leave period – see further Chapter 2, 'Health and safety protection'.

Furthermore, the European Union has adopted a Directive ensuring equal treatment for the self-employed: the EU Equal Treatment of Self-Employed Workers Directive (No.2010/41). Under this Directive, which had to be implemented by 5 August 2012, Member States must provide maternity leave rights equivalent to those provided under the Pregnant Workers Directive to self-employed women and 'assisting spouses' (meaning the spouses and 'life partners' of self-employed workers who are involved in the same work). In the

UK Maternity Allowance is available for self-employed workers, subject to the worker having made sufficient national insurance contributions – see Chapter 5, 'Statutory maternity pay', under 'Maternity Allowance'.

3.19 Relationship with other statutory leave rights

A period of leave guaranteed by EC law cannot affect the right to take another period of leave also guaranteed by that law – Commission v Luxembourg 2005 ECR I-3067, ECJ (a case on maternity, adoption and parental leave). So where a Finnish employer refused to allow an employee to interrupt her pre-arranged parental leave in order to take up paid maternity leave, it was depriving her of her rights attaching to maternity leave under Articles 8 and 11 of the Pregnant Workers Directive and was also discriminating against her contrary to the EU Equal Treatment Directive (No.76/207) (now consolidated into the recast Equal Treatment Directive) – Kiiski v Tampereen Kaupunki 2008 1 CMLR 5, ECJ. Thus, an employer will be obliged to allow an employee to cancel or rearrange her parental leave dates in order to take maternity leave. The same principle would apply where any other period of statutory leave overlaps with maternity leave; for example, statutory annual leave – see further 'Terms and conditions during maternity leave – annual leave' below.

It is possible that the principle laid down in the Commission v Luxembourg case (above) could be relied upon in this country by a woman who conceives again within three months of giving birth. According to the MPL Regulations (see 'Commencement of ordinary maternity leave' below), her second period of SML would start before her first period had finished (assuming she does not return to work early), given that the gestation period is around 40 weeks and the latest date SML can start is the day following the birth. But as she would thus be sacrificing part of her first SML entitlement, she might argue that her second period of SML should be delayed to start immediately after the end of her first period of SML in order to comply with European law. Whether this argument would be successful would depend on whether the court or tribunal considered the principle in the above cases to be limited to the minimum entitlement under EC law, or extended to more generous domestic statutory provisions.

3.20 Notice provisions

In order to qualify for SML an employee must notify her employer no later than the end of the 15th week before the expected week of childbirth (EWC) (or if that is not reasonably practicable, as soon as is reasonably practicable) of the following:

- her pregnancy – Reg 4(1)(a)(i) MPL Regulations

- her EWC – Reg 4(1)(a)(ii). The EWC is the week, beginning with midnight between Saturday and Sunday, in which it is expected that childbirth will occur – Reg 2(1). The employer may request a medical certificate as evidence of the EWC – see 'Medical certificate' below

- the date on which she intends her ordinary maternity leave (OML) to start – Reg 4(1)(a)(iii). Note, however, that that date cannot be earlier than the beginning of the 11th week before the EWC – Reg 4(2)(b). Notice under this provision must be in writing if the employer so requests – Reg 4(2)(a).

This information may be given at different times if the employee so wishes.

The notice of pregnancy does not need to be in writing and there is no requirement that the employee state whether she wishes to take additional maternity leave (AML) – it is presumed that she will take it. Furthermore, the employee does not at this stage have to inform her employer of whether or not she intends to tack a period of unpaid parental leave onto the end of her SML or to curtail her SML and take shared parental leave instead.

Personalised information. The Government's public service information **3.21** website (www.gov.uk) provides a link to a tool giving employees personalised information about their maternity rights and responsibilities, including a calendar of key dates.

Changing the start date. An employee who has given notice under Reg 4(1) **3.22** can revise the date on which she intends to start her OML by giving a further notice – Reg 4(1A). The further notice does not have to be in writing unless the employer so requests – Reg 4(2)(a). If the employee wants to delay the start of her OML, she must tell the employer 28 days before the date previously notified. If she wants to bring the start date forward, she must tell the employer 28 days before the new start date (which must be no earlier than the beginning of the 11th week before the EWC). However, if it is not reasonably practicable to give the requisite 28 days' notice, then the employee must tell her employer of the change as soon as is reasonably practicable – Reg 4(1A).

Time limits. The information required under Reg 4(1)(a) should normally be **3.23** given by the end of the 15th week before the EWC (often referred to as the 'qualifying week' when talking about SMP, since an employee must have 26 weeks' service at the end of this week to qualify). The EWC starts at midnight on a Saturday night – Reg 2(1). Therefore, to calculate the latest possible date for giving notice, start with the Saturday immediately before the date on which childbirth is expected and count back a further 14 Saturdays.

Notification later than the end of the 15th week before the EWC will not disentitle an employee from taking SML if it was 'not reasonably practicable' for her to give notice by that date and she gave notice as soon as it was reasonably practicable to do so. For example, it may not be reasonably practicable to give notice by the required date if the employee did not start working for the employer until a later date. Alternatively, the employee herself may not have been aware that she was pregnant. The 'not reasonably practicable' formula is frequently used in connection with the time limits for bringing claims under a wide range of employment rights and the relevant law is discussed in more detail in IDS Employment Law Handbook, 'Employment Tribunal Practice and Procedure' (2014), Chapter 5, 'Time limits', under '"Not reasonably practicable" extension'.

3.24 **Medical certificate.** In order to qualify for SML the employee must, if requested to do so by her employer, produce a certificate from a doctor or a registered midwife stating the EWC – Reg 4(1)(b). There is no required form for the certificate but it will normally be a MAT B1 form, which is that prescribed under the Schedule to the Statutory Maternity Pay (Medical Evidence) Regulations 1987 SI 1987/235 for proving entitlement to SMP. The employee will lose her right to SML if she fails to comply with the employer's request. However, no time limit is specified for the production of a certificate, and so in theory an employee could produce this certificate at any time before – or even after – starting her maternity leave. (The MPL Regulations do not provide an exception in the case of employees who give birth prematurely before they have been able to produce a certificate. Presumably, the employer could agree to accept the certificate retrospectively in such circumstances.)

The employer must make it clear that it is asking for a certificate. In Eagles v Cadman t/a Baby Days ET Case No.20154/82 the employer's request read: 'Please supply as requested under the [ERA] the expected week of confinement date.' The employee produced a card from a midwife that was not a certificate, but the tribunal pointed out that she had not been asked for a certificate as such, and so had not lost her rights.

3.25 To safeguard her right to SML, an employee only has to produce a medical certificate if the employer asks for one. But if the same employee is claiming SMP she must produce medical evidence of the expected week of childbirth in any event by the end of the third week of the maternity pay period. This time limit can be extended to the end of the 13th week of the maternity pay period in special circumstances – see Chapter 5, 'Statutory maternity pay', under 'Medical evidence'. In practice, the medical evidence necessary for SMP, which will usually be a MAT B1 form issued by a doctor or midwife, will suffice as the certificate that the employer can request before granting maternity leave. Note, however, that for the purpose of claiming SMP the MAT B1 form cannot be dated earlier than the 20th week before the expected week of confinement. There is no such requirement if the certificate is only being used as evidence of entitlement to SML.

3.26 **Exceptions.** There are two exceptions to the requirement in Reg 4(1)(a)(iii) that an employee must give notice of the date on which she intends her OML to commence. These are where:

- her OML commences automatically by virtue of Reg 6(1)(b) on the day following any day after the beginning of the fourth week before the EWC on which she has been absent from work wholly or mainly because of pregnancy – Reg 4(3)(a). The employee must notify the employer, as soon as is reasonably practicable, of the fact that she is absent wholly or partly because of pregnancy, and of the date that absence commenced – Reg 4(3)(b)

- her OML commences automatically on the day following childbirth by virtue of Reg 6(2) – Reg 4(4)(a). The employee must notify the employer, as soon as is reasonably practicable, that she has given birth, and of the date on which it occurred – Reg 4(4)(b).

The employee does not have to give the above information in writing unless the employer so requests – Reg 4(5). For further details, see 'Commencement of ordinary maternity leave' below.

In either of the above situations, the employee is entitled to take SML regardless **3.27** of whether she gave the requisite notice of the date on which she intended her OML to start in accordance with Reg 4(1)(a)(iii). However, the employee must still have complied with Reg 4(1)(a)(i) and (ii), which require her to have notified the employer of the fact that she is pregnant and of her EWC no later than the end of the 15th week before the EWC or as soon as reasonably practicable thereafter; and with Reg 4(3)(b) or Reg 4(4)(b) as appropriate (see above). She must also have produced a medical certificate as evidence of the EWC if so requested by the employer under Reg 4(1)(b) – see 'Medical certificate' above.

Failure to give correct notice. If an employee fails to give any or all of the **3.28** required notifications under Reg 4, or has given the notifications late and is unable to satisfy the 'not reasonably practicable' test, she will lose her right to SML. However, it is not entirely clear what rights the employee and employer have in this situation. A DTI consultation paper issued prior to the enactment of the MPL Regulations in 1999 proposed that a woman who started her maternity leave without giving the required notifications should be treated as being on unauthorised absence. However, this proposal did not make it into the Regulations themselves and there has been no further legislative clarification. The Pregnant Workers Directive is of no assistance in resolving the issue: by virtue of Article 2, the rights in that Directive are only available to a worker who 'informs her employer of her condition, in accordance with national legislation and/or national practice'. In other words, the Directive is subordinate to the UK rules on notification.

What is clear is that the employment contract will not come to an end simply by virtue of the woman taking unauthorised maternity leave, unless she resigns or is dismissed. However, under S.99 ERA and Reg 20(3), a dismissal is automatically unfair if the reason or principal reason for it relates to pregnancy, childbirth, or the fact that the employee sought to take maternity leave (among other things). Although we are not aware of any tribunal cases on the point, this would arguably cover the situation where an employee is dismissed for taking maternity leave despite having failed to comply with the notice provisions. Even if tribunals were not to take this view, it would still be open to an employee who has two years' service to argue that the dismissal was unfair on ordinary principles – see Chapter 12, 'Detriment and unfair dismissal', under '"Ordinary" unfair dismissal'. In Thurisamy v Alma Enterprises Ltd ET Case No.27627/94, for instance, T failed to give her employer the relevant notices until just before she left on maternity leave. Her employer wrote to her once she had started leave stating that since she had not complied with the statutory requirements her job would not be kept open for her. In finding the dismissal unfair, the tribunal took into account the unsatisfactory arrangements made by the company to keep its female employees (many of whom spoke English as a second language) aware of their rights, the action the claimant took before taking leave, and the very swift action taken by the employer to terminate the employment on the technical ground that T had not provided the necessary information.

3.29 In addition to claiming unfair dismissal, an employee who is dismissed in these circumstances or who suffers any unfavourable treatment may also have grounds for a complaint of pregnancy and maternity discrimination, or sex discrimination. See Chapter 13, 'Discrimination and equal pay', under 'Direct discrimination – pregnancy and maternity discrimination', for a detailed discussion of discrimination law in relation to pregnancy and childbirth.

While it is by no means certain that an employee in a particular case would succeed in any of the above claims if she was dismissed or suffered a detriment through not giving the requisite notice to take SML, until the law is clarified there does not appear to be any action that an employer can take against the employee without running a serious risk. The most likely position is that an employee who has failed to give the required notices loses nothing more than the special rights associated with being on SML, such as the benefit of her contractual terms and conditions by virtue of Ss.71 and 73 ERA and Reg 9. However, this is by no means certain, and the safest and simplest course for employers to take in these circumstances is probably to ignore the breach altogether.

3.30 **Employer's notice of end date**

An employer must notify the employee of the date her AML (and hence her SML) will end – Reg 7(6) MPL Regulations. The notice does not have to be in writing, although employers would be well advised to give it in writing in order to provide evidence of the requirement having been complied with. Indeed, the latest guidance issued by the Department of Business, Innovation and Skills states that the employer must write to the employee, within 28 days, informing her when she is due back at work (see 'Pregnancy at Work: what you need to know as an employer. Babies due on or after 3 April 2011'). This is obviously good advice but, strictly speaking, it goes beyond what is actually required by Reg 7(6).

The obligation to give notice of the date SML will end is triggered where:

- the employee gives notice under Reg 4(1) of the date she intends to start OML

- the employee gives notice under Reg 4(1A) of a variation in the date she intends to start OML

- the employee gives notice under Reg 4(3) that she has been absent for a pregnancy-related reason four weeks or less before the EWC, and of the date that absence started

- the employee gives notice under Reg 4(4) that she has given birth and the date of birth.

3.31 The employer has to respond within 28 days of the date on which it receives notification from the employee, except in the case of a variation notice under Reg 4(1A), when the employer has 28 days from the date OML actually starts in which to respond – Reg 7(7). There does not seem to be any explanation for this anomaly.

Note that, even if the employer has already notified the employee of the end date, the obligation will be triggered again if the employee gives another notice.

3.32 **Employer's failure to give notice.** If the employer fails to inform the employee of the date SML will end, it will not be able to complain if the employee comes back from maternity leave too early or too late.

Normally speaking, an employee who wishes to return to work earlier than the end of her SML period must give at least eight weeks' notice of the date on which she intends to return – Reg 11(1). However, this obligation does not apply if her employer failed to give her notice in accordance with Reg 7(6) and (7) of the date on which her SML period would end – Reg 11(5) (see Chapter 4, 'Returning to work after maternity leave', under 'Date of return to work').

3.33 Similarly, any detriment suffered by the employee as a result of coming back too late will be unlawful under Reg 19 and any dismissal will be automatically unfair under Reg 20. These provisions apply if either of the following conditions are met:

- the employer did not notify the employee, 'in accordance with Reg 7(6) and (7) or otherwise', of the date her SML period would end and she reasonably believed that SML had not ended – Regs 19(2)(ee)(i) and 20(3)(ee)(i), or

- the employer gave the employee less than 28 days' notice of the date on which SML would end and it was not reasonably practicable for her to return on that date – Regs 19(2)(ee)(ii) and 20(3)(ee)(ii).

Note that the first of the above conditions refers to a failure to notify the employee 'in accordance with Reg 7(6) and (7) *or otherwise*' (our stress). For the purposes of avoiding a finding of automatically unfair dismissal or unlawful detriment, it is not therefore necessary for notice of the end date to be given within the 28-day time limit prescribed by Reg 7(7), provided it is given 28 days or more before the end of the SML period. In Sethi v Greentech International Ltd ET Case No.1900752/07 an employer confirmed an employee's maternity leave expiry date belatedly, but nevertheless thereby avoided a finding of automatic unfair dismissal or unlawful detriment under the MPL Regulations. However, on the facts of the case, the employer's failure to make proper arrangements for the employee's return and assumption that it would not be 'appropriate' for her to return amounted to a fundamental breach of the implied term of trust and confidence, entitling her to resign and claim unfair constructive dismissal. For further details on detriment and unfair dismissal, see Chapter 12, 'Detriment and unfair dismissal'.

3.34 In some cases the employee may give notice of her intention to return to work early at the same time as she notifies her employer of the fact of her pregnancy, her EWC and the date on which she wishes to start her leave (she may, for example, be intending to take shared parental leave with the father (or her spouse/partner) – see Chapter 8, 'Shared parental leave and pay'). There is no suggestion in the MPL Regulations that in such circumstances the employer is released from the obligation to notify the employee of the date her SML would normally be expected to end. The employee is at liberty to change her mind as to her return date subject to giving proper notice, and so both parties need to be sure of the length of her legal entitlement. Best practice in such cases would probably be for the employer to notify the employee of the date SML would have ended had she not notified it of her intention to return early, but to acknowledge the date on which she intends to return.

3.35 Commencement of ordinary maternity leave

An employee's OML commences on the earliest of:

- the date she has notified to her employer as the date she intends her OML to start under Reg 4(1)(a)(iii) or 4(1A) MPL Regulations (see under 'Entitlement to maternity leave – notice provisions' above) – Reg 6(1)(a)

- the day which follows the first day, after the beginning of the fourth week before the EWC, on which she is absent from work wholly or partly because of pregnancy – Reg 6(1)(b) (see 'Pregnancy-related absence' below), or

- the day which follows the day on which childbirth occurs – Reg 6(2) ('childbirth' meaning the birth of a living child at any time or a stillborn child after 24 weeks of pregnancy – Reg 2(1)). In such circumstances the

OML period starts automatically on the day following childbirth even when that day falls before the beginning of the 11th week before the EWC.

The effect of these provisions is that, subject to certain restrictions, a woman can choose when she starts her OML. The restrictions are that leave cannot commence earlier than the 11th week before the EWC (see Reg 4(2)(b)) – except following a premature birth – or later than the day following the actual date of birth. Leave begins automatically on the day after the child is born, or earlier if the employee is absent from work because of pregnancy at any time during the four weeks before the EWC. Note that if the employer tries to specify the date on which leave must start, e.g. by way of a term in the contract of employment, this can be overridden by the employee's statutory right to choose – Inner London Education Authority v Nash 1979 ICR 229, EAT. Where a woman's OML is triggered automatically under Reg 6(1)(b) or 6(2), she must inform her employer of the reason for her absence, or of the birth, as soon as is reasonably practicable – see 'Entitlement to maternity leave – notice provisions' above. Problems may arise where the employee is absent from work after the fourth week before the EWC but does not give notice under Reg 4(3)(b) because she takes the view that her absence was not due wholly or partly to pregnancy. If a dispute then arises as to the reason for her absence, she could theoretically find herself excluded from the right to SML on the ground that she failed to comply with the statutory notice requirements. However, where the employee's failure to give notice arose from her genuine and reasonable belief that she was not on pregnancy-related absence, we suspect that the courts would take a sympathetic approach to avoid depriving her of her statutory rights.

Compulsory maternity leave. Note that where OML is triggered by early **3.36** childbirth under Reg 6(2), it begins on the day following the birth. Compulsory maternity leave, on the other hand, starts on the same day as childbirth, a day earlier than OML – see 'Compulsory maternity leave' below.

Pregnancy-related absence
3.37
An employee who is absent from work due to illness will normally be able to take sick leave until she starts her SML. If the illness is unrelated to her pregnancy, she can continue taking sick leave up to the date that she has notified her employer as being the date she intends to start OML (even if this is after the beginning of the fourth week before the EWC). If, however, the employee is absent from work in the four-week period (starting with a Sunday) before the start of the EWC 'wholly or partly because of pregnancy', the OML period starts automatically on the following day – Reg 6(1)(b).

On a strict reading of this provision, a woman who has any time off on account of her pregnancy in the last four weeks before the EWC will find that her OML will be deemed to have commenced even though she is, after the absence, fit to continue work. It is not clear from the wording of the Regulations whether the

81

employee must be absent for a whole working day in order for her leave to be triggered. Reg 6(1)(b) merely provides that OML commences on 'the day which follows the first day... on which she is absent from work... because of pregnancy'. Arguably, any period of absence, however short, would be sufficient. If this interpretation is correct, an employee who comes into work a few minutes late for a reason connected with her pregnancy, e.g. fatigue or morning sickness, or who leaves work a few minutes early for a pregnancy-related reason, may find that her OML period is triggered under Reg 6(1)(b) – although in practice many employers will make a distinction between 'absence' and 'lateness' in their employment policies. Without the benefit of any case law on this point, it seems that it will be up to the parties how they choose to interpret the meaning of 'the first day... on which she is absent from work'. Note, though, that the HMRC guidance on an employer's liability to pay SMP in certain circumstances, 'Statutory Maternity Pay: employee circumstances that affect payment', states that the statutory maternity pay period and maternity leave start on 'the day after the first *complete* day of absence from work because of [the employee's] pregnancy within the four-week period' (our stress). However, Reg 2(4) of the Statutory Maternity Pay (General) Regulations 1986 SI 1986/1960, which deals with the issue, lacks this specificity.

3.38 Given that a woman's SML may be automatically triggered by pregnancy-related absence at any time after she has reached the fourth week before the EWC, the crucial question arises as to what will be regarded as absence 'wholly or partly because of pregnancy'. On the face of it, the phrase would appear to cover a wide range of ailments including morning sickness, back-pain, high blood pressure, anaemia, fatigue and urinary tract infections. However, in some cases a medical certificate will be needed to confirm whether or not the absence is pregnancy-related.

The automatic triggering of SML under Reg 6(1)(b) was introduced to prevent employees effectively extending their maternity leave period by taking a period of pregnancy-related sick leave so as to delay the start of OML. However, Reg 6(1)(b) has been drafted widely and appears to go further than this. It seems that OML can also be triggered by a suspension from work on health and safety grounds, or even by the employee exercising her right to take time off work to attend an ante-natal appointment – see Chapter 1, 'Time off for ante-natal care', and Chapter 2, 'Health and safety protection'. But given the administrative difficulties involved in changing the start date of SML at late notice, the employer may agree to waive the absence – see 'Waiving days of pregnancy-related absence' below.

3.39 **Effect of triggering provisions.** An employee who finds that her OML has been triggered by Reg 6(1)(b) is likely to find herself starting maternity leave earlier than she intended, and consequently her maternity leave will end sooner.

This may cause particular inconvenience to women who planned to start their maternity leave at the last possible moment.

Problems may also arise where an employee who is unaware of the triggering effect of Reg 6(1)(b) takes a short period of pregnancy-related absence after the beginning of the fourth week before the EWC but then returns to work. When her employer discovers that her absence was pregnancy-related the employee may be informed that her OML has already started and be sent home again. Since her maternity pay period would also have been automatically triggered by her absence, she may additionally lose SMP at the prescribed rate for any week in which she has worked after the start of the maternity pay period – see Chapter 5, 'Statutory maternity pay', under 'Disentitlement to statutory maternity pay'.

Alternatively, the employee may inform her employer of the reason for her **3.40** absence but, ignorant of the law, may continue to work up to the birth (or her intended leaving date, if earlier) without any objection by her employer. In this situation, the employee is likely to assume that her OML runs from the date on which she left work to have her baby. This raises the question of whether the employer, having failed to alert the employee to the effect of the triggering provision at the time of the pregnancy-related absence, may nevertheless insist at a later date that the OML period began to run when the employee was first absent from work on account of her pregnancy. In this situation it may be arguable, depending on the facts of the case, that the employer, by its conduct, has impliedly waived the effect of the triggering provision, thus giving rise to a 'composite right' to maternity leave – see 'Waiving days of pregnancy-related absence' below. However, there may still be implications for the employee's right to statutory maternity pay.

Working beyond a pregnancy-related absence in the last four weeks of **3.41** **pregnancy.** The law is unclear as to whether an employee is entitled to carry on working after OML has been triggered under Reg 6(1)(b) where her employer does not agree to a waiver (see 'Waiving days of pregnancy-related absence' below). One view suggests that once OML has started, in the absence of agreement with the employer an employee can only return to work before the end of the SML period if she gives eight weeks' notice in accordance with Reg 11 ('Requirement to notify intention to return during a maternity leave period'). If she attempts to return to work without giving that notice the employer is not obliged to pay her. But if this is the case, it would not in any event avoid the automatic trigger because the eight weeks' notice would take the employee beyond the expected date of birth. The giving of such notice would therefore be of no use to the employee in these circumstances.

An alternative view is that the OML period, like AML, is in effect a protected period during which the employee is entitled, but not obliged, to be absent from work. This proposition is derived from S.71(1) ERA, which provides that 'an employee may... be absent from work at any time during an ordinary maternity leave period'. (S.73(1) makes a similar provision with regard to AML.) S.71(4)(a) and (5) (and S.73(4)(a) and (5)), read in conjunction with Reg 9, then goes on to explain that an employee who 'exercises her right under subsection (1)' – i.e. the right to be absent – is entitled to the benefit of her terms and conditions of employment that would have applied if she had not been absent, except those relating to remuneration. The implication of this is that if she does not exercise her right to be absent she should still be entitled to remuneration. With the exception of the requirement to take compulsory maternity leave in S.72 and Reg 8, there is nothing in the ERA or the MPL Regulations to compel the employee to exercise her right to be absent during the OML period, the only exception being Reg 11, described above, whereby the employee must give at least eight weeks' notice if she intends to return to work before the end of the SML period (although there would be nothing to prevent the employee giving such notice well before her SML had started). An employee who is fit and willing to work and who has not yet exercised her right to be absent during maternity leave could potentially complain of pregnancy discrimination under S.18 of the Equality Act 2010 (EqA) or, alternatively, deduction of wages if her employer refuses to pay her. Of course, even if the employer does pay her, the employee would lose a day of leave for every day she works after SML has started (unless the employer agrees to extend the maternity leave period, giving rise to a 'composite right' – see 'Waiving days of pregnancy-related absence' below), and she would lose a week's statutory maternity pay at the prescribed rate of £138.18 – or at the earnings-related rate, if lower – for every week in which she does any work after the start of the maternity pay period.

3.42 **Waiving days of pregnancy-related absence.** The Government's guidance for employers on an employee's rights to maternity leave and pay used to state that employers '*may* start an employee's SML as soon as she is absent from work for a pregnancy-related reason' after the beginning of the fourth week before the EWC (our stress). Additional guidance on 'Managing expectant and new mothers at work' stated: 'You are entitled (though not obliged) to start her maternity leave automatically.' In other words, the advice was that pregnancy-related absence in the four weeks before the due date did not start the employee's maternity leave automatically. However, the Government's guidance on this point has now changed. In its current guidance for employers on 'Pregnant employees' rights', it states that 'if the employee is off work for a pregnancy-related illness in the four weeks before the baby is due, maternity leave... *will start automatically*' (our stress). Similarly, the employees' guide, 'Maternity pay and leave', states that SML '*starts automatically* if you're off work for a pregnancy-related illness in the four weeks before the week... that your baby is due' (our stress).

However, the fact that there is no explicit statutory authority allowing an employer to ignore any pregnancy-related absence in the four-week period, the discretion to do so might nevertheless be seen as implicit within the 'composite right' provisions of Reg 21. This regulation provides that, where an employee has a statutory right to maternity leave and also a 'right which corresponds to that right and which arises under the employee's contract of employment or otherwise', the employee can take advantage of whichever right is more favourable to her. This is known as a composite right. It means that, where an employee's OML would normally have been triggered by a pregnancy-related absence, the employer can offer her the opportunity to delay the start of maternity leave without any loss in the overall period of leave.

The employer cannot, however, insist on the employee delaying the start of her **3.43** leave as it is her choice whether she starts leave in accordance with her statutory entitlement or on terms offered by her employer. Conversely, the employee cannot insist on delaying her maternity leave if her employer does not agree. Note that there is no need for a specific contractual provision or variation to cover this, since under Reg 21 the right can arise 'under the employee's contract of employment *or otherwise*' (our stress), and so an ad hoc arrangement between the parties will suffice. However, it would be advisable to record the agreement in writing to avoid any misunderstanding. See 'Contractual and composite maternity rights' below for further details on the operation of Reg 21.

Pregnancy-related absence and maternity pay. Unfortunately, where an **3.44** employer and an employee agree to ignore a period of pregnancy-related absence so as to defer the start of OML, a problem arises in relation to the payment of SMP. The statutory provisions that cause the triggering of the maternity leave period apply in precisely the same way to trigger the SMP period. In other words, entitlement to SMP is automatically triggered by premature childbirth or by pregnancy-related absence occurring during or after the fourth week before the EWC. But, whereas maternity leave entitlement is governed by the ERA and the MPL Regulations, SMP entitlement is governed by the Social Security Contributions and Benefits Act 1992 (SSCBA) and various statutory instruments made under that Act. The 'composite right' provisions in Reg 21 MPL Regulations do *not* apply to SMP and any agreement between the parties to exclude or modify the operation of the SSCBA is void – S.164(6) SSCBA. It follows that, while any agreement by the parties to ignore short periods of pregnancy-related absence may validly delay the start of maternity leave, it will not be effective to prevent the automatic triggering of the maternity pay period. As maternity pay is not payable during any week in which the employee works for the employer after the start of the maternity pay period, the employee could lose out financially – S.165(4) SSCBA. She will still have her full six weeks' payment at the 'earnings-related rate' of 90 per cent of her salary, since payment at this rate will simply be deferred to the next week in which she does no work – S.166(1) SSCBA. However, she will lose one week of her 20 weeks' entitlement to SMP at the prescribed rate of £138.18 – or at the earnings-related rate, if lower – for each week she works after the maternity pay period has been triggered. See Chapter 5, 'Statutory maternity pay', under 'Disentitlement to statutory maternity pay', for a fuller explanation.

In practice, though, the issue is frequently ignored because the employer will simply disregard the trigger date for SMP, start paying it from the date maternity leave actually starts, and claim reimbursement in the normal way from HMRC, which will be unaware of any irregularity. Indeed, many employers in this situation will not be aware that there is a problem either.

3.45 Note that a contractual provision similar to the triggering provisions contained in Reg 6(1)(b) (before it was amended in 2002) was challenged in Boyle and ors v Equal Opportunities Commission 1999 ICR 360, ECJ, as being contrary to the Pregnant Workers Directive and the Equal Treatment Directive (now consolidated into the recast Equal Treatment Directive). However, the European Court held that nothing in those Directives precluded such a clause, notwithstanding that it forced the employee to start her paid maternity leave from a date earlier than that which she had envisaged, and would exclude her from the right to contractual sick leave after the beginning of the sixth week before the EWC.

3.46 **Dismissal or resignation before intended start date**

If an employee is dismissed or resigns before the date she has notified to her employer as that on which she intends to start her OML, or before she notifies any date, she will lose her right to SML. (However, any dismissal for a pregnancy-related reason will be automatically unfair – see Chapter 12, 'Detriment and unfair dismissal', under 'Automatically unfair dismissal'. The employee may also be able to claim pregnancy discrimination under S.18 EqA – see Chapter 13, 'Discrimination and equal pay', under 'Direct discrimination – pregnancy and maternity discrimination', for more details.) Even if the employee has lost her right to OML, she will still be able to claim SMP if she has qualified for it – see Chapter 5, 'Statutory maternity pay', under 'Continuous employment – weeks that count'.

Employers should be cautious about treating any intimation on the employee's part that she does not intend to return to work after her maternity leave as a resignation. Since an employee's contract of employment continues during her SML, the employee's intimation may at most indicate an intention to resign at the end of the maternity leave period. It would be wise for an employer to assume that an employee on maternity leave remains employed unless and until she gives very clear notice that she is resigning, preferably in writing.

3.47 ## Commencement of additional maternity leave

An employee's AML commences on the day after the last day of her OML – Reg 6(3) MPL Regulations (see 'Duration of maternity leave – duration of ordinary maternity leave' below for discussion of the day OML ends). It is important to pinpoint the day AML starts as the rules relating to an employee's right to return to work after maternity leave differ depending on whether she is returning from OML or AML – see Chapter 4, 'Returning to work after maternity leave'. However, there is no longer any distinction between the terms and conditions of employment applicable during OML and AML.

Duration of maternity leave   3.48

In the vast majority of cases an employee's SML will be for a period of 52 weeks (assuming she does not elect to return to work early or take shared parental leave with the father (or her spouse/partner)). This is made up of 26 weeks' OML and 26 weeks' AML.

Duration of ordinary maternity leave   3.49
An employee's OML lasts:

- for a period of 26 weeks from its commencement – Reg 7(1), or

- until the end of the compulsory leave period if later (see 'Compulsory maternity leave' below) – Reg 7(1), or

- until the end of any later period during which she is prohibited by any statutory provision from working by reason of having recently given birth – Reg 7(2) (any provision specified in an order under S.66(2) ERA suspending the employee from work for health and safety reasons is not covered by this paragraph – Reg 7(3) – see further Chapter 2, 'Health and safety protection', under 'Suspension on maternity grounds'), or

- until the employee is dismissed, where she is dismissed during her OML period before it would otherwise have ended – Reg 7(5).

Where an employee's OML ends by reason of dismissal, the employee is entitled to a written statement of reasons for dismissal without having to request one and irrespective of her length of service – S.92(4) ERA.

Note that Reg 7 does not refer to the employee's resignation. However, if an   3.50 employee resigns during her OML period this would inevitably bring that period to an end. This is because the continuation of OML would be inconsistent with the termination of the employment contract. However, as noted under 'Commencement of ordinary maternity leave – dismissal or resignation before intended start date' above, employers should be cautious about treating any intimation on the employee's part that she does not intend to return to work as a resignation. In Wilkinson v RKR Associates Ltd ET Case No.2407150/07, for example, an employee on maternity leave for the second time suggested to her employer that 'she did not think that she would be [able] to continue working whilst looking after two young children'. The tribunal was 'wholly satisfied' that the employee had not thereby given notice of her resignation, and found that she was unfairly dismissed and discriminated against when her employer refused to pay her or give her any work to do upon the expiry of her maternity leave.

Note also that an employee who has resigned or been dismissed is likely to continue to be entitled to statutory maternity pay. See Chapter 5, 'Statutory maternity pay', under 'Continuous employment', for details of the circumstances in which SMP entitlement comes to an end.

3.51 Duration of additional maternity leave

AML lasts for a fixed period of 26 weeks from the end of OML – Reg 7(4). The exception is where the employee is dismissed before the time when her AML would otherwise have ended, in which case AML terminates at the time of the dismissal – Reg 7(5). An employee dismissed during maternity leave is entitled to a written statement of reasons for dismissal without having to request one – S.92(4) ERA.

As with OML, there is no mention in Reg 7 of AML ending upon the employee's resignation. If the employee does resign this would inevitably also bring her AML to an end, because the continuation of AML would be inconsistent with the termination of the employment contract.

3.52 Multiple leave periods?

It is notable that the list of circumstances in Reg 7 which bring OML and AML to an end does not refer to an employee's return to work early from maternity leave. In fact, nowhere in the MPL Regulations does it state, explicitly, that OML and AML end upon the employee returning to work prematurely. Reg 12A (which covers work during the maternity leave period) states that an employee may carry out up to ten days' work for her employer during her statutory maternity leave period 'without bringing her maternity leave to an end', which implies that a return to work for more than ten days will bring maternity leave to an end. But it does not specifically state this. In fact, Reg 11, which deals with the employee's obligation to notify her employer if she decides to return to work early from maternity leave, is entitled 'Requirement to notify intention to return *during* a maternity leave period' (our stress). Although titles do not have substantive legal effect, the choice of wording is illuminating. Reg 11 also refers to an employee returning 'earlier than the end' of her maternity leave period – see, for example, Reg 11(1). (For more on Reg 11, see Chapter 4, 'Returning to work after maternity leave'.)

If the maternity leave period is not, technically, terminated by the employee's return to work, the unavoidable implication is that her entitlement to take maternity leave continues for the full 52-week period despite her early return. It is therefore arguable that she could return to work during OML, for example, and then change her mind and leave again to take AML (though she might sacrifice some SMP in respect of her working time – see Chapter 5, 'Statutory maternity pay'). This analysis of the maternity leave period as a protected period during which the employee is entitled to be absent from work is supported by the wording of the primary legislation from which the maternity leave scheme derives. Ss.71(1) and 73(1) ERA provide that 'an employee may... be absent from work *at any time*' (our stress) during the OML and AML periods, so long as she complies with any prescribed conditions. Neither the statutory wording, nor the 'prescribed conditions' in the secondary legislation, indicate that the employee may be absent only for a single, continuous period of time during OML and AML. On the contrary, the natural reading of the phrase 'at any time' might well lead an employee to believe that she could be absent whenever she chose during SML, provided she complied with any conditions in the MPL Regulations. However, this is not quite as straightforward as one might expect – see 'Difficulties with the "prescribed conditions"' below.

European law. The above argument does not apply in respect of European law. **3.53** The Pregnant Workers Directive states that 'Member States shall take the necessary measures to ensure that workers... are entitled to a *continuous* period of maternity leave of at least 14 weeks allocated before and/or after confinement in accordance with national legislation and/or practice' (our stress) – Article 8(1). But EC law cannot be relied upon to reduce the protection afforded by existing domestic legislation – a point made explicit in Article 1(3) of the Directive. It is, on the contrary, instructive that the UK Government has apparently chosen not to incorporate the 'continuous period' phrase into the domestic legislation. This may be because the SMP scheme, which was in existence at the time the Directive was brought into force in October 1992, clearly envisages that once an employee qualifies for statutory maternity pay, she does not cease to be entitled to it if she carries out any work (though she sacrifices her pay for any week in which she does such work) – see Chapter 5, 'Statutory maternity pay'.

Difficulties with the 'prescribed conditions'. It has to be said, however, that **3.54** no matter how persuasive our argument first appears, the MPL Regulations very clearly do not cater for an employee seeking to take multiple periods of maternity leave during the 52-week SML period. In order to qualify for maternity leave the employee must notify her employer of various matters in accordance with Reg 4 (see 'Entitlement to maternity leave – notice provisions' above). But once the employee has complied with Reg 4, no further notification requirements seem to apply if she wishes to go back onto leave, having previously returned to work. If she goes back onto AML, this is certainly the case – as we noted above, AML simply starts when the OML period ends: there is no need for the employee to 'do' anything. Arguably, however, if the employee were to go back onto leave again during a period of OML, she could be caught by the requirement in Reg 4(1A) that she must give 28 days' notice if she wishes to start OML later than previously notified (or as soon as reasonably practicable if it is not reasonably practicable to give 28 days' notice). However, given that

89

such an employee would have started her earlier period of OML on the date previously notified, it is unclear whether she would, indeed, need to 'vary' that date within the meaning of Reg 4(1A) in order to go back onto leave within the same OML period.

The 'prescribed conditions' might also cause practical difficulties in other respects. In particular, Reg 11 sets out various notification requirements for an employee wishing to return early from maternity leave. Under Reg 11(1), she must give her employer at least eight weeks' notice of the date on which she intends to return, if this is earlier than the end of her AML period. If she subsequently decides that she wishes to return at a later date, she must, again, give eight weeks' notice, ending with the original return date – Reg 11(2A)(b). Clearly, if the employee did, in fact, return on the original return date she notified to her employer, it will be impossible for her to give the notice required by Reg 11(2A)(b) of her return date from a second period of leave. However, this problem might be overcome in cases where the employer had failed to notify the employee of the date on which her AML period would end under Reg 7(6) and (7). This is because Reg 11(5) expressly states that Reg 11 does not apply in such cases – leaving the employee free to give her employer as much, or as little, notice of her planned return(s) to work as she wishes (see Chapter 4, 'Returning to work after maternity leave', for more detail). Even if Reg 11 does apply, the employer might still run the risk of the employee bringing a claim of unlawful detriment, discrimination or unfair dismissal if it sought to penalise her for having taken a further period of maternity leave – see Chapter 12, 'Detriment and unfair dismissal', and Chapter 13, 'Discrimination and equal pay'.

3.55 However, it is clear that the Government's view is that the employee's return to work from SML automatically ends her entitlement to take maternity leave. The Regulations simply do not envisage a situation where an employee may wish to revert to being on maternity leave – hence the many practical difficulties facing employees wishing to do so. This view is supported by the provisions of the new shared parental leave scheme. The Shared Parental Leave Regulations 2014 SI 2014/3050 appear to operate to end an employee's entitlement to maternity leave in any circumstances where she returns to work early. Reg 4(2)(d) provides that in order to be entitled to take shared parental leave, the mother must bring her maternity leave entitlement to an end by submitting a leave curtailment notice in accordance with the provisions of the Maternity and Adoption Leave (Curtailment of Statutory Rights to Leave) Regulations 2014 SI 2014/3052, or by 'return[ing] to work before the end of her statutory maternity leave'.

So while it is clear that an employee cannot take multiple periods of maternity leave during the SML period under the MPL Regulations, an employee whose child is born on or after 5 April 2015 may be able to take multiple leave periods under the new shared parental leave scheme. This scheme provides express provision for employees to take what it calls 'discontinuous' periods of leave. (For more information about the shared parental leave scheme, see Chapter 8, 'Shared parental leave and pay', under 'Planning and booking periods of leave – continuous periods of leave'.)

Compulsory maternity leave 3.56

Section 72(1) ERA states that an employer 'shall not permit an employee... to work during a compulsory maternity leave period'. This is defined in Reg 8 MPL Regulations as the two-week period commencing with the date of birth and it applies to all employees who are entitled to take OML.

The prohibition against working during the compulsory leave period applies to all work, including any work done from home (or a hospital bed). It places the onus on the employer to ensure that an employee does not work during this period and a breach of S.72 by the employer amounts to a criminal offence – S.72(5). It should be noted, however, that the offence is not one of strict liability and the employer will not be guilty of an offence if it did not intend to breach S.72 (Ian McCartney, Standing Committee E, Hansard, 23 February 1999).

Although S.72(3)(b) states that the compulsory maternity leave period should **3.57** fall within the OML period, there is one circumstance in which the compulsory leave will start a day earlier than the OML period. This is where childbirth occurs prematurely, before the employee's notified maternity leave start date, and before her OML has been triggered by any absence. In such circumstances, OML starts 'on the day which follows the day on which childbirth occurs' – Reg 6(2) (see 'Commencement of ordinary maternity leave' above). Her compulsory maternity leave, however, would have started on the day on which childbirth occurred by virtue of Reg 8. The practical significance of this is that the employee in such circumstances would continue to be entitled to receive remuneration as normal on the day on which she gives birth; the requirement to pay SMP does not start until OML starts (see Chapter 5, 'Statutory maternity pay', for a full discussion of SMP).

Otherwise, for all practical purposes, the compulsory maternity leave period will fall within the OML period. If an employee had, in theory, taken all her OML before the baby was born, or had less than 2 weeks remaining, her OML period would be extended until the end of her compulsory maternity leave period by virtue of Reg 7(1) – see 'Duration of maternity leave – duration of ordinary maternity leave' above. This provision was introduced at a time when the OML period was only 14 weeks. Since OML cannot start more than 11 weeks before the EWC, a woman could have used up her entire maternity leave before the end of the compulsory leave period if she started her leave 11 weeks before the EWC and the baby was born more than a week late. Now that a woman has 26 weeks' OML entitlement, the baby would need to be born more than 13 weeks late before this provision would be triggered. Even if such a late birth were physically possible, in practice the woman would almost certainly be induced or have a caesarean well before this time. Therefore the only occasion on which this provision is likely to have any practical effect is in the event of a serious mistake by the doctor or midwife in calculating the EWC.

Note that under S.205 of the Public Health Act 1936 factory workers are prohibited from working for *four* weeks after giving birth.

3.58 Terms and conditions during maternity leave

Sections 71(4) and 73(4) ERA and Reg 9(1) MPL Regulations provide that an employee who takes OML or AML is:

- entitled to the benefit of all the terms and conditions of employment which would have applied if she had not been absent, and

- bound by any obligations arising under those terms and conditions (except in so far as they are inconsistent with the employee's right to take OML or AML).

'Terms and conditions of employment' for these purposes includes 'matters connected with an employee's employment whether or not they arise under her contract of employment, but... does not include terms and conditions about remuneration' – Ss.71(5) and 73(5).

3.59 In other words, an employee's contract of employment continues during her entire SML (unless either party brings it to an end) and she must be treated in all respects as if she were not absent, both in terms of the benefits to which she is entitled and the obligations she owes her employer. The only exceptions to this are that she is not entitled to receive remuneration (unless, of course, her contract expressly states that she will continue to be paid during her SML – see 'Contractual and composite maternity rights' below) and she is not bound by any obligations inconsistent with the taking of SML (e.g. the obligation to turn up and work).

As a result of the Maternity and Parental Leave etc and the Paternity and Adoption Leave (Amendment) Regulations 2008 SI 2008/1966 the previous distinction between OML and AML with respect to terms and conditions of employment no longer applies. These changes were necessary following the High Court's decision in R (Equal Opportunities Commission) v Secretary of State for Trade and Industry 2007 ICR 1234, QBD, that the Sex Discrimination Act 1975 (SDA) did not fully implement the law. Mr Justice Burton, sitting alone, held that certain parts of the SDA – including S.6A (exceptions from the right to claim discrimination in respect of terms and conditions during maternity leave) – did not fully implement the corresponding provisions of the Equal Treatment Directive (now consolidated into the recast Equal Treatment Directive). He accepted the EOC's argument that, applying the decision of the ECJ in Land Brandenburg v Sass 2005 IRLR 147, ECJ, there is no reason why OML and AML should be treated differently. Given that it was not possible to interpret the domestic provisions in line with the Directive, he called for them to be recast. The Government duly complied and on 14 March 2008 the Sex Discrimination Act 1975 (Amendment) Regulations 2008 SI 2008/656 were published.

Section 6A as recast (now para 17 of Schedule 9 to the Equality Act 2010 **3.60** (EqA)) eliminated the distinction between OML (i.e. the first 26 weeks) and AML (i.e. weeks 27 to 52) in respect of non-pay benefits under the contract of employment. As a result, employers who remove non-cash benefits from employees during AML will be laying themselves open to pregnancy and maternity discrimination claims under S.18 EqA – as well as to detriment claims under the MPL Regulations. These changes were reflected in the Maternity and Parental Leave etc and the Paternity and Adoption Leave (Amendment) Regulations, which made the necessary changes to the MPL Regulations to bring them into line with the SDA.

Remuneration
3.61

As we saw above, an employee on maternity leave is entitled to benefit from all of her terms and conditions of employment, with the exception of those relating to remuneration. It is therefore important to determine what exactly is meant by 'remuneration'.

Regulation 9(3) provides that 'only sums payable to an employee by way of wages or salary are to be treated as remuneration'. This definition seems to cover only the actual monetary payments that an employee receives from her employer for her work (i.e. the monetary elements of a woman's contract that are replaced by SMP, Maternity Allowance or contractual maternity pay) and not other benefits which the employee receives through her employment. However, HMRC takes the view that benefits which have a transferable cash value should also be treated as remuneration (in contrast to non-cash benefits in kind) – see its guidance document, 'Statutory maternity leave – salary sacrifice and non-cash benefits'. (Note that this guidance is now only available on the Government's national archive site.) Such benefits with a transferable cash value might include:

- cash allowances such as housing allowance, car allowance, fuel allowance or first aid allowance

- vouchers, such as luncheon vouchers or retail vouchers, that have a transferable cash value.

In addition, benefits that are provided for business use only (such as a **3.62** company car or mobile phone) may be withdrawn during SML, even if they do not have a transferable cash value. This is not because they amount to remuneration – they do not – but because they are provided for the sole purpose of enabling the employee to carry out her duties – duties from which she is exempt while on SML.

3.63 **Non-cash benefits.** In contrast, an employee should continue to receive any non-cash benefits throughout her SML that she would have received had she not been absent, as these do not count as remuneration within the meaning of Reg 9(3). This is the case even if these benefits were provided as part of a salary sacrifice arrangement. Such non-cash benefits might include:

- life assurance (but note our comments under 'Pensions' below)
- private medical, dental or permanent health insurance (but, again, note our comments under 'Pensions' below)
- private use of a company car, laptop or mobile phone
- pension contributions (again, see 'Pensions' below)
- participation in a share ownership scheme
- living accommodation
- membership of a health club
- childcare vouchers, in so far as these can only be used by the employee for qualifying childcare and are not transferable (see below)
- mortgage subsidies
- reimbursement of professional subscriptions.

3.64 *Childcare vouchers.* The HMRC guidance lists the provision of childcare vouchers as an example of a non-cash benefit that must be provided throughout SML, as they do not amount to remuneration under Reg 9. However, this raises potential problems for employers. While an employee is earning, she sacrifices part of her salary in return for the receipt of tax-efficient childcare vouchers – thus there is no loss to the employer. But where an employee is receiving only SMP, or is on unpaid leave, the employer must continue to provide the vouchers and cannot deduct the value of the vouchers against SMP. The cost to the employer could therefore be significant. It is suggested that one way round the problem could be for employers to agree with employees that childcare vouchers will not be provided while they are on maternity leave, and that their salary will revert to normal for this period. It may be in employees' interests to agree: partly because they are less likely to use childcare while they are on maternity leave, and partly because the earnings-related part of their SMP will then be based on their full salary, without deduction for childcare vouchers.

3.65 **Pay rises.** Although not entitled to receive remuneration during SML, employees must not be denied the benefit of any pay rises awarded during their absence – Alabaster v Woolwich plc 2005 ICR 695, ECJ. This is now provided for by S.74 EqA: see Chapter 5, 'Statutory maternity pay', under 'Normal weekly earnings – pay rises', for the impact of pay rises upon the calculation of statutory maternity pay, and Chapter 13, 'Discrimination and equal pay', under 'Equal pay – pay rises during maternity leave', for further discussion of this important case.

Profit-related pay, bonuses and commission. There are certain benefits/ **3.66** payments that, depending on the circumstances, may or may not fall within the scope of 'wages or salary'. These include profit-related pay, bonuses and commission. (Note that the issues surrounding the payment of bonuses during periods of family-related leave are also relevant to questions of sex discrimination and equal pay, which are discussed further in Chapter 13, 'Discrimination and equal pay'.)

The purpose for which and the terms under which these payments are made and the period over which they are calculated will determine how they are labelled for the purposes of the maternity leave provisions. If, for instance, the payment relates to work the employee did before she commenced SML, she should be entitled to it regardless of the fact that she is absent from work when it is actually paid. If, however, the payment relates to work that would have been done during the SML period if the employee had not been absent, it amounts to 'wages or salary' for that period and need not be paid (except in so far as it relates to work that would have been done during compulsory maternity leave – see below).

In Hoyland v Asda Stores Ltd 2005 ICR 1235, EAT, the Appeal Tribunal **3.67** considered how a bonus should be paid where it is designed to reward work done over the course of the year, during part of which the employee was absent on maternity leave. (Note that this case was subsequently considered by the Court of Session on the issue of whether or not the bonus scheme in question was discretionary – 2006 IRLR 468, Ct Sess (Inner House).) The EAT concluded that the claimant did not suffer a pregnancy-related detriment under Reg 19 when her employer made a pro rata reduction in her annual bonus to reflect the period when she was absent from work on maternity leave, according to the terms of the scheme. The bonus was designed to reward attendance at work which contributed to the overall performance of the business during the bonus year. As such, the EAT concluded that it formed part of the claimant's 'wages or salary' within the meaning of Reg 9 and thus fell within the category of 'remuneration' to which an employee ceases to be entitled during maternity leave.

Note that, depending upon the rules of the scheme, days spent 'keeping in touch' ('KIT days') during maternity leave under Reg 12A may need to be counted as days worked for the purposes of calculating any pro rata reduction in an annual bonus to reflect absence – see 'Work during maternity leave' below. Where payment of a bonus is dependent solely on a condition that the employee

95

is in active employment on the date on which it is awarded, an employee on maternity leave might be well advised to arrange a KIT day for the date in question to avoid losing out on the bonus altogether.

3.68 *Bonuses and compulsory maternity leave.* In Hoyland v Asda Stores Ltd (above) the EAT upheld the tribunal's decision that Asda's failure to pay a bonus in respect of the two-week period of compulsory maternity leave did amount to a pregnancy-related detriment. This conclusion was based on the decision in Lewen v Denda 2000 ICR 648, ECJ (a case concerned with equal pay in the context of parental leave and discussed in further detail in Chapter 13, 'Discrimination and equal pay', under 'Equal pay – bonuses'), where the ECJ held that an employer can make a pro rata reduction in a bonus which constitutes retroactive pay for work performed in the course of the scheme year to take account of absence on parental leave. But the ECJ went on to note that Article 119 of the EC Treaty (now Article 157 of the Treaty on the Functioning of the European Union) – which enshrines the principle of equal pay – precludes an employer from taking into account periods in which the worker was statutorily prohibited from working by the legislation protecting pregnant women and new mothers. These periods must be treated as periods worked: to hold otherwise would amount to discrimination against female workers.

Following Lewen, therefore, time spent on compulsory maternity leave must count as time spent working for the purpose of calculating whether, or how much of, a bonus or profit-related pay dividend should be paid to an employee. As a result, S.74(7) EqA provides that a maternity equality clause will operate to ensure that a woman is paid any bonus in respect of the period during which she is on compulsory maternity leave.

3.69 Consequently:

- if a bonus scheme rewards work done over a period, the two-week compulsory maternity leave period should be treated as time spent working when reducing the bonus on a pro rata basis to take account of absence on maternity leave

- if a bonus is awarded subject only to a condition that the employee is in active employment on the date at which it is awarded, time spent on compulsory maternity leave must be treated as 'active employment' (although Lewen implies that subsequent absence on maternity leave need not be).

3.70 *Bonuses dependent on qualifying service.* As for payments which are dependent upon a period of qualifying service, both OML and AML periods must count towards that service.

3.71 **Discretionary/ex gratia benefits.** Sections 71(5) and 73(5) ERA state that 'terms and conditions of employment' include 'matters connected with an employee's employment *whether or not* they arise under her contract of employment' (our stress). This appears to cover non-contractual and discretionary benefits as well as benefits stipulated in the contract of employment. (Note that withholding a non-contractual benefit which does not amount to wages or salary from a woman because she is on maternity leave would also be discriminatory – see Chapter 13, 'Discrimination and equal pay'.)

Private medical insurance. As mentioned above, an employee will be entitled **3.72** to continue in membership of any private health insurance (PHI), long-term disability insurance or private medical insurance scheme during her SML.

Sick pay
3.73

What is the position with regard to the payment of sick pay during periods of maternity leave?

Statutory sick pay. Employees may not claim statutory sick pay during the **3.74** maternity pay period – para 1, Sch 13 SSCBA.

Contractual sick pay. Similarly, employees on maternity leave cannot claim **3.75** contractual sick pay, as this amounts to remuneration. The EAT emphasised this point in Department of Work and Pensions v Sutcliffe EAT 0319/07. In that case S notified her employer of her intention to take maternity leave from 1 August 2006. However, from the beginning of June she was signed off sick with a pregnancy-related illness. Her medical certificate ran until 1 January 2007. S's contract stated that she was allowed full pay for sickness absence of up to six months in any 12-month period. S received full pay for June and July, but from August onwards she only received Maternity Allowance. She brought a claim to an employment tribunal, arguing that her employer had made an unlawful deduction from her wages by not paying her sick pay until January 2007. The tribunal determined that, on a proper construction of her contract, S was entitled to receive full pay while signed off sick. This entitlement, the tribunal continued, was not affected by S.71(5)(b) ERA or Reg 9(3) MPL Regulations, since (in its view) sick pay was not remuneration. The EAT, however, held that the tribunal had erred in its conclusion as to what amounted to 'remuneration'. On a proper construction of S.71(5) and Reg 9(3), 'remuneration' does include contractual sick pay, and thus an employee is not entitled to claim such pay while on maternity leave. It would be strange, the EAT argued, to find otherwise, given that, under S.27(1) ERA, contractual sick pay can constitute part of a worker's wages in a claim for unlawful deductions from wages. S's claim therefore failed.

Annual leave
3.76

The relationship between maternity leave and annual leave is complex and has been the subject of numerous cases, in both the domestic courts and the ECJ.

Accrual of leave. Paid annual leave (both contractual and statutory) that **3.77** would normally accrue while the employee was at work should continue to

97

accrue during her SML (as should any other benefits that accrue over a period of time, such as seniority rights and pensionable service). Statutory annual leave entitlement is governed by Reg 13 of the Working Time Regulations 1998 SI 1998/1833 ('the Working Time Regulations') – see IDS Employment Law Handbook, 'Working Time' (2013), Chapter 4, 'Annual leave', in the section 'Right to paid annual leave', under 'Basic annual leave' and 'Additional annual leave'.

3.78 **'Holiday credits' systems.** In Adcock and ors v H Flude and Co (Hinckley) Ltd EAT 521/97 the EAT held that holiday credits paid under a system for calculating the holiday entitlement of pieceworkers constituted 'remuneration'. Accordingly, employees had no right to continue to accumulate the credits during maternity leave since employees on maternity leave have no right to remuneration. However, this case may no longer be good law and should be treated with considerable caution for two reasons. First, it was decided before the strict definition of remuneration contained in Reg 9 was formulated; and secondly, it was decided before the Working Time Regulations came into force. Paid annual leave now accrues in accordance with those Regulations regardless of whether the worker is paid a piecework rate or a fixed salary.

3.79 **Can an employee take paid holiday during maternity leave?** The current legal position appears to be that the two rights cannot be exercised at the same time. In other words, a woman has to bring her maternity leave to an end if she wants to take paid annual leave, or take her annual leave before she starts maternity leave.

This position is based, partly, on the Court of Appeal's decision in Inland Revenue Commissioners v Ainsworth and ors 2005 ICR 1149, CA, that workers absent due to sickness may not take annual leave at the same time as sick leave. Although the Court did not explicitly extend its reasoning to other types of leave, it drew its conclusion from the premise that annual leave must be construed as a release from what would otherwise be an obligation to work. The Court concurred with the employer's observations that 'it would be contrary to all ordinary usage for a worker who is off work for a year or more as a result of serious illness to say that during some arbitrarily chosen part of that period he is taking "leave" – leave from what?' Consideration had to be given to the underlying basis of the EU Working Time Directive (No.2003/88) ('the Working Time Directive') (which the Working Time Regulations implement) – that is, the protection of workers' health and safety. Allowing workers on long-term sick leave to take leave would not, in the Court's view, serve any health and safety purpose, since an employee who is not required to work during the period in question stands to gain no benefit to his or her health by taking leave.

3.80 Given the Court of Appeal's construction of leave as a release from what would otherwise be an obligation, the principle that workers on sick leave cannot simultaneously take annual leave appears to be equally applicable in the context of other forms of leave – such as maternity leave. Although, following a reference to the ECJ, the Court's decision was subsequently overturned by the House of Lords on other grounds (namely, that contrary to the Court of Appeal's decision, workers on long-term sick leave were entitled to claim holiday pay in lieu – see Revenue and Customs Commissioners v Stringer and ors 2009 ICR 985, HL), it was clear from the ECJ's ruling that it was not contrary to the Working Time Directive for a worker on sick leave to be prevented from taking annual leave at the same time: the purpose of annual leave was to allow a worker to benefit from a period of rest and, accordingly, it was legitimate to conclude that a period of rest could not be taken by a worker who was on sick leave – see Stringer and ors v Revenue and Customs Commissioners; Schultz-Hoff v Deutsche Rentenversicherung Bund 2009 ICR 932, ECJ.

In any event, it almost certainly remains the case that employees on maternity **3.81** leave may not simultaneously take annual leave. This is as a result of another ECJ decision that preceded the Court of Appeal's ruling in Ainsworth – Merino Gómez v Continental Industrias del Caucho SA 2005 ICR 1040, ECJ. The issue in that case was whether an employer can require a worker on maternity leave to take annual leave during the maternity leave period where, for example, there is an annual shutdown. The facts were that a collective agreement between a Spanish factory and its workers specified two periods in which annual leave had to be taken. For 2001, the first ran from 16 July to 12 August, and the second from 6 August to 2 September. G took maternity leave from 5 May 2001 until 24 August 2001 and subsequently asked to take annual leave from 25 August (the day after her maternity leave ended) to 21 September, or alternatively from 1 September to 27 September. Her employer refused and G brought proceedings that were, in time, referred to the ECJ. The European Court reiterated its position, set out in R v Secretary of State for Trade and Industry ex parte BECTU 2001 ICR 1152, ECJ, that the entitlement to annual leave under the Working Time Directive is a particularly important principle of EU social law from which there can be no derogation. The ECJ in BECTU had also noted that the Directive requires that workers should normally be entitled to 'actual rest' to ensure effective protection of their health and safety – since it is only where the employment relationship is terminated that Article 7 allows paid annual leave to be replaced by a payment in lieu. The ECJ in Merino Gómez concluded from this that the right to take annual leave under the Directive cannot be satisfied where a worker's maternity leave coincides with the annual leave period fixed for the workforce. Compelling her to take leave during a period of maternity leave would lead to either her right to annual leave or her right to maternity leave being lost, which would be unlawful – the purposes of the two types of leave being very different. Maternity leave is intended to protect a woman's biological condition and the special relationship between a woman and her child over the period that follows pregnancy and childbirth. The ECJ also relied upon Article 11(2)(a) of the Pregnant Workers Directive – which provides that the rights connected with a worker's contract must be ensured during maternity leave – for the principle that the entitlement to paid annual leave must be ensured during maternity leave.

The consequence of the Merino Gómez case is that an employee must be able to take annual leave before or after her maternity leave. She cannot take it, or be compelled to take it, at the same time as her maternity leave. Although the Directive prescribes only four weeks' minimum annual leave, the ECJ in Merino Gómez ruled that the principle is applicable to the longer period of minimum annual leave provided by statute in some Member States (such as the UK).

3.82 The ECJ's reasoning is also likely to apply where employers offset paid bank and public holidays against the statutory annual leave period. In these circumstances, women on maternity leave should not be made to 'take' bank holidays during their maternity leave, but should be permitted to take time off in lieu of those days at another time.

3.83 **'Lost' holiday.** Given that employees may not take annual leave concurrently with maternity leave, the question arises as to when they may take their annual leave entitlement. The difficulty is that Reg 13(9)(a) of the Working Time Regulations states that the basic four-week statutory leave entitlement is to be taken in the same year to which it relates. Statutory maternity leave may last for up to 52 weeks. Unless an employee's maternity leave starts and ends in the same leave year, and ends with enough time left to allow the leave to be taken, she will be unable to take her basic statutory annual leave entitlement after her maternity leave (although a relevant agreement may allow her to carry over the 1.6 weeks of additional statutory leave, or enhanced contractual leave, into the following leave year – see Reg 13A(7)). An employee whose maternity leave is due to end around the same time as the leave year could come back from maternity leave early (see Chapter 4, 'Returning to work after maternity leave', under 'Date of return to work') and then take an immediate period of paid annual leave. However, for many employees this would not be a suitable option as it would involve cutting maternity leave short, sometimes by several months, simply in order to gain a couple of weeks' paid holiday before the end of the leave year.

An alternative might be for her to take her annual leave for that year before she commences her maternity leave. However, she may be unable to do this where her maternity leave commences soon after the beginning of the employer's annual leave year. Payment in lieu may not be made for any accrued but untaken statutory holiday entitlement, apart from on termination of employment.

3.84 An obvious solution would be for an employee on maternity leave to be allowed to carry forward her annual leave entitlement into the following leave year. The carrying forward of a certain portion of statutory annual leave is permitted under the Working Time Directive – Federatie Nederlandse Vakbeweging v Netherlands State 2006 ICR 962, ECJ. In that case the ECJ held that, while a Dutch law allowing workers to receive payment in lieu of annual leave carried over from the previous year's minimum leave entitlement was a violation of the Working Time Directive, nothing in the Directive precluded an agreement to carry over part or all of the four-week minimum annual leave entitlement to be redeemed in subsequent years. The ECJ observed that the positive effect of the leave entitlement on the health and safety of the worker is maximised if the leave is taken in the year in which it accrues. However, the ECJ considered that the significance of the rest period in terms of health, safety and welfare still remains where the leave is taken in a subsequent period. It was not, therefore, contrary to the purpose of the Working Time Directive that the minimum leave entitlement could be carried over and taken in a later year.

The ECJ drew support for its decision from another European case – Commission v Luxembourg 2005 ECR I-3067, ECJ – which concerned the interrelation of maternity leave and parental leave. The Court there held that a period of leave guaranteed by Community law cannot affect the right to take another period of leave also guaranteed by that law. Thus a Member State cannot require that a period of parental leave comes to an end on the date it was interrupted by maternity leave or adoption leave, without it being possible to defer the portion not taken. On this basis, the ECJ in Federatie Nederlandse Vakbeweging concluded that in the event of the aggregation of several periods of leave guaranteed by Community law at the end of a leave year, it 'may be inevitable', under the Directive, that annual leave will need to be carried forward to the following year.

This view has since been confirmed by the ECJ in Stringer and ors v Revenue **3.85** and Customs Commissioners; Schultz-Hoff v Deutsche Rentenversicherung Bund 2009 ICR 932, ECJ. There, the European Court held that where a worker has been unable to take his or her full annual leave entitlement because of his or her absence on sick leave for all or part of the leave year, it is contrary to the Working Time Directive for his or her leave entitlement to be extinguished at the end of the leave year under national law. It is highly probable that the ECJ would take a similar view where an employee has been prevented from taking her annual leave due to her absence on maternity leave, particularly given that this is a period of leave guaranteed by Community law (whereas sick leave is not). The ECJ noted in Stringer that whereas national law may allow a worker to take paid annual leave during a period of sick leave, this was not the case in relation to maternity leave – a right guaranteed by Community law – where the two periods of leave must be taken at separate times.

Given the wording of Reg 13(9)(a) (that 'leave to which a worker is entitled... may only be taken in the leave year in respect of which it is due'), the ECJ's ruling raises questions as to whether the UK's approach is compatible with the Working Time Directive. Applying Merino Gómez v Continental Industrias del Caucho SA 2005 ICR 1040, ECJ (see 'Can an employee take paid holiday during maternity?' above), it seems likely that an employee who loses her annual leave because she is prevented from carrying it over due to her absence on maternity leave will have been discriminated against. A woman absent for an entire leave year on pregnancy-related sick leave followed by a period of maternity leave could raise a similar argument.

3.86 Although Reg 13(9)(a) appears to preclude employees taking annual leave outside the leave year in respect of which it is due, public sector workers can rely directly on the interpretation accorded to the Working Time Directive by the ECJ in the Stringer case (above) in order to carry over annual leave into the following leave year. With regard to private sector workers, in Shah v First West Yorkshire Ltd ET Case No.1809311/09 an employment tribunal inserted additional wording into Reg 13(9)(a) in order to give effect to the Working Time Directive as construed by the ECJ, thus allowing such workers to take their annual leave entitlement after the end of the leave year. In the light of this, it may well be prudent to allow employees in both the public and private sectors to take their full annual leave entitlement before and/or after their maternity leave, regardless of the leave year in which it accrued.

Note that Merino Gómez v Continental Industrias del Caucho SA (above) did not hold that a woman is entitled to tack her annual leave entitlement onto the end of her maternity leave. An employer still has the right under Reg 15(2) of the Working Time Regulations to object to a worker taking leave on particular days, provided that the employer permits her to take that leave at a time separate from her maternity leave (irrespective of any agreement for fixed periods of holiday leave). However, if the objection means that the worker is no longer able to exercise her right to annual leave for that leave year (because of the operation of Reg 13(9)(a)), the employer is likely to be in breach of the Working Time Regulations.

Notice rights

3.87 The pay and other benefits to which an employee who gives or is given notice of dismissal while on maternity leave is entitled will depend on the length of the notice contractually due.

3.88 **Statutory notice pay.** The amount payable during the statutory notice period to an employee who gives notice or is given notice while on maternity leave depends upon the length of the notice contractually due by the employer. Ss.87–89 ERA provide for full salary to be paid to employees where they are given notice, or give notice, in certain specified situations. One of these is where the notice is given to, or by, an employee during her maternity leave (Ss.87(1)–(3), 88(1)(c) and 89(3)(b)). These provisions only apply, however, where the notice due by the employer does not exceed the statutory minimum – set out in S.86(1) – by one week or more (S.87(4)). If the notice due by the employer does exceed the statutory minimum by one week or more, then an employee who is given notice (or who gives notice) during her SML period will be entitled to no more during the notice period than the normal statutory or contractual maternity pay that would otherwise have applied.

The EAT has confirmed that where the period of notice to be given by the employer under the contract is at least one week more than the statutory notice, S.87(4) operates to disapply entirely the employer's liability to pay the employee during both the contractual and the statutory elements of the notice period – The Scotts Co (UK) Ltd v Budd 2004 ICR 299, EAT. This achieves the curious result that someone entitled to a long contractual notice period is actually financially worse off than someone who is only entitled to the statutory minimum. While the latter employee is entitled to be paid in full for the statutory notice period, the employee in the former case is only entitled to receive statutory maternity pay (if it is still due) or any other sums specifically provided for under the contract such as contractual maternity pay, but not ordinary remuneration.

3.89 The amount of pay due under Ss.88 and 89 is calculated by reference to 'a week's pay', which is determined according to the formula set out in Ss.220–229 ERA – see IDS Employment Law Handbook, 'Wages' (2011), Chapter 10, 'A week's pay'. Broadly speaking, for employees who have 'normal working hours', the amount of a week's pay is the amount payable by the employer to an employee who works his or her normal working hours for a week. For employees who have no normal working hours, the 'average weekly remuneration' over the previous 12 weeks of active employment is taken. There is no statutory maximum on a week's pay for these purposes. Any payments actually made by the employer in respect of the statutory notice period (e.g. statutory or contractual maternity pay) will go towards discharging the employer's statutory liability for notice pay – Ss.88(2) and 89(4).

Note that if an employee's contract ends before the end of the SMP period, the employer must continue to pay her SMP for the duration of that period (currently 39 weeks in total), provided she has not started work for another employer – see Chapter 5, 'Statutory maternity pay', under 'Stopping work', and also under 'Disentitlement to statutory maternity pay – working during the maternity pay period'.

3.90 Some examples:

- an employee has six years' continuous service and is therefore entitled to a minimum of six weeks' statutory notice of dismissal under S.86(1) ERA. However, under her contract the employer is obliged to give her three months' notice of dismissal, while she must give three months' notice if she wishes to resign. While on SML, she is given three months' notice of her dismissal. Because the notice to which she is contractually entitled exceeds statutory notice by at least one week, S.87(4) disapplies the special provisions in Ss.87–89 ERA. This means that she is entitled only to SMP and/or any contractual maternity pay, to the extent that they are still due, for the three-month notice period

- an employee has six years' continuous service. Under S.86(1), she is entitled to six weeks' statutory notice of dismissal from her employer, and under S.86(2) she is obliged to give one week's notice if she wishes to resign. There are no contractual provisions increasing these notice periods. While on SML, the employee gives her employer one week's notice of her resignation. Under S.88(1) her employer is obliged to pay her normal salary for the week's notice period

- an employee has six years' continuous service. She is contractually entitled to six weeks' notice of dismissal and is contractually obliged to give four weeks' notice if she wishes to resign. While on SML, she gives her employer four weeks' notice of her resignation. S.88(1) still applies, because although the notice she is contractually obliged to give exceeds the statutory minimum by at least one week, the notice contractually due by her employer does not. Therefore she is due her normal salary for the one week's notice to which she is statutorily entitled, and SMP and/or any contractual maternity pay, to the extent that they are still due, for the remaining three weeks of her contractual notice period.

Statutory notice rights are considered in greater detail in IDS Employment Law Supplement, 'Notice Rights' (2006).

3.91 **Contractual notice.** An employee is entitled to the benefit of all her terms and conditions of employment during SML except for those relating to remuneration. This includes terms and conditions relating to contractual notice. As a result, a woman on SML is entitled to the same amount of contractual notice that she would have received had she been at work. However, since notice pay is in effect the wages or salary payable for the weeks of notice, it falls within the definition of 'remuneration' and is therefore not payable during the contractual notice period. The employee would, however, be entitled to any statutory or contractual maternity pay that she would normally have received in that period. Furthermore, she may be entitled to her full salary for as much of her contractual notice period as is equivalent to the statutory minimum – see 'Statutory notice pay' above.

3.92 Continuity of employment

Since an employee's contract of employment continues during her SML, the period of leave will count towards her period of continuous employment for the purposes of her statutory employment rights (see S.212(1) ERA). SML will also count for the purposes of any contractual rights that are dependent on a period of qualifying service (for example, pay increments and rights dependent on seniority). Reg 18A(1) makes it clear that an employee has the right to return from SML 'with her seniority, pension rights and similar rights as they would have been if she had not been absent' – see Chapter 4, 'Returning to work after maternity leave', for details of the right to return to work.

Note that the ECJ has held that where a woman was appointed to a post as a civil servant while on maternity leave, the date of her appointment, not the date on which she actually took up her post at the end of that leave, should be used for the purpose of calculating her seniority under what is now the recast Equal Treatment Directive – Herrero v Instituto Madrileňo de la Salud 2006 IRLR 296, ECJ.

Pensions
The employer's obligations in respect of pensions depend on whether the employee is on a paid or unpaid period of maternity absence. 'Paid maternity absence' in this sense covers any period of OML or AML during which SMP is paid, and/or any period during which the employee is entitled to be paid under a contractual maternity scheme.

Pension rights during paid maternity leave. A woman on maternity leave benefits from protection in relation to her rights under an occupational pension scheme. The protection is given effect by S.75 EqA, which provides for the deemed inclusion of a 'maternity equality rule' in an occupational pension scheme. In brief, the rule has the effect that any term of the scheme, or any discretion capable of being exercised under it, that purports to treat a woman differently in respect of time when she is on maternity leave compared with time when she is not, is modified so that both periods fall to be treated in the same way – S.75(3) and (4). Any term or discretion relating to membership of the scheme, accrual of rights or determination of benefits payable under the scheme falls within the scope of the maternity equality rule – S.75(5) and (6).

The effect of this is that any period when a woman is on paid maternity leave (OML or AML) should be treated as if she is not on such leave – i.e. the woman's maternity leave must be treated as if it were a period during which she was working normally for occupational pension purposes. This applies to both final salary schemes and money purchase schemes and regardless of whether or not the woman returns to work after maternity leave. The protection covers scheme membership, accrual of rights and determination of benefits, and extends to any discretion under the rules of a scheme that might be exercised in a way that treats a period of maternity leave differently from periods when the woman is not on such leave. (Similar but not identical provisions apply with respect to paid adoption leave – see Chapter 6, 'Adoption leave and pay', under 'Terms and conditions during adoption leave – pensions and other service-related

3.93

3.94

benefits'; paid paternity leave – see Chapter 7, 'Paternity leave and pay', in the section 'Employment protection during and after paternity leave', under 'Terms and conditions during paternity leave – pension and other service-related benefits'; and paid shared parental leave – see Chapter 8, 'Shared parental leave and pay', in the section 'Employment protection during and after SPL', under 'Terms and conditions during shared parental leave – pensions and other service-related benefits during paid leave'.)

3.95 It should be noted that S.75 EqA replaced (as from 1 October 2010) para 5 of Schedule 5 to the Social Security Act 1989. The repealed provision referred not simply to occupational pension schemes but to all 'service related benefits' paid in the form of a pension or otherwise, including personal pensions. However, S.75 only expressly relates to occupational pension schemes. It is unclear whether this change was deliberate or inadvertent. However, the effect of the change is that a more limited statutory entitlement operates in this context than previously. That being said, in practice employers may decide to maintain the pre-EqA position, despite not being obliged to do so.

3.96 *Employer's contributions.* The employer's contributions to a pension or other employment-related benefit scheme must be paid on a level based on the employee's notional pay (i.e. the pay she would have received had she been working normally, taking into account any pay rise she would have received) as opposed to contributions based on the actual pay she receives during maternity leave.

In final salary schemes an employee is guaranteed a pension based on final salary and it is the actuary who decides from time to time what level of contributions are needed from employers to fund the liabilities of the pension scheme as a whole. In such schemes an employer's contributions are not specifically designated to any one employee. Accordingly (depending upon the actuary's advice), an employer may or may not have to pay more contributions to take account of women in the scheme taking maternity leave.

3.97 *Employee's contributions.* It is made clear, by S.75(7) EqA, that the maternity equality rule does not require the *woman's* contributions to the scheme in respect of the time when she is on maternity leave to be determined other than by reference to the amount she is actually paid (in the form of SMP or contractual maternity pay) during that time. Thus, while there is a requirement under the general rule to treat a woman on maternity leave as if she were not on maternity leave (and so on full pay) for the purpose of pension contributions, she may not be required to continue making the contributions she would otherwise have made. The employer must make up the woman's contributions in this respect. The Explanatory Notes to the EqA state that 'a woman who is paid while on maternity leave *will be entitled to accrue rights in a scheme as though she were paid her usual salary* but she will only be required to make contributions based on her actual pay' (our stress). Guidance from The Pensions Trust is even more categorical. In its 'Pensions Bulletin – Fact Sheet 3' (Spring 2012, Issue 13) it states that 'the employer is required to pay the shortfall in the member's contributions to ensure that the scheme receives the right amount of funding for the benefits being accrued'. Therefore, given that the full accrual of rights, at least under a defined contribution scheme, depends on full contributions from employer and employee, the employer must foot the bill for what would be the woman's normal contributions during paid maternity leave.

Pension rights during unpaid OML. Section 75 EqA applies to unpaid OML **3.98** in the same way as it applies to paid OML in respect of all cases where the EWC began on or after 6 April 2003 – S.75(8). This means that the employer should continue to make contributions to any occupational pension scheme during unpaid OML as if the employee were working normally and on the basis of her normal remuneration. This is confirmed in the HMRC guide, 'Statutory maternity leave – salary sacrifice and non-cash benefits', which states that 'the law... requires that employers continue pension contributions during OML, regardless of whether the employee is in receipt of maternity pay'. (Note that this guidance is now only available on the Government's national archive site.)

This approach accords with the ECJ's decision in Boyle and ors v Equal Opportunities Commission 1999 ICR 360, ECJ, to the effect that the accrual of pension rights under an occupational scheme is one of the rights connected with the employment contracts of workers within the meaning of Article 11(2)(a) of the Pregnant Workers Directive. This led the ECJ to conclude that pension accrual must be maintained during the minimum period of maternity leave referred to in Article 8 of the Directive (then, as now, 14 weeks), even if the woman is not in receipt of any pay during that period.

In practice, most employees who do not qualify for SMP are also ineligible to **3.99** join an occupational pension scheme, either because they do not meet a minimum earnings criterion specified by the rules of the scheme or because they do not have sufficient continuous service. If, however, an employer's pension scheme does permit access to membership to those employees with low earnings or who have less than six months' service, then although such employees may not qualify for SMP during the 26-week period of OML, they will be entitled to the benefit of continued pension contributions by their employer throughout that period.

Pension rights during unpaid AML. Section 75 EqA provides that the **3.100** maternity equality rule does not apply to the accrual of rights under an occupational pension scheme in respect of periods of unpaid AML – S.75(9)(a). However, the rule does apply for all other purposes, but only where the EWC began on or after 5 October 2008 – S.75(9)(b).

In the Government's guidance notes, 'Employee rights when on leave', it states that 'pension contributions usually stop if a period of leave is unpaid, unless your contract says otherwise'. However, this is misleading as it suggests that an employer need not continue to make pension contributions during any period of unpaid OML, which is incorrect – see 'Pension rights during unpaid OML' above. It is only during unpaid periods of *AML* that the employer is not required to make contributions to the employee's occupational pension scheme (unless of course the contract provides otherwise). The employee's contributions may also stop during any such period of unpaid maternity leave. However, the occupational pension scheme rules may allow her to make voluntary contributions.

3.101 The MPL Regulations reflect this position. As we have seen under 'Terms and conditions during maternity leave', Reg 9(1)(a) provides that an employee who takes OML or AML is entitled to the benefit of all the terms and conditions of employment that would have applied if she had not been absent (except for those relating to remuneration). However, Reg 9(4) clarifies this, stating that in the case of accrual of rights under an employment-related benefit scheme during AML, nothing in Reg 9(1)(a) should be taken to impose a requirement which exceeds the requirements of para 5 of Schedule 5 to the Social Security Act 1989 (now repealed and replaced by S.75 EqA).

(Note that any days in respect of which the employee is paid for carrying out work during a period of unpaid AML under the 'keeping-in-touch' scheme will fall within the scope of S.75, and therefore employers must make contributions to any applicable occupational pension scheme in respect of such days – see 'Work during maternity leave' below.)

3.102 At first sight, this distinction between OML and AML appears to be inconsistent with the ECJ's decision in Land Brandenburg v Sass 2005 IRLR 147, ECJ, as interpreted by the High Court in R (Equal Opportunities Commission) v Secretary of State for Trade and Industry 2007 ICR 1234, QBD. The ECJ in Sass held that the fact that domestic legislation grants women maternity leave of more than 14 weeks does not preclude that leave from being considered to be maternity leave within the meaning of Article 8 of the Pregnant Workers Directive, and therefore a period during which the rights connected with the employment contract must be ensured under Article 11. In other words, there is no justification for distinguishing between the first 14 weeks of maternity leave and the rest of the statutory maternity leave period in terms of ensuring that employees are not deprived of their rights under the Directive. And thus – as the High Court held – there is no justification for giving employees on AML less protection from sex discrimination than those on OML in respect of the provision of contractual benefits. However, the SDA did not apply to 'benefits consisting of the payment of money when the provision of those benefits is regulated by the woman's contract of employment' – S.6(6). So the Government, applying the High Court's interpretation of EU case law restrictively, took the view that the accrual of rights under employment-related benefit schemes is a monetary benefit provided by the employment contract – and therefore that it is still lawful to discriminate against employees on AML in regard to pension benefit provision. This is now reflected in S.75 EqA.

However, although the Government's distinction between OML and AML with regard to the provision of rights under occupational pension schemes may be reconciled with the High Court's decision in R (Equal Opportunities Commission) v Secretary of State for Trade and Industry (above), it is arguable that it contravenes the ECJ's decisions in Boyle and ors v Equal Opportunities Commission (above) and Land Brandenburg v Sass (above). This argument is supported (to some extent) by the Equality and Human Rights Commission in its statutory Code of Practice on Equal Pay, para 101 of which states that 'the only time a woman on maternity leave may be treated differently is when she is on a period of unpaid additional maternity leave, when she is not entitled to accrue occupational pension benefits as of right'. But, rather unhelpfully, there is a footnote to this provision that throws in the following caveat: 'However, this is a developing area of domestic and EU law, so advice should be sought on whether pension accrual should be maintained throughout the entire maternity leave period.' This suggests that the EHRC is not as certain as the Government that the distinction in treatment between paid and unpaid AML with regard to occupational pensions is sustainable.

3.103 Of course, the treatment of unpaid AML would cease to be a live issue were the Government to extend the maternity pay period to cover the full length of the maternity leave period. However, this proposal has been postponed 'indefinitely', and there seems little likelihood that it will happen in the near future. Furthermore, even if the maternity pay period were to be extended, it would remain the case that some women would not qualify for statutory or contractual maternity pay at all, so further guidance from the courts would still be needed.

3.104 **Continuity for 'pensionable service' purposes.** One important aspect of the protection of pension and other employment-related benefit rights is the extent to which periods of maternity leave count towards computing lengths of service for the purpose of calculating benefit entitlement. S.75 EqA provides that a woman's paid maternity leave (whether OML or AML) should be treated as if it were a period during which she was working normally for the purposes of occupational pension schemes. Thus, in respect of the period of absence covered by SMP and/or contractual maternity pay, a woman is entitled to add the length of that period to the periods on either side of her maternity absence when computing her pensionable service.

In addition, as pointed out in Chapter 4, 'Returning to work after maternity leave', under 'Returning after additional maternity leave – seniority, pensions and similar rights', Regs 18 and 18A(1)(a) MPL Regulations make specific provision for an employee's 'seniority, pension rights and similar rights' to be

109

preserved during her OML and AML. However, Reg 18A(2) provides that this is subject to the requirements of para 5 of Schedule 5 to the Social Security Act 1989 (now repealed and replaced by S.75 EqA). In other words, a period of unpaid OML does count as pensionable service, but a period of unpaid AML need not (unless, of course, the rules of the particular pension or employment-related benefit scheme expressly provide that the entire period of maternity absence will count in this regard). As the HMRC guide, 'Statutory maternity leave – salary sacrifice and non-cash benefits', states: 'Employers need not continue during unpaid AML to make employers' occupational pension contributions, or to count unpaid AML as reckonable service for the purposes of occupational pension contributions.'

3.105 However, as maternity leave does not break the employee's continuity of service (see under 'Continuity of employment' above), the employee's pensionable service before and after any unpaid AML must be treated as continuous – i.e. she must not be treated as having left and then rejoined the scheme.

3.106 **Remedies**

An employee who is denied the non-remuneration benefits of her contract during SML may bring a claim for breach of contract in the county court. She may also be able to bring a breach of contract claim in an employment tribunal where the claim arises or is outstanding on the termination of the employee's employment. Furthermore, if the breach amounts to an unauthorised deduction from wages she will be able to bring a claim under the protection of wages provisions contained in Part II of the ERA. 'Wages' in this context could include bonuses, commissions and maternity pay but not benefits in kind such as medical insurance or use of a company car – S.27 ERA. Breach of contract claims are dealt with in IDS Employment Law Handbook, 'Contracts of Employment' (2014), Chapter 10, 'Breach of contract', while deduction of wages claims are dealt with in IDS Employment Law Handbook, 'Wages' (2011), Chapter 3, 'Protection of wages – 1', and Chapter 4, 'Protection of wages – 2'. An employee on SML denied the terms and conditions to which she is entitled will also be able to rely on Reg 19 MPL Regulations, which provides that an employee is entitled not to be subjected to any detriment by any act, or deliberate failure to act, by her employer done because she took or sought to take, or availed herself of the benefits of, OML or AML. She may also be entitled to resign and claim unfair constructive dismissal under Reg 20. Regs 19 and 20 are discussed in detail in Chapter 12, 'Detriment and unfair dismissal'.

3.107 **Sex discrimination/equal pay.** Any unfavourable treatment of an employee on SML may give rise to a claim under the EqA, either for pregnancy and maternity discrimination (S.18) or for breach of the maternity equality clause (Ss.72–76), and/or under European equality law. Discrimination law, and its relevance to maternity rights, is discussed in detail in Chapter 13, 'Discrimination and equal pay'.

110

Employee's obligations

Sections 71(4)(b) and 73(4)(b) ERA and Reg 9(1)(b) MPL Regulations provide that an employee taking OML and/or AML is bound by any obligations arising under her terms and conditions of employment, except in so far as they are inconsistent with her right to take OML or AML. In other words, she is not bound by her usual obligation to turn up and work, but is still bound by all the other terms and conditions of her contract, including any implied terms such as the implied term of mutual trust and confidence or the implied obligation of good faith. (A full discussion of these and other implied terms can be found in IDS Employment Law Handbook, 'Contracts of Employment' (2014), Chapter 3, 'Contractual terms', under 'Principal implied terms', and Chapter 4, 'Implied term of mutual trust and confidence'.)

If an employee breaches any of the terms or conditions of her contract during her SML her employer may treat her in the same way as it would treat any other employee in these circumstances. It should, however, be careful not to treat her less favourably because of the fact that she is on SML, as this could amount to an unlawful detriment or sex discrimination – see Chapter 12, 'Detriment and unfair dismissal', under 'Right not to suffer detriment', and Chapter 13, 'Discrimination and equal pay', under 'Direct discrimination'. An employer should be particularly wary of penalising an employee for unauthorised absence in circumstances where it neglected to inform her of the date on which she is due to return to work and she therefore fails to return on time, or because it gave her less than 28 days' notice of the date on which her leave was due to end and it was not reasonably practicable for the employee to return on that date – see Reg 19(2)(ee).

'Reasonable contact' during maternity leave

Given the fact that women are entitled to take up to 52 weeks' SML, it is not entirely surprising that employers sometimes forget to keep them informed of important changes in their work, or for employees to feel isolated from the workplace. As part of the Government's move to encourage better communication during maternity and adoption leave, it amended the MPL Regulations in 2006 to clarify that 'reasonable contact' from time to time made by either party during the SML period will not bring that period to an end – Reg 12A(4) MPL Regulations. The provision gives the example of reasonable contact 'to discuss an employee's return to work'.

Despite the wording of Reg 12A(4), it seems unlikely that 'reasonable contact' would, in any event, have had the effect of bringing the maternity leave period to an end, so Reg 12A(4) seems somewhat otiose. The DTI (the predecessor to what is now the Department for Business, Innovation and Skills) stated in its consultation document on the issue: 'Contact between employers and women during maternity leave can... be beneficial and there is nothing in law to prevent it' ('Work and Families: choice and flexibility' – February 2005). It appears therefore that the 'reasonable contact' provision was introduced not to amend the law, but primarily to remove the uncertainty felt by some employers over whether it was lawful for them to make contact with an employee on maternity or adoption leave, and to encourage better communication during leave with a view to encouraging more women to return to work afterwards.

3.110 From a legal point of view, while making contact with an employee while she is on maternity leave is unlikely to bring the statutory period to an end, there are dangers in making unreasonable contact – whether not enough or too much. On the one hand, a failure to inform an employee on maternity leave of important matters such as a change in the workplace, a redundancy situation or a promotion or training opportunity could give rise to a claim of detriment, sex discrimination and/or unfair dismissal, depending on the circumstances. On the other hand, pestering an employee while she is lawfully absent from work could cause her stress and might amount to harassment on the ground of sex and/or lead to constructive dismissal. It is for this reason that it can be useful for an employer to discuss with the employee, before she goes on maternity leave, how much contact she would find helpful or acceptable. Reasonable contact could be made by telephone, e-mail or letter, or by having a face-to-face meeting either in the workplace or at a mutually convenient location. The frequency and nature of the contact that is reasonable might depend on factors such as the type of work involved and the employee's position, and whether either party needs to communicate important information to the other, e.g. changes in the workplace that might affect the employee on her return.

An employer must keep the employee informed of promotion opportunities and other information relating to her job that she would have been made aware of if she had been at work, e.g. organisation changes or redundancy situations. In Visa International Service Association v Paul 2004 IRLR 42, EAT, VISA fundamentally breached the implied term of mutual trust and confidence by failing to keep P informed of developments and job opportunities in her department during her maternity leave. More specifically, VISA failed to inform P of a vacancy that she would have applied for had she been aware of. It did not matter that the employment tribunal had found as fact that P was not suitable to be shortlisted for the post. P's complaint was not that she had not been informed of a job opportunity which turned out to be illusory. It was that she believed that she was suitable for the post and that VISA's failure to notify her of the opportunity fatally undermined her trust and confidence. P was entitled to treat herself as having been constructively dismissed and that dismissal was automatically unfair under S.99 ERA on the basis that P was dismissed for a reason related to maternity leave. P was also found to have been subjected to a detriment for a reason related to maternity leave under S.47C ERA.

112

(Detriment and dismissal rights are discussed in Chapter 12, 'Detriment and unfair dismissal', while discrimination is dealt with in Chapter 13, 'Discrimination and equal pay'.)

Work during maternity leave

3.111

An employee can work for her employer on up to ten days during SML without bringing that leave to an end, and without extending the total duration of the SML period – Reg 12A(1) and (7) MPL Regulations. These days are called 'keeping in touch' (KIT) days. It does not matter how long the employee actually takes as maternity leave, she is still entitled to ten KIT days. More significantly, perhaps, Reg 9A of the Statutory Maternity Pay (General) Regulations 1986 SI 1986/1960, added by the Statutory Maternity Pay, Social Security (Maternity Allowance) and Social Security (Overlapping Benefits) (Amendment) Regulations 2006 SI 2006/2379, provides that work an employee carries out under the KIT provisions will not involve her losing any SMP – see Chapter 5, 'Statutory maternity pay'. These provisions are mirrored in the adoption leave and pay schemes – see Chapter 6, 'Adoption leave and pay'. Note also that an employee who shares his or her leave with a partner under the shared parental leave (SPL) scheme (discussed in detail in Chapter 8, 'Shared parental leave and pay') is entitled to take up to 20 'shared parental leave in touch' days (SPLIT days) while absent on SPL without bringing his or her entitlement to SPL or shared parental pay to an end. SPLIT days can be taken in addition to KIT days, so a woman may be able to work for her employer for up to 30 days in total if she takes both SML and SPL.

Regulation 12A(3) MPL Regulations provides that 'work' means any work done under the contract of employment and may include training or any activity undertaken for the purpose of the employee keeping in touch with the workplace. Work for only part of a day will still constitute 'a day's work' for the purposes of the KIT provisions – Reg 12A(2). The work can be carried out at any time during the statutory leave period, except during the two-week compulsory leave period immediately following childbirth – Reg 12A(5). (Reg 12A does not refer to the four-week compulsory leave period applicable to factory workers, but such employees should certainly be prevented from taking KIT days during that period.) Since the Regulations do not specify whether KIT days should be taken as a single block or separately, this issue is left to be agreed between the parties.

As with the 'reasonable contact' provision in Reg 12A(4) (see '"Reasonable contact" during maternity leave' above), the purpose of the KIT scheme is to facilitate communication between employees and employers during SML. Previously, if an employee did even as little as one day's work, she would be barred from receiving statutory maternity or adoption pay for that entire week. KIT days are aimed at overcoming this obstacle in recognition of the benefits to

3.112

employers and employees alike of communicating during SML and preparing the employee for her return to work.

The Regulations make it clear, however, that KIT days must be agreed between the parties. The employee has no right to work during SML and the employer has no right to require an employee to carry out work during SML – Reg 12A(6). In fact, pressuring an employee to work during SML is liable to amount to discrimination. In Chigboh-Anyadi v Wickramapathirana t/a Edmunds Solicitors ET Case No.3200926/05, for example, C-A worked as an assistant solicitor for a small firm that was highly dependent on publicly funded legal work. While C-A was on maternity leave, her employer needed to prepare to face an audit conducted by the Legal Services Commission. He put pressure on C-A to continue to work during her maternity leave, on the basis that if she did not, the business would suffer and her job would be 'on the line'. She felt a sense of obligation to help and carried out paid work on 30 days during her leave. A tribunal found that she was denied 'the full benefit of maternity leave', and that her perception of having suffered a real loss was genuine and 'exacerbated by the discovery that her sacrifice had been in vain when, without due process, she was dismissed as redundant'. It upheld her claim of unlawful discrimination on the ground of her pregnancy in being pressured into working while on maternity leave.

3.113 There is no provision for KIT days to be paid, so payment will be a matter for agreement between the employer and the employee. However, the employer must ensure that the employee receives at least the national minimum wage. SMP may be offset against any contractual pay agreed. Any payment for KIT days during a period of otherwise unpaid AML may have effects with regard to pension contributions. In its guidance note, 'Statutory maternity leave – salary sacrifice and non-cash benefits' (available on the Government's national archive site), HMRC advises that if an employee receives pay for any KIT days during a period which would otherwise be unpaid AML, the employer must make pension contributions in respect of those remunerated KIT days – see 'Terms and conditions during maternity leave – pensions' above.

The Government's commitment to ensuring that employees on maternity leave are genuinely free to choose whether or not to make use of KIT days is underlined by the fact that the MPL Regulations provide that an employee who undertook, considered undertaking, or refused to undertake KIT days is entitled to the protection against detriment offered by S.47C ERA – Reg 19. Furthermore, Reg 20 provides that the dismissal of an employee because she undertook, considered undertaking, or refused to undertake KIT days will be automatically unfair under S.99 ERA (see Chapter 12, 'Detriment and unfair dismissal', for more detail).

3.114 **'Without bringing her maternity leave to an end'.** The express statement in Reg 12A that an employee may take up to ten KIT days 'without bringing her maternity leave to an end' could be taken to imply that her maternity leave will end if she works for more than ten days. This is the assumption made in HMRC's guide, 'Statutory Maternity Pay: employee circumstances that affect payment', which states: 'If your employee does more than ten days' work for you in her SMP pay period you cannot pay SMP to her for any week in which she does such work and her maternity leave will come to an end.' However, nothing in the legislation expressly states this. Maternity leave may only be ended early by the employee:

- giving the employer eight weeks' notice of her return to work under the provisions of Reg 11 (see Chapter 4, 'Returning to work after maternity leave', under 'Date of return to work – notice of intention to return early'), or

- if she intends to take shared parental leave, by following the procedure set out in Reg 5(1) of the Maternity and Adoption Leave (Curtailment of Statutory Rights to Leave) Regulations 2014 SI 2014/3052 to curtail the amount of maternity leave she intends to take, which again requires her to give at least eight weeks' notice – Reg 6(2)(b). Curtailment notices are dealt with in Chapter 8, 'Shared parental leave', under 'Curtailing maternity or adoption leave'.

That said, under Reg 11(2) MPL Regulations the employer may accept less or no notice of an employee's return to work at its discretion. It provides that if an employee attempts to return without giving eight weeks' notice, or by giving shorter notice, the employer 'is entitled' to postpone her return – the implication being that it need not exercise that entitlement. This raises a danger that where an employee carries out work during the maternity leave period, this could be perceived as an attempt to return from maternity leave, and, where the employer does not exercise its Reg 11(2) entitlement to postpone that return, the maternity leave comes to an end. Thus, Reg 12A was drafted to make it clear that taking up to ten KIT days will not inadvertently end the employee's maternity leave.

3.115 The position where an employee works in excess of the statutory ten KIT days remains ambiguous. Arguably, working for more than ten days during maternity leave will, in the circumstances described above, bring the maternity leave period to an end. However, we suggest that this outcome may be prevented. The simplest route, if the maternity leave has eight weeks or less to run, would be for the employer formally to exercise its entitlement under Reg 11(2) to postpone the employee's return to the end of the maternity leave period, while in practice allowing her to work occasional days. Alternatively, the employee may provide a written statement that in working additional days she is not attempting to return from maternity leave early. The difficulty with the latter approach is that maternity leave, being a statutory right, is governed by legislation and not by the parties' agreement, except to the extent that the legislation provides for such agreement. Thus, a tribunal might interpret the maternity leave legislation to the effect that working during maternity leave, over and above KIT days, constitutes an attempt to return to work, regardless of the parties' intentions. In practice, however, we envisage that tribunals will rarely be called upon to decide the question as the parties are likely to simply assume that maternity leave continues in the absence of any clear authority to the contrary. Disagreement is most likely to arise where, for example, an employee considers that she has agreed to work extra 'KIT' days, but the employer is under the impression that it has negotiated an early return.

The position regarding payment of SMP must be considered separately – see Chapter 5, 'Statutory maternity pay', under 'Disentitlement to Statutory Maternity Pay – working during the maternity pay period'.

3.116 Contractual and composite maternity rights

The rights under the SML scheme set a minimum standard. However, many employers offer contractual rights which are more favourable than those under the statutory scheme. For example, the contract may allow for more favourable notice requirements than those provided by the Regulations, or for a longer period of leave. Alternatively, it may allow the employee more flexibility in choosing the dates for starting and ending maternity leave.

3.117 Composite rights

An employee who is entitled to SML and has a corresponding contractual right relating to maternity leave may not exercise the two rights separately but may take advantage of whichever is the more favourable in any particular respect – Reg 21. If any aspect of an employee's contractual maternity rights is *less* favourable than the equivalent statutory right, then the statutory right applies as an irreducible minimum. Where an employee combines elements of a contractual right and a statutory right, the result is referred to as a 'composite right' – Reg 21(2)(b).

Imagine, for example, a contractual scheme that is more favourable than the statutory scheme in treating a period of unpaid AML as pensionable service under an occupational pension scheme (normally only OML and paid AML are pensionable), but seeks to impose harsh restrictions on the employee's right to return to work in the same job. The effect of Reg 21 is that the employee can take advantage of the enhanced pension rights without losing any of her statutory protection on the right to return. There is no need for an all-or-nothing choice between the statutory and contractual schemes.

3.118 Note that use of the word 'contractual' is not strictly accurate since Reg 21 is drafted more widely. It applies not just to maternity schemes set out in a contractual document, but to any right which corresponds to the statutory right and which 'arises under the employee's contract of employment *or otherwise*' (our stress). The use of the words 'or otherwise' suggests that a right does not need to be expressly set out in a contractual document for the employee to be able to take advantage of it. It could, for example, include a separate oral agreement reached with the employer or an implied or tacit understanding.

Where the contract is silent on a particular point, the statutory rules are assumed to apply. Thus, the various statutory notice requirements will still govern the exercise of the employee's composite right to return unless it can be shown that there was an express or implied agreement between employer and employee to modify them – see Kolfor Plant Ltd v Wright 1982 IRLR 311, EAT, and Lavery v Plessey Telecommunications Ltd 1983 ICR 534, CA.

Modification of statutory provisions. If the employee does combine elements **3.119** of a contractual right and the statutory right, the various statutory provisions that apply to the statutory right are modified to give effect to the more favourable contractual terms – Reg 21(2)(b).

Inadvertent composite right. Where an employer's contractual maternity **3.120** terms attempt to mirror the statutory scheme, problems can arise if the wording does not precisely reflect the statutory rules. In Watson v Marylebone Optical Co Ltd ET Case No.1404/89 (a case decided under an old maternity rights scheme) the employee postponed her return to work on medical grounds on two occasions. The employer argued that she could only postpone her return once in accordance with the provisions then in force. In support of her claim for unfair dismissal, the employee pointed to the employer's statement of maternity rights. The relevant paragraph omitted the statutory provision that a medical postponement could only be made on one occasion and for a period of not more than four weeks. Accordingly, the employee was entitled to rely on the more favourable contractual provision.

Maternity pay and composite rights. Maternity schemes often provide **3.121** employees with greater entitlement to maternity pay than provided for under the Statutory Maternity Pay (General) Regulations 1986 SI 1986/1960 (see Chapter 5, 'Statutory maternity pay'). However, there is no general right to modify the operation of the Social Security Contributions and Benefits Act 1992 (the enabling Act for the 1986 Regulations) even if this is to the employee's advantage – S.164(6) SSCBA. An illustration of the problems this strict view might cause can be found earlier in this chapter under 'Commencement of ordinary maternity leave – pregnancy-related absence', which shows how any attempt to modify the date from which SMP is payable may affect the right of the employer to recover payments of SMP from HMRC.

However, this is not to say that no composite right to maternity pay can arise. Those provisions of the ERA and the MPL Regulations which provide that the employee has no right to remuneration can be modified by a contractual clause which provides for specific payments during maternity leave. Para 3 of Schedule 13 to the SSCBA provides that any SMP payable will count towards

117

any contractual maternity pay and vice versa, so that in any given week the employee will be entitled to whichever is the greater of her contractual and statutory entitlements.

4 Returning to work after maternity leave

Returning after ordinary maternity leave

Returning after additional maternity leave

Date of return to work

Returning on different terms

Failure to allow employee to return

Combining different types of leave

Redundancy during maternity leave

This chapter deals with an employee's right to return to work after a period of **4.1** maternity leave, as set out in Regs 18 and 18A of the Maternity and Parental Leave etc Regulations 1999 SI 1999/3312 ('the MPL Regulations'). This right is similar to the rights of employees to return to work after periods of adoption, paternity, unpaid parental and shared parental leave (see Regs 13 and 14 of the Paternity and Adoption Leave Regulations 2002 SI 2002/2788 with regard to paternity leave; Regs 26 and 27 of those Regulations with regard to adoption leave; Regs 18 and 18A MPL Regulations with regard to unpaid parental leave; and Regs 40 and 41 of the Shared Parental Leave Regulations 2014 SI 2014/3050 with regard to shared parental leave). Adoption leave is discussed in Chapter 6, 'Adoption leave and pay', while paternity leave is dealt with in Chapter 7, 'Paternity leave and pay'. Unpaid parental leave is covered in Chapter 10, 'Unpaid parental leave', and shared parental leave is examined in Chapter 8, 'Shared parental leave and pay'.

As we discussed in Chapter 3, 'Maternity leave', many of the differences between ordinary maternity leave (OML) and additional maternity leave (AML) were eliminated by amendments made by the Maternity and Parental Leave etc and the Paternity and Adoption Leave (Amendment) Regulations 2008 SI 2008/1966. However, two important differences still exist in respect of the right to return to work, as we discuss later in this chapter under 'Returning after additional maternity leave'. These concern the accrual of rights under an occupational pension scheme and the employer's options where reinstatement in the old job is not reasonably practicable.

Note that all statutory references in this chapter are to the Employment Rights **4.2** Act 1996 (ERA) and all references to Regulations are to the MPL Regulations (as amended), unless otherwise stated. The equivalent Regulations in Northern Ireland are the Maternity and Parental Leave etc Regulations (Northern Ireland) 1999 SR 1999/471 (as amended).

4.3 Returning after ordinary maternity leave

An employee returning to work after taking OML 'is entitled to return to the job in which she was employed before her absence', with 'her seniority, pension rights and similar rights as they would have been if she had not been absent' and 'on terms and conditions not less favourable than those which would have applied if she had not been absent' – Regs 18(1) and 18A(1)(a) and (b) MPL Regulations.

Thus, an employee is entitled to return to exactly the same job she left and to be treated as if she had never been absent. She should be paid the same rate of pay that would have been payable had she not taken leave, including any pay increases which would have been awarded during the period of leave. Furthermore, her period of OML should count as continuous employment for the purpose of any rights or benefits that are dependent on the employee's length of service; for example, service-related pay increments.

4.4 A refusal to allow the employee to return following maternity leave would count as a dismissal, which, depending on the reasons for it, may be unfair, and may also amount to direct pregnancy and maternity discrimination or sex discrimination. This is dealt with under 'Failure to allow employee to return' below.

4.5 Exceptions

There are three exceptions to an employee's right to return to the same job following OML. The first applies where the employee is returning to work having taken two or more consecutive periods of statutory leave which include the OML and any period of unpaid parental leave of more than four weeks, or any period of statutory leave which when added to any other period of statutory leave (excluding unpaid parental leave) taken in relation to the same child means that the total amount of leave taken in relation to that child totals more than 26 weeks. In these circumstances, the employee has the same rights as someone returning directly from AML – see further 'Combining different types of leave' below.

The second exception applies where a redundancy situation has arisen during maternity leave and for that reason it is not practicable to continue to employ the employee under her existing contract. The employee is entitled to be offered any suitable alternative vacancy on terms and conditions which are 'not substantially less favourable to her' – Regs 18(4) and 10 MPL Regulations.

This exception is considered in greater detail under 'Redundancy during maternity leave' below.

Finally, the employee may voluntarily relinquish her right to return to the same **4.6** job. In Akintoye v Sutton and Merton Primary Care Trust ET Case No.2301458/05, for example, A informed her employer that she wanted to work closer to home on her return to work after maternity leave. As A did not want to return to her previous location, her job was filled on a permanent basis. It transpired that A was unable to work at the office where she had hoped to be located on her return from maternity leave and she accepted a secondment at a hospital near her home. At the end of the secondment, the employer made it clear that there were limited posts that could be offered to her and she applied for and obtained the post she had carried out on secondment on a permanent basis. However, she claimed that she had suffered unfair dismissal and sex discrimination in that her permanent post was filled because she took maternity leave and that put her at risk of redundancy. A tribunal dismissed her claim. Her permanent post had been filled, with her knowledge, because she had been adamant that she did not wish to return to her role at that particular location. Her wish to work closer to home was a constant theme of her evidence. A could have returned to a comparable job to that which she held before going on maternity leave, but chose not to do so and instead elected to take up the secondment because that would allow her to work closer to home. It was her decision to accept the secondment that placed her at risk of redundancy, not the fact that her employer had filled her permanent post.

Below, we look at the different elements that make up the employee's right to return to the same job on no less favourable terms and conditions assuming none of the above exceptions applies.

Employee's 'job'   4.7

Regulation 18(1) MPL Regulations entitles an employee to return to the 'job in which she was employed' before her absence. 'Job' means 'the nature of the work which she is employed to do in accordance with her contract and the capacity and place in which she is so employed' – Reg 2(1). In Blundell v Governing Body of St Andrew's Catholic Primary School and anor 2007 ICR 1451, EAT, the EAT stated that the level of specificity with which the three elements contained in this definition – 'nature', 'capacity' and 'place' – were addressed was likely to be critical and should be determined as a question of fact by the employment tribunal. The EAT went on to say that in determining the appropriate level of specificity, the tribunal should have in mind both the purpose of the legislation – to ensure that there is as little dislocation as reasonably possible in the employee's working life – and the fact that the MPL Regulations themselves provide for exceptional cases where it is not reasonably practicable for the employer to permit the employee to return to her previous

121

job, in which case the employer may provide a job which is not the same job, but is nonetheless suitable and appropriate.

The problem with this aspect of the EAT's decision is that the 'suitable and appropriate' job option only applies where the employee is returning from AML. An employee returning from OML has the right simply to return to the same job. This would seem to lead to the very unsatisfactory conclusion that the interpretation of 'job' may differ depending upon whether the employee is returning from OML or AML.

4.8 **'Nature' of work.** The first element of the definition of 'job' in Reg 2(1) is 'the nature of the work which she is employed to do in accordance with her contract'. Thus it is important to establish what the employee was contractually employed to do, as this may be wider than what she actually did. What seems to be a different job to an employee may in fact simply be a different element of the job that she was contractually employed to do. Two examples:

- **Blundell v Governing Body of St Andrew's Catholic Primary School and anor** 2007 ICR 1451, EAT: B taught at a primary school where teachers usually teach pupils of a particular age for two years and then move on to another class. Shortly before her return from maternity leave, B was offered either a floating role or a 'year two' class. B complained that that was not the 'same job' she had performed before she went on leave, when she had taught a reception class. The tribunal disagreed and the EAT upheld its decision. Where a role varies, this can be taken into account. In B's case, the EAT concluded that the nature of her work, according to her contract, was that of a teacher

- **Edgell v Lloyd's Register of Shipping** 1977 IRLR 463, ET: before her maternity leave E was a bookkeeper, grade 13, who reported directly to a manager and who had authority to sign cheques. During her absence there was a reorganisation and on her return she was asked to report to a supervisor and she lost her cheque-signing duties. The tribunal held that her right to return had not been infringed. There was still an offer of employment in the same grade, despite some minor administrative changes.

4.9 If there is no detail in the contract beyond the job title it may be more difficult for an employee to argue that the job has changed. In Rowan v Bertrams Ltd ET Case No.S/1830/78, for example, R's contract described her as 'canteen manager'. During her absence stringent economy measures were taken and she returned to find the canteen providing only snacks, instead of a full meals service, and the staff reduced to one. But there had been no infringement of her right to return: she was still a canteen manager and there was no difference in her terms and conditions of employment.

The statutory definition of 'job' in Reg 2(1) is not limited to the contractual definition of the work. It also includes the employee's capacity and the place in which she is employed. Whereas 'the nature of the work' is determined in accordance with the employee's contract, 'capacity' and 'place' are not restricted to any contractual definitions.

'Capacity'. According to the EAT in Blundell v Governing Body of St Andrew's **4.10** Catholic Primary School and anor (above), 'capacity' describes 'the function in which the employee serves in doing work of the nature she does'. It is thus a matter of fact for the tribunal to decide. It is not merely equivalent to status but can include it. As noted above, unlike the 'nature of the work', capacity is not defined by the contract of employment.

In the following cases, the employee's capacity was held to be unchanged on her return from maternity leave:

- **Blundell v Governing Body of St Andrew's Catholic Primary School and anor** (above): the EAT considered that as the head teacher's policy was to move teachers to a new class every two years, B's 'capacity' was viewed more realistically as a class teacher than as teacher of the reception class that she had taught before going on maternity leave. The EAT held that where a position is variable, it is not necessary for the tribunal to freeze time at the precise moment the position's occupant takes maternity leave, but it may have regard to the normal range within which variation has previously occurred

- **Banks v Carter Hodge and anor** ET Case No.28362/94: before taking maternity leave B was employed as a secretary in the financial services department. When she discussed her return to work with her employer she was offered the position of a 'floating' secretary, to work in whichever department required her services. The tribunal held that B had been offered her old job back, albeit in a different department. It did not think that the work which the claimant had done prior to her maternity leave gave her enhanced status over floating secretaries. She was a secretary in the financial services department but she did not actually service any financial contract; she merely did secretarial work in connection with it. The tribunal accepted that if an employee had a position before maternity leave of a highly confidential secretarial nature with considerable responsibility, say to a managing director or a similar executive, and after maternity leave she was offered a position as a floater in the typing pool, it might come to the conclusion that that was not an offer to return to the same job. However, such was not the position in this case.

The following cases illustrate a change in capacity: **4.11**

- **Hayman v Constant and Constant Services Ltd** ET Case No.34384/83: H was described in her contract simply as a 'secretary' but she had risen to become a secretary grade 1 and was employed as a personal secretary to a

123

partner. On her return she was only offered a job as a 'floater'. The tribunal held that being a personal secretary had become a term of H's contract and that refusal to re-employ her as a personal secretary was an unfair dismissal (note that this case was decided before the EAT in Blundell made it clear that capacity was not qualified by the contract of employment. However, it remains a valid example of the sort of issues tribunals will take into account when determining capacity)

- **Taylor v Staffordshire Building Society** ET Case No.15127/82: T had been confidential secretary to the managing director. On her return from maternity leave she was offered the job of secretary to the manager of the premises department. This involved working in a basement next to the post room, instead of on the top executive floor, and personally checking the fire extinguishers and filling the sanitary machines in the ladies' lavatories. The tribunal held that the job on offer was completely different in capacity and status from T's old job and that refusal to re-employ her in her old job was an unfair dismissal.

Note that there was no reduction in pay or other employment benefits in either of these cases. It was simply the capacity of employment that had changed.

4.12 **'Place' of work.** An employee can only be expected to work at the place where she was recruited to work (unless there is a redundancy situation, in which case it may be reasonable for the employer to offer her a job in another location and the employee may be acting unreasonably if she refuses it – see 'Redundancy during maternity leave' below). For example, in Rawlings v McDonalds Restaurants Ltd ET Case No.2511279/04 R was the manager of one of her employer's restaurants in Barrow until she left to go on maternity leave in July 2002. On her return in 2003 she gave notice that she intended to take a further period of maternity leave starting in September. Her employer had concerns about her performance and at a meeting in August told her that when she returned to work after her second period of maternity leave she would not be allowed to return to the Barrow restaurant. Shortly before she was due to return to work, R's employer confirmed that she would have to take a non-managerial post or work part time if she wished to remain in Barrow – otherwise she was offered a co-managerial position in Kendal, some 35 miles away. R resigned and a tribunal upheld her claims of sex discrimination and constructive unfair dismissal. The only reason that R was not allowed to return to Barrow was that she had taken maternity leave. Had she not been taking maternity leave, performance measures would have been put in place in order to help her to achieve the required standards.

As with the concept of 'capacity', the 'place' in which the employee worked is not qualified by the contract. The question arises as to whether, if there is a mobility term in the contract, the employee may be moved in accordance with it on her return to work from maternity leave. According to the EAT in Blundell v Governing Body of St Andrew's Catholic Primary School and anor (above), if a contract has a mobility clause by virtue of which the returnee could be assigned to a different workplace, the employer cannot make her transfer upon her return from maternity leave because 'she would suffer the dislocation and the unsettling need to familiarise herself with that workplace at a time when she was vulnerable, and still learning to accommodate the needs of her newborn alongside those of work'. In the EAT's view, the aim of the MPL Regulations is to ensure that a returnee comes back to a work situation as similar as possible to the one she left. Nevertheless, on the facts of Blundell, the claimant's place of work could not be said to be the reception classroom, but the school.

However, it is arguable that the primary purpose of the MPL Regulations is **4.13** simply to ensure that the pregnant employee suffers no disadvantage in the workplace as a result of her pregnancy and that is why she is entitled to return to the same job she performed before going on maternity leave. It is possibly overstating matters to say that the MPL Regulations are concerned with not adding to the burdens placed on private and family life by the presence of a newborn child. As for a mobility clause, one would have thought that, even though 'place' of work is not to be determined solely by reference to the contract of employment, the existence of such a clause in the employee's contract would nevertheless be a relevant factor in deciding 'the place in which she is... employed' within the meaning of Reg 2(1). It is not apparent why an employee returning from maternity leave should be in any better position than any other employee whose contract contains a mobility clause, provided, of course, that the decision to relocate the employee is not in any way taken on pregnancy or maternity grounds.

Terms and conditions 'not less favourable'   4.14
As we have seen above, an employee's right to return to work under the MPL Regulations is a right to return 'on terms and conditions not less favourable than those which would have applied if she had not been absent' – Reg 18A(1)(b). This is not the same as saying that she is entitled to the terms and conditions which applied before she went on maternity leave. What it means is that the employee is entitled on her return to the benefit of any changes in terms and conditions at work which took place during her absence and which would have applied to her if she had been at work during that time. The most obvious example would be a general pay increase during her leave. Another example might be an increase in annual holiday entitlement.

Some examples of less favourable terms and conditions on return from maternity leave:

- offering only 1.5 days' work a week to an employee who had worked full time prior to going on leave (and in a different capacity, as a workshop

125

trainer as opposed to an assessor) – Jones-Fraser v First Rung Ltd ET Case No.3302366/02

- allowing an employee who had worked 13.5 hours a week before her maternity leave to return on only two 2.5-hour shifts a week – Pearson v Griffiths t/a RGB Leisure ET Case No.2800509/04

- offering to pay a previously full-time employee for only 21 hours' work per week – Abate v Davish Enterprise Development Centre Ltd ET Case No.3200683/06

- reducing an employee's entitlement to contractual sick pay – Mewes v Hilary Florek PR Ltd ET Case No.2502421/11.

In the above cases the employer was found to have unfairly constructively dismissed the employee and discriminated against her on the ground of her sex.

4.15 Of course, whether or not the terms offered upon return are genuinely less favourable will depend on the circumstances. In Dye v CCL Peacehaven Ltd t/a Community Careline Services Brighton and Hove ET Case No.3101746/06, for example, D was employed as a carer. Her contract stated that her hours of work were variable depending on the needs of clients, and that the availability and continuity of work could not be assured. She was provided with clients on a regular basis and her working hours exceeded 16 hours a week. Within two weeks of her return to work from maternity leave, she was concerned that she was not being offered 16 hours' work a week. She lodged a grievance regarding her employer's failure to provide her with sufficient hours' work, and subsequently resigned and claimed that she had been constructively dismissed and subjected to unlawful sex discrimination in being refused the right to return to her original job after her period of maternity leave. The tribunal dismissed her claim. Having regard to the reduction in the number of days on which D was willing to work, and the fact that she was geographically limited in respect of the areas where she could work since she did not have her own transport, it was not possible for her employer to find her 16 hours' work a week immediately, but the tribunal was satisfied that she was permitted to return to her old job on the same terms and conditions of employment. The only alteration after her return was the change in hours brought about by her own limited availability.

It is important to note that entitlement to return on terms and conditions not less favourable than those that would have applied if the employee had not been absent cuts both ways. Provided that any changes to terms and conditions that took place during her absence were lawfully made and would have applied to her had she not been absent, they will apply to the employee on her return even if those changes are to her disadvantage. Two contrasting examples:

- **Acteson v Silent Channel Products Ltd** ET Case No.15826/79: the employee worked a daytime shift from 8 am to 4.30 pm. During her maternity leave the employer decided to phase out this shift in favour of alternating weekly shifts of 6 am – 2 pm and 2 pm – 10 pm. But rather than ask existing workers on this shift to change to the early and late shifts, the employer decided to put all new employees on the early and late shifts and let the daytime shift phase out by 'natural wastage', i.e. until all employees on that shift had left employment. However, when A returned from maternity leave she was not allowed to go back onto the daytime shift and was only offered early and late shifts, even though a significant number of people were still working the daytime shift. The tribunal held that the employer was not entitled to change A's terms and conditions unilaterally, and that the failure to allow her to work her old shift was an infringement of her right to return and amounted to a dismissal. The dismissal was automatically unfair since the employer admitted that A's shift would not have been changed had she not become pregnant and taken maternity leave

- **Tighe v Midland Magazine Representation Services Ltd** ET Case No.5172/82: before her maternity leave T worked from 9 am to 4 pm with a 30-minute lunch break. The employer subsequently changed the working hours with the agreement of the other employees and when she returned T was asked to work from 9 am to 5 pm with a one-hour lunch break. She refused but a tribunal said that the new terms would have applied to T if she had not been on maternity leave and so there had been no infringement of her right to return to work.

The tribunal's reasoning in the Tighe case is open to criticism, however. An **4.16** employer does not have the right unilaterally to change an employee's terms and conditions unless the contract of employment allows it to do so. So, unless there was a term in the contract to that effect or the employee had given consent to the change, the employee's terms and conditions should have remained the same. This is so regardless of the fact that the rest of the workforce had agreed to the changes.

Circumstances in which a valid change in terms and conditions to the employee's detriment may occur include where the employee's terms and conditions can be varied by collective agreement with a trade union (see IDS Employment Law Handbook, 'Contracts of Employment' (2014), Chapter 9, 'Variation of contract', under 'Collective agreements'), or where the employee's contract contains an express power for unilateral variation of certain terms by the employer (see IDS Employment Law Handbook, 'Contracts of Employment' (2014), Chapter 9, 'Variation of contract', under 'Contractual right to vary'). In these situations an employee would have no right to insist on her old terms upon her return from maternity leave. However, where the employer consults with the workforce prior to implementing changes, the employee may nevertheless be able to argue that her effective exclusion from the consultation process while on maternity leave amounted to a detriment under Reg 19 MPL

127

Regulations or to discrimination under the Equality Act 2010 – see Chapter 12, 'Detriment and unfair dismissal', under 'Right not to suffer detriment', and Chapter 13, 'Discrimination and equal pay'.

4.17 Breastfeeding on returning to work

One issue of concern to many women returning to work after maternity leave – particularly if they are returning early – is whether to continue breastfeeding and, if so, how to combine breastfeeding and work. The National Health Service recommends exclusive breastfeeding for around the first six months of an infant's life, and continued breastfeeding alongside other foods beyond that. The Health and Safety Executive (HSE) guidance, 'New and expectant mothers', reassures employees that 'there are no legal restrictions on breastfeeding at work or any time limit for doing so. This is something for you to decide but it should not prevent you from returning to work.' This raises the question: What are an employee's rights – and an employer's obligations – with respect to breastfeeding?

4.18 Breastfeeding facilities.
As discussed in Chapter 2, 'Health and safety protection', employers are obliged to conduct a health and safety risk assessment with respect to breastfeeding mothers at work, and to provide 'suitable facilities' for breastfeeding mothers to rest – Reg 25(4) Workplace (Health, Safety and Welfare) Regulations 1992 SI 1992/3004. These health and safety protections are not subject to any time constraint – so long as the employee is breastfeeding, the employer's specific health and safety responsibilities towards her continue.

However, at present, there is no statutory right to time off work for breastfeeding or expressing milk. Nor is there any legislation that requires facilities to be provided specifically for breastfeeding or expressing milk. The HSE guidance advises employers that they 'are legally required to provide somewhere for pregnant and breastfeeding employees to rest. Where necessary, this should include somewhere for them to lie down. It is not suitable for new mothers to use toilets for expressing milk. You may provide a private, healthy and safe environment for employees to express and store milk, although there is no legal requirement for you to do so.'

4.19
The Department of Health White Paper, 'Healthy Lives, Healthy People' (November 2010), stated that the Government wished to work in partnership with employers to encourage breastfeeding-friendly employment policies, and promised to set up pilot schemes, but this initiative has yet to lead to the introduction of any new legal rights. Proposed amendments to the EU Pregnant Workers Directive (No.92/85) included the right to two separate one-hour periods of time off for breastfeeding, unless another arrangement was agreed with the employer. However, Member States were unable to reach agreement and the proposals were withdrawn in June 2014 – see Chapter 3, 'Maternity leave', under 'General considerations – European law reform'.

Sex discrimination. As discussed in Chapter 13, 'Discrimination and equal 4.20 pay', under 'Pregnancy and maternity discrimination – protected period', the period covering an employee's pregnancy and statutory maternity leave is regarded as a 'protected' period under European law, and this is reflected in UK law. As a result, an employee can claim discrimination if she is treated unfavourably because of her pregnancy, or a pregnancy-related illness, or on the ground that she is exercising or seeking to exercise (or has exercised or sought to exercise) her right to statutory maternity leave, without the need to compare her treatment with that afforded to a comparator – see S.18 of the Equality Act 2010 (EqA). However, this free-standing protection does not extend beyond the end of the protected period – which begins with pregnancy and finishes either at the end of additional maternity leave or, where she returns to work earlier, when the woman returns to work. In the case of a woman who is not entitled to statutory maternity leave, the protected period ends two weeks after the end of the pregnancy (S.18(6) EqA). S.18(5) provides that where a woman is treated unfavourably because of pregnancy or a related illness after the end of the protected period, but due to the implementation of a decision taken during the protected period, then this is also treated as pregnancy or maternity discrimination, with no need for a comparator. But otherwise, when the protected period ends (i.e. on return to work) then any unfavourable treatment because of pregnancy or maternity will be considered direct sex discrimination under S.13 EqA, rather than pregnancy or maternity discrimination, with the usual requirement for a comparator (namely, a man or non-pregnant woman).

Because there is potential for overlap between pregnancy and maternity discrimination and sex discrimination, S.18(7) EqA specifically precludes claims being based on the direct sex discrimination provisions in S.13 where they can just as well be based on the pregnancy and maternity discrimination provisions in S.18. However, there is an argument that S.13 might permit direct pregnancy and maternity discrimination (as opposed to sex discrimination) claims occurring during the protected period. The relationship of S.18 claims to those brought under S.13 is discussed in further detail in Chapter 13, 'Discrimination and equal pay', under 'Direct discrimination'.

Employees who wish to continue breastfeeding or expressing milk while at 4.21 work and are either prevented from returning because of this or are inhibited from doing so because of their working arrangements will need to demonstrate in the usual way that they have been discriminated against, directly or indirectly, because of sex. In so far as direct sex discrimination claims are concerned, S.13(6) EqA specifically provides that less favourable treatment of a woman includes less favourable treatment of her because she is breastfeeding. A claim of indirect discrimination would have to be brought under S.19 EqA – see further Chapter 13, 'Discrimination and equal pay', under 'Indirect sex discrimination'.

129

4.22 Some examples:

- **Squillaci v WS Atkins (Services) Ltd** ET Case No.68108/94: S went on maternity leave in January 1994. Because her baby suffered from eczema she wanted to breastfeed her for at least a year. In August she spoke to her employer about returning part time but was told that that would not be possible. No explanation was given. S responded by setting out the difficulties involved in working full time while breastfeeding. She pointed out that the arrangement would only be necessary for up to six months and suggested that a job share might be a way forward. However, the employer refused her request without explaining why part-time or job-share arrangements would not be allowed. A tribunal upheld S's claim of unlawful indirect discrimination. Her employer's refusal was not justified. Any difficulties could have been satisfactorily overcome with a proper and planned approach to organising S's work schedule and hours of work

- **Marshall v Governing Body of Langtree Community School and anor** ET Case No.1701005/00: M was employed as a head teacher. She took maternity leave from May 1999 and her child was born in July. Her baby suffered from an allergic reaction to formula milk and other dairy products and she was advised to breastfeed him until he was at least 18 months old. She asked her employer if she could return to work on a job-share basis in February, as full-time work was not practicable while she was breastfeeding her baby four times a day and needing to rest. However, during her maternity leave an OFSTED inspection had taken place which identified significant weaknesses in the leadership and management of the school and, largely because of this, the employer refused M's request, believing that the head teacher post had to be filled by one person in order to demonstrate unambiguous leadership. A tribunal upheld her claim of indirect sex discrimination. The employer had not considered whether the post could be undertaken on a part-time, as opposed to a job-share, basis, or looked at ways of avoiding the discriminatory impact of the requirement to work full time. The tribunal made a declaration that the condition of five-day working was discriminatory and was not justified and recommended that the employer consult with M within 28 days to seek a way of obviating or reducing the adverse effect on her of the discriminatory condition

- **Ministry of Defence v Williams** EAT 0833/02: W was a highly regarded flight lieutenant in the RAF. On her return from maternity leave she was aggrieved at the RAF's policy on breastfeeding, which stated that 'local circumstances may permit a return to duty whilst still breastfeeding, however, service women have no right to this and will be expected to go on exercise, take part in operational deployments, be drafted to seas service (if so liable), and undertake unaccompanied or emergency tours... service women who wish to be certain of being able to breastfeed beyond their

18 weeks' ordinary maternity leave should take [occupational maternity absence] to cover this period'. A tribunal held that the MoD's requirement that W return to full duties after her OML had expired despite the fact that she was still breastfeeding constituted direct, or alternatively indirect, sex discrimination. The MoD appealed to the EAT. W conceded that the tribunal's finding that a breastfeeding mother was entitled to 'free-standing protection' after maternity leave could not stand. Such protection was limited to the maternity leave period or where health and safety issues arose. In W's case, the maternity leave period had expired and health and safety issues had not been considered by the tribunal. In relation to the claim of indirect sex discrimination, the EAT accepted that it was not clear that the tribunal had considered the following relevant issues: whether the MoD had imposed a requirement that W undertake the full range of duties upon her return to work; whether she could comply with this requirement; whether such a requirement had an adverse impact on women; whether she suffered detriment in that she left the service; and whether there was any justification for the prima facie discrimination. The EAT allowed the MoD's appeal in relation to the claims arising from the breastfeeding policy and remitted those claims to be heard by a fresh tribunal

- **Pryce v Blair Travel and Leisure Ltd** ET Case No.2202973/00: P was employed as a senior travel consultant. She took maternity leave in 1999 and requested a return to work on a part-time basis because she was still breastfeeding and was having difficulty finding suitable childcare. Her employer refused, claiming it was impracticable because of the need to provide clients with a seamless, highly personalised service. P's claim of indirect discrimination on the ground of sex failed because she was unable to show that the proportion of female travel consultants who could comply with the requirement to work full time was considerably smaller than the proportion of male travel consultants who could comply with it – and the tribunal thought that the requirement to work full time was justifiable on the facts.

Returning after additional maternity leave   4.23

With two exceptions, an employee returning from AML has the same rights as someone returning from OML. She is 'entitled to return from leave to the job in which she was employed before her absence' with her seniority, pension rights and similar rights as they would have been had she not been absent and on terms and conditions not less favourable than those which would have applied had she not been absent – Regs 18(2)(a) and 18A(1)(a) and (b) MPL Regulations. (For what is meant by 'terms and conditions not less favourable', see 'Returning after ordinary maternity leave – terms and conditions "not less favourable"' above.) The period of AML also counts towards continuity of

131

employment for the purposes of statutory employment rights such as unfair dismissal, redundancy and minimum notice periods.

The two exceptions to the general rule that an employee returning from AML has the same rights as someone returning from OML concern:

- the accrual of rights under an occupational pension scheme during unpaid AML – Reg 18A(2) (see 'Seniority, pensions and similar rights' below)

- the employer's options where reinstatement in the old job is not reasonably practicable – Reg 18(2) (see 'Reinstatement not reasonably practicable' below).

4.24 Seniority, pensions and similar rights

Regulation 18A(1)(a) MPL Regulations provides that an employee's right to return after statutory maternity leave is a right to return 'with her seniority, pension rights and similar rights as they would have been if she had not been absent'. However, this is subject to Reg 18A(2), which states that nothing in Reg 18A(1)(a) concerning the treatment of AML is to be 'taken to impose a requirement which exceeds the requirements of [S.75 EqA]'. (Note that Reg 18A(2) actually refers to paras 5 and 6 of Schedule 5 to the Social Security Act 1989. However, para 5 – the relevant paragraph for present purposes – was repealed by the EqA and replaced by S.75 EqA.) As discussed in Chapter 3, 'Maternity leave', S.75 provides for the preservation, during paid maternity leave, of any term or discretion relating to the accrual of rights under an occupational pension scheme (whereas para 5 referred to employee benefit-related schemes). (Para 6 of the 1989 Act – which remains in force – applies similar provisions during periods of paid 'family leave'.) The effect of Reg 18A(2) therefore appears to be that an employee is not entitled to return with her seniority, pensions and similar rights as they would have been if she had not been absent in so far as these constitute rights under an occupational pension scheme during unpaid AML. However, the employee is entitled to the occupational pension scheme rights that would have applied had the two periods either side of the unpaid AML been continuous. In other words, the employee's rights are preserved exactly as they were at the beginning of the unpaid AML period. See Chapter 3, 'Maternity leave', under 'Terms and conditions during maternity leave – pensions', for a full discussion of the effect of unpaid AML on occupational pension benefits.

4.25 Reinstatement not reasonably practicable

Where it is not reasonably practicable, for a reason *other than redundancy*, for an employer to permit the employee to return to her old job after taking AML, the employer can offer her 'another job which is both *suitable* for her and *appropriate* for her to do in the circumstances' – Reg 18(2) MPL Regulations (our stress). As explained above, this option is not available to the employer where the employee is returning to work after taking OML. (Note that where, during an employee's AML, it is not practicable by reason of *redundancy* for her employer to continue to employ her under her existing contract of employment, the employee is entitled to be offered any suitable alternative vacancy on terms and conditions which are 'not substantially less favourable to her' – Reg 10. This provision, which also applies to OML, is considered in greater detail under 'Redundancy during maternity leave' below.)

The requirements in Reg 18A(1)(a) and (b) (subject to Reg 18A(2)) – for the employee to return with her seniority and pension rights and similar rights as they would have been if she had not been absent and on 'terms and conditions not less favourable than those which would have applied if she had not been absent' – still apply even if the employer cannot offer the same job. Therefore the terms and conditions of the new job offered under Reg 18(2) must be no less favourable than those that applied (or would have applied) to the old job.

Before considering whether the new job on offer is suitable, the employer must **4.26** first show that it was not reasonably practicable to reinstate the employee in her old job. In Stelfox v Westco Building Components Ltd ET Case No.15083/95 the claimant's temporary replacement proved to be exceptionally good at his job and was made permanent (at his request) during the maternity leave. When S approached her employer to discuss her proposed return to work she was offered a different job at a protected rate of pay. The tribunal held that as the replacement employee had originally been engaged on a temporary basis and since the employer had failed to consider any alternative strategy for dealing with the situation when he had refused to continue on that basis, the employer had failed to demonstrate that it was not reasonably practicable to reinstate S in her old job. This was particularly so since the employer had failed even to consider whether S ought in any case to be allowed to return to her old job once she had approached the company about her return. Her dismissal was therefore automatically unfair.

Once it is shown that it was not reasonably practicable to allow an employee to return to her old job, she must be allowed to return to another job which is both 'suitable for her and appropriate for her to do in the circumstances' – Reg 18(2). It is not open to the employer to refuse to offer any job at all, unless there is a genuine redundancy situation – see 'Redundancy during maternity leave' below, which also includes a discussion of some of the considerations that apply in determining what is a suitable and appropriate alternative job.

The question of whether the new job on offer is suitable and appropriate cannot **4.27** be decided simply by reference to the employee's job title. In Kelly v Secretary of State for Justice EAT 0227/13 K had worked as a healthcare officer at a prison for 15 years. Her contract of employment stated that her job title was 'prison officer' but she had in fact only worked in that capacity during the first two weeks of her employment when she was carrying out training. After this,

133

only approximately 5 per cent of her duties had been as an ordinary prison officer. When K returned to work following AML, she found that the healthcare work had been outsourced to the National Health Service and the only job available for her was that of prison officer. She claimed that her employer was in breach of Reg 18(2). However, an employment tribunal dismissed her claim, concluding that since her contractual position was as a prison officer it was therefore suitable and appropriate in all the circumstances for her to return to that role. Allowing K's appeal and remitting the case to a fresh tribunal, the EAT held that the tribunal had 'fettered its discretion by concluding that, effectively, once a prison officer, always a prison officer'. The tribunal should have asked itself whether the job offered of prison officer – without any mental health or nursing involvement – was suitable and appropriate. This could not be decided simply by reference to K's job title. On remission, there would be various factors for the tribunal to consider, including whether the absence of nursing duties might affect K's professional qualification as a nurse and the likelihood of her having to carry out some weekend work for the first time in 15 years. It was also relevant that K was used to a prison environment and coping with prisoners; had received pay and benefits comparable with a prison officer; and had received training (and more was offered) on issues like restraint, so would or could be qualified for the post.

4.28 An example of a case in which an employee was prevented from returning to an alternative suitable and appropriate job following AML:

- **Raithatha v Addleshaw Goddard** ET Case No.2406019/05: R was employed as a part-time construction solicitor working in Manchester, involved predominantly in contentious work. She went on maternity leave in 2004. In June 2005, she was informed that on her return she would be working in a newly formed construction litigation department. However, shortly before her return to work a new team of construction litigation lawyers based in Leeds joined the firm and it was agreed that all contentious construction work would be centred there. R was told that it would not be possible for her to work for the new team as they needed someone who was readily available at all times, which would be impossible for her given that she lived in Bolton and worked part time. On her return, she would therefore have to undertake purely non-contentious work in the Manchester office. R went on sick leave suffering from stress and anxiety, and resigned three months later when her grievance (in so far as it related to the nature of the work she would be offered on her return to work) was dismissed. A tribunal held that R had been unfairly constructively dismissed as a result of the employer's failure to make any effort to provide her with contentious work or to consult her about how this might be achieved and had suffered sex discrimination. Although it was not reasonably practicable for her to return as a construction litigator in the Manchester office, given the absence of contentious work there, she had a right under Reg 18 to return to another job which was suitable and appropriate for her to do in the circumstances. The tribunal found that such a job would have involved her return to the Manchester office with a view to securing her at least some contentious work in conjunction with the new litigation team in Leeds, but this possibility was never offered to her. Had she not been on maternity leave at the time the new construction team joined, it is more likely than not that some accommodation would have been reached with the Leeds team.

Date of return to work 4.29

Statutory maternity leave (SML) normally lasts 52 weeks in total (i.e. 26 weeks' OML and 26 weeks' AML). Therefore, assuming the employee has taken her full leave entitlement, the first day back to work should fall on the same day of the week as the first day of maternity leave.

Normally, this means that an employee whose last working day before taking SML was, for example, a Tuesday, and whose leave started on a Wednesday, would be obliged to return to work on the Wednesday 52 weeks later. (If that is not normally a working day, or if the employee is then on sick leave or annual leave, her physical attendance at work would not be expected until the next working day or the next working day following the period of sick leave or annual leave.) Note, however, that a slightly more complicated rule applies where the woman's maternity leave was triggered by childbirth under Reg 6(2) MPL Regulations or by a pregnancy-related absence in the four weeks before the expected week of confinement (EWC) under Reg 6(1)(b). In these circumstances, the employee effectively gets a day's grace because maternity leave starts on the day after the birth or absence. Therefore if, for example, the employee's last working day was a Tuesday and she gave birth on the Wednesday, her OML would not actually start until the Thursday and she would be obliged to return to work on the Thursday 52 weeks later.

An employee has an automatic right to come back to work following maternity 4.30 leave and it is assumed that she will do so unless she says otherwise. Thus, a woman returning to work at the end of her full entitlement to SML is not required to give her employer any notice of her intention to return. She can simply turn up for work the day after her 52-week leave period has ended. In Parkin v Self t/a Barbot Sandwiches ET Case No.2801754/04 P went on maternity leave in January 2004. On 15 May her employer wrote to her asking her to let him know by the end of May whether she intended to return to work. She did not reply and on 1 June he sent a text message saying that he was disappointed that she had not replied, that he presumed that she had no intention of returning to work, and that her job was no longer left open. He followed that up with a letter confirming his position and saying that her employment would end on 3 July. A tribunal upheld P's claim of automatically unfair dismissal for exercising her right to take maternity leave. Her employer

135

sought to impose a further condition, over and above the then statutory regime. She was also awarded damages for unlawful direct sex discrimination.

Notice provisions do apply, however, where the employee intends to return to work before the end of her SML – see 'Notice of intention to return early' below, or where she wishes to curtail her maternity leave in order to share the balance with the father of her child (or her spouse, civil partner or partner) under the shared parental leave regime – see Chapter 8, 'Shared parental leave and pay', under 'Curtailing maternity or adoption leave'.

4.31 Notice of resignation
There is no specific provision in the MPL Regulations dealing with the position of an employee who does not wish to return after the end of her maternity leave. However, Reg 9(1)(b) provides that an employee on maternity leave (OML and AML) is bound by the contractual obligation to give notice to terminate her employment. Therefore a woman who does not intend to return to work must notify her employer before the end of her leave period, in accordance with the notice period specified in her contract, which cannot be less than the statutory minimum of one week under S.86 ERA. An employee should, however, exercise caution before telling her employer that she will not be returning to work. An unambiguous notice of resignation, once given, cannot be withdrawn and the employee will not be able to change her mind unless the employer agrees to take her back – Harris and Russell Ltd v Slingsby 1973 ICR 454, NIRC. On the other hand, employers should be cautious about accepting purported resignations unless they are clear and unambiguous – see Chapter 3, 'Maternity leave', under 'Commencement of ordinary maternity leave – dismissal or resignation before intended start date', and 'Duration of maternity leave – duration of ordinary maternity leave'.

4.32 Notice of intention to return early
If the employee wishes to return to work before the end of her full maternity leave entitlement, she must give her employer at least eight weeks' notice of the date on which she intends to return – Reg 11(1) MPL Regulations (unless she is an 'employee shareholder' within the meaning of S.205A(1) ERA, in which case she must give at least 16 weeks' notice – see 'Employee shareholders' below). There is no requirement that this notice be in writing. The employer may accept less or no notice at its discretion.

If an employee attempts to return to work early without having given eight weeks' notice, her employer is entitled to postpone her return to a date that will secure the full eight-week notice period – Reg 11(2). The employer may not, however, delay the employee's return beyond the end of the full 52-week maternity leave period – Reg 11(3). If the employer notifies the employee that her return date is being deferred because she did not give enough notice, then she has no right to be paid her contractual remuneration until the date to which her return was postponed, even if she insists on turning up for work – Reg 11(4). This allows the employer enough time to make any necessary arrangements, such as giving notice of dismissal to a replacement employee so that the employer does not have to pay both employees at the same time. The law governing the employment of replacement employees is discussed in Chapter 14, 'Replacement employees'.

An employee must also give eight weeks' notice where she changes her mind as **4.33** to her return date having previously given notice of early return, or where she decides to return later than any date to which her employer has postponed her return under Reg 11(2). If she wishes to return to work earlier than her original return date, she must give her employer not less than eight weeks' notice of her new intended return date; if she wishes to return later than the original return date, she must give her employer at least eight weeks' notice ending with the original return date – Reg 11(2A)(a) and (b). (The 'original return date' means either the date the employee notified her employer as being the date of her return to work under Reg 11(1), or the date to which it was postponed by her employer under Reg 11(2), as applicable – Reg 11(2B).) Thus, once an employee has given notice of early return under Reg 11(1), and then decides to take her full 52-week SML entitlement after all, she may no longer rely on her automatic right to return at the end of the 52 weeks – she must give eight weeks' notice. The MPL Regulations place no limit on the number of times an employee may change her mind as to her return date, provided she complies with Reg 11.

Exception. The employee's obligation to give eight weeks' notice to return to **4.34** work early does not apply if the employer has failed to notify the employee in accordance with Reg 7(6) and (7) of the date when her AML will come to an end (see Chapter 3, 'Maternity leave', in the section 'Entitlement to maternity leave', under 'Employer's notice of end date – employer's failure to give notice') – Reg 11(5). Therefore an employer who has not given this notice at the proper time has no right to prevent an employee from returning to work early without prior warning and must pay her if she does so. In addition, it cannot prevent an employee who changes her mind as to her return date giving less than eight weeks' notice – or no notice at all – of her new return date. However, an employee's freedom in this respect may be curtailed to some extent by the implied term of mutual trust and confidence or the implied obligation of good faith found in every contract of employment, which (as discussed in Chapter 3, 'Maternity leave', under 'Terms and conditions during maternity leave – employee's obligations') subsist throughout the maternity leave period. An employee who informs her employer that she is going to return on a particular date may be in breach of such a term if she fails to turn up without explanation. In theory, the employer could then treat her in the same way as it would treat any other employee in similar circumstances. It should, however, be careful not to treat her less favourably because she is on SML, as this may render it liable to claims for unlawful detriment or pregnancy and maternity

137

discrimination – see Chapter 12, 'Detriment and unfair dismissal', under 'Right not to suffer detriment', and Chapter 13, 'Discrimination and equal pay', under 'Direct discrimination – pregnancy and maternity discrimination'.

4.35 **Employee shareholders.** The notification requirements applicable to employees who are 'employee shareholders' within the meaning of S.205A(1) ERA are slightly different. S.205A(3) provides that in the case of employee shareholders, all references in Reg 11 to 'eight weeks' notice' are to be read as if there were substituted '16 weeks' notice'. In other words, employee shareholders who wish to return early must give 16 weeks' notice of the date on which they wish to return from maternity leave under Reg 11(1), and, if they change their mind in the circumstances described in Reg 11(2) or (2A), they must give 16 weeks' notice of the revised date.

The law governing employee shareholders is considered in detail in IDS Employment Law Handbook, 'Atypical and Flexible Working' (2014), Chapter 7, 'Employee shareholders'.

4.36 Postponing return

An employer can only postpone an employee's return if the employee wishes to return early but has failed to give the requisite eight weeks' notice (see 'Notice of intention to return early' above). The employer cannot postpone the employee's return for any reason if maternity leave has come to an end or if the employee has given proper notice and wants to return early.

However, there are a few circumstances in which an employee may herself postpone her return beyond the end of the SML period. These exceptions apply where:

- the employer has failed to notify the employee at the appropriate time of the date her leave should end

- the employee is sick

- the employee is entitled to take another period of leave – for example, annual leave or another type of family-related leave.

4.37 **Employer's failure to notify end of leave.** Where the employer failed to notify the employee, in accordance with Reg 7(6) and (7) MPL Regulations or otherwise, of the date when her leave would end, and the employee reasonably believed that the leave period had not ended, the employer cannot dismiss the employee or subject her to any detriment if she does not return to work by the correct date – Regs 19(2)(ee)(i) and 20(3)(ee)(i). The same applies where the employer gave the employee less than 28 days' notice of the date on which her leave would end, and it was not reasonably practicable for her to return on that date – Regs 19(2)(ee)(ii) and 20(3)(ee)(ii). See Chapter 3, 'Maternity leave', under 'Entitlement to maternity leave – employer's notice of end date', and Chapter 12, 'Detriment and unfair dismissal', on detriment and unfair dismissal in general.

Sickness. If the employee is too sick to return at the end of her maternity **4.38** leave period (or after her notified date of return if she has given notice to return earlier), she does not lose her right to return but should be treated as if she has returned and is currently on sick leave. She should comply with any contractual requirements for notifying her employer of her illness, and the employer should treat her in the same way as any other employee off sick and pay her whatever sick pay she would normally be entitled to. A failure to pay sick pay in these circumstances is likely to amount to a detriment and an unlawful deduction from wages as well as a breach of contract and sex discrimination. It may also lead to an unfair constructive dismissal claim if the employee resigns as a result. Detriment and unfair dismissal are discussed in Chapter 12, 'Detriment and unfair dismissal', and sex discrimination is covered in Chapter 13, 'Discrimination and equal pay'. Breach of contract claims are dealt with in IDS Employment Law Handbook, 'Contracts of Employment' (2014), Chapter 10, 'Breach of contract', while deduction from wages claims are dealt with in IDS Employment Law Handbook, 'Wages' (2011), Chapter 3, 'Protection of wages – 1', and Chapter 4, 'Protection of wages – 2'.

Long-term sick leave. If the employee is absent on long-term sick leave after **4.39** the end of her leave period and the employer is considering dismissal, it must adopt a fair procedure involving consultation with the employee and a thorough medical investigation and should consider, where appropriate, alternative employment (see IDS Employment Law Handbook, 'Unfair Dismissal' (2010), Chapter 5, 'Ill health', under 'Long-term ill health'). When considering the employee's absence record, the employer must ignore the maternity leave period itself and any periods of absence connected with the employee's pregnancy that occurred before her maternity leave, as to do otherwise would amount to sex discrimination – see Brown v Rentokil Ltd 1998 ICR 790, ECJ. However, the ECJ also held in that case that, for the purposes of sex discrimination law, any periods of absence related to pregnancy or childbirth that occurred *after* the end of an employee's leave can be taken into account provided they are treated in the same way as any period of sickness absence taken by a male employee. The impact of the ECJ's ruling in the Brown case is illustrated by Lyons v DWP Jobcentre Plus 2014 ICR 668, EAT, where L, who had a history of depressive illness, suffered post-natal depression after the birth of her daughter. She was unable to return to work after the end of her maternity leave and an agreed period of annual leave, and she remained absent until her dismissal for long-term absence. The EAT held that, while L had been treated unfavourably, her dismissal had taken place after her maternity leave, when the 'protected period', as defined in S.18(6) EqA, had ended. She had not, therefore, suffered pregnancy and

139

maternity discrimination. L's claim of direct sex discrimination also failed. The EAT rejected L's argument that because her post-natal depression had arisen during her maternity leave her dismissal was discriminatory even though it had taken place after the end of the protected period.

(Note that it has been held that a dismissal for a pregnancy-related reason which takes place after maternity leave may nonetheless amount to an automatically unfair dismissal under S.99 ERA – see Caledonia Bureau Investment and Property v Caffrey 1998 ICR 603, EAT – but it is questionable whether Reg 20 would support such a decision today – see Chapter 12, 'Detriment and unfair dismissal', under 'Automatically unfair dismissal – pregnancy, childbirth and maternity', and Chapter 13, 'Discrimination and equal pay', under 'Direct discrimination – pregnancy-related illness', for further discussion of this case.)

4.40 There is, of course, nothing to prevent an employer and employee from agreeing between themselves to postpone the employee's date of return. Such an agreement would become part of the employee's composite maternity rights – see Chapter 3, 'Maternity leave', under 'Contractual and composite maternity rights'.

4.41 **Other types of leave.** An employee may be entitled to postpone her return by taking an immediate period of unpaid parental leave at the end of her maternity leave – see 'Combining different types of leave' below. She may also be entitled to take annual leave under her contract or under the Working Time Regulations 1998 SI 1998/1833, in which case she would have to give the requisite notice and, at least in so far as statutory leave is concerned, the employer may have the right to object to her taking leave at that time for any reason (or no reason at all). For further information on the right to annual leave under the Working Time Regulations, see IDS Employment Law Handbook, 'Working Time' (2013), Chapter 4, 'Annual leave'.

Note that paid annual leave (both contractual and statutory) which would normally accrue while the employee was at work continues to accrue during her SML. Holiday rights during maternity leave are discussed in Chapter 3, 'Maternity leave', under 'Terms and conditions during maternity leave – annual leave'.

4.42 **Unauthorised late return.** A woman who has no lawful excuse (as set out above) for delaying her return from maternity leave may be treated as any other employee who takes unauthorised leave and dealt with under the employer's disciplinary procedure. However, it does not always follow that an employee's failure to return by the due date will constitute a repudiatory breach entitling the employer to dismiss her without notice – Rashid v Asian Community Care Services Ltd EAT 480/99.

Returning on different terms 4.43

An employee's right to return from maternity leave is a right to return to her old job on terms and conditions no less favourable than those which would have applied had she not been absent – unless, in the case of AML, it is not reasonably practicable for her to return to that job, in which case she has a right to return to a suitable and appropriate alternative job, but still on no less favourable terms and conditions – Regs 18 and 18A MPL Regulations (see 'Returning after ordinary maternity leave' and 'Returning after additional maternity leave' above). However, an employee may wish to return to work on different terms and conditions – e.g. part time or with different hours – to fit in with her family responsibilities.

Contractual right to return on different terms 4.44

Some employers, particularly in the public sector, expressly allow employees to return to work on different terms, e.g. on a part-time basis or working different hours. If an employee who worked full time before her maternity leave has this sort of provision in her contract, she may choose to return part time (or on different hours) if she wishes. Her freedom of choice derives from the 'composite right' conferred on her by Reg 21 MPL Regulations, which provides that if an employee has statutory maternity leave rights and corresponding maternity leave rights 'under [her] contract of employment or otherwise' she may not exercise the two rights separately but may take advantage of whichever right is, in any particular respect, the more favourable – see Chapter 3, 'Maternity leave', under 'Contractual and composite maternity rights'.

However, there are limits to how far an employee can pick and choose. In Bovey v Board of Governors of the Hospital for Sick Children 1978 ICR 934, EAT, B was employed as a full-time physiotherapist, grade 1. Before starting maternity leave she said that she wanted to return to work part time. The employer said that she could but only as a physiotherapist, basic grade. B agreed but later claimed that she was entitled to exercise a composite right to return part time at grade 1. No such job was available and B claimed that she had been unfairly dismissed when the employer refused to allow her to return on her own terms. The EAT said that her right to return part time was not a contractual one: this was true, but it was a right under an agreement separate from her contract and was still covered by the then equivalent of Reg 21. The EAT went on to say that B's rights, such as they were, were essentially indivisible. B had a statutory right to return full time in grade 1 and she also had a contractual right to return part time in the basic grade. B could not subdivide her rights further and claim a right to return part time but at a better grade than that provided by her agreement with the employer.

141

4.45 'Flexible working' and indirect sex discrimination

Even where an employee has no contractual right to opt to return part time (or with different working hours), she has the right to request 'flexible working' – in effect, to request a change in her terms and conditions of employment. From 30 June 2014, this 'right to request' became available to all employees with 26 weeks' continuous service (not just those with caring responsibilities as was the case before this date). For more information about the right to request flexible working, see IDS Employment Law Handbook, 'Atypical and Flexible Working' (2014), Chapter 4, 'Flexible working'.

In addition, an employee may succeed in a complaint of indirect sex discrimination if the employer cannot show any objective justification for its refusal to allow her to return on different terms. This is dealt with in Chapter 13, 'Discrimination and equal pay', under 'Indirect sex discrimination', and in IDS Employment Law Handbook, 'Atypical and Flexible Working' (2014), Chapter 4, 'Flexible working', under 'Discrimination claims'. Two examples:

- **Sidpra v Smile Publishing Ltd** ET Case No.3202027/03: during her maternity leave S raised the possibility of returning part time, working for one day a week. Her employer replied in writing saying that it was not able to accommodate her wish to return for one day a week, and the letter concluded with thanks for her work for them and wishing her well for the future. The letter was followed two weeks later by a cheque for holiday pay and her P45. S had tried on many occasions to contact her employer by telephone, but nobody was available to speak to her until shortly before she received her P45. At no time did the employer discuss with S whether she would be able to work for more than one day a week. A tribunal upheld her discrimination and unfair dismissal claims. Having made up its mind that one day a week would not work, the employer made a conscious decision that it was not going to discuss the matter further with S to see if a mutually acceptable compromise could be reached. That amounted to direct discrimination. There was also indirect discrimination in that the employer might have had grounds for not accepting S's request to work for just one day a week, but that was not the same as showing that the requirement to work full time was justified. The employer was not prepared to consider whether S could have been employed for something between one and five days a week

- **Warren v Maple House Independent Montessori School Ltd** ET Case No.2300997/04: W worked as a full-time teacher until she went on maternity leave in summer 2003. She hoped to return to teaching at the school on a part-time basis. By November 2003 the employer had decided that part-time work could only be offered to W for three months, after which time she would have to revert to full-time working. She refused to accept that condition and the employer withdrew the offer of three months' part-time work. A tribunal upheld W's discrimination claim. Her employer had failed to investigate the possibility of making part-time working feasible, and by insisting that W could only come back on a part-time basis if she agreed to revert to full-time working after three months, it removed the possibility of carrying out an empirical trial. The employer thus failed to establish justification.

However, whether or not a discrimination claim can be made out will depend **4.46** entirely on the circumstances, as the following cases demonstrate:

- **Riggs v Parker Bath Ltd** ET Case No.3103163/02: R was employed full time until 2001 when she went on maternity leave. She asked her employer if she could return part time, working mornings. Her employer had no objection in principle, provided appropriate arrangements could be made, and sought to employ another person to work on a job-share basis. However, by the time R was due to return from maternity leave, her employer had been unable to recruit anyone. Her employer informed her that part-time work was not available and that if she did not return to work she would be in repudiatory breach of contract. R refused to return to full-time employment and her employer regarded her as having resigned. R's sex discrimination claim failed because her employer had a genuine need that outweighed the discriminatory effect of the refusal to accede to her request. Her claims of unfair dismissal and breach of contract also failed. Since her contract required her to work full time, her refusal to do so amounted to a repudiation of the contract. Her employer was entitled to accept the breach as discharging it from further performance of the contract

- **Browning v HSBC Bank Ltd** ET Case No.1101477/07: B was employed as a commercial manager. She indicated that on her return to work following maternity leave she wanted to work only three days a week, but the employer said that this would not be possible because of the need to meet customer demands. She declined an offer to work reduced hours over five days. She was subsequently offered a senior clerical role on a temporary basis, pending a suitable managerial role becoming available and was told she would retain her managerial status, pay and benefits. She rejected the offer. Her manager was determined not to lose her and persuaded the employer to create a new role for her. She accepted the post and it was agreed that she would begin work on 2 March 2007. However, she resigned soon afterwards and claimed discrimination and constructive unfair dismissal in relation to her employer's handling of her return to work. The tribunal dismissed her claims. The employer had applied a criterion that commercial manager posts had to be carried out over five days a week, but that was legitimate given the need to provide customer satisfaction: the tribunal accepted that business customers expected instant access to their commercial manager, especially when they had urgent matters to discuss. The employer attempted

143

to employ B in a suitable alternative role, and the tribunal concluded that the employer had acted reasonably in this regard

- **Andrews v Rapid Electronics Ltd** ET Case No.1500748/03: A asked to work for 24 hours a week on her return from maternity leave. Her employer replied that it would need to discuss and agree the precise job content with her. On her return, and as a result of the change in hours, her role had changed somewhat and she subsequently resigned and claimed unfair constructive dismissal, sex discrimination and breach of Reg 18. She said she would have considered returning on a full-time basis had she been told that was the only way she could maintain her position. The tribunal decided that on the facts A had never sought to exercise her right to return to her original job and it was justifiable for the employer to feel that it was unreasonable for her to 'cherry pick the best parts' of her previous job. However, she had been unfairly constructively dismissed as a result of the way she was treated during meetings to discuss the issue on her return.

4.47 Failure to allow employee to return

If the employer refuses to take the employee back after her maternity leave, this will amount to a dismissal. Employers need to be wary of making assumptions about an employee's intentions in this regard. If it is wrongly assumed that she does not intend to return, she is likely to have a strong case for unfair dismissal and/or sex discrimination. Some illustrations:

- **Musgrove v Horizons Health and Leisure** ET Case No.2601700/04: M worked as an administrator at the leisure centre where her partner was a general manager. While she was on maternity leave, he resigned. Although M had notified her employer of her intention to return to work at the end of her maternity leave, it appeared that her employer believed that because her partner had left, she was also leaving. Her employer took steps to fill her job and merged it with a receptionist role. Even if her job no longer existed, the tribunal found that she should have been offered the new position. She had been unfairly dismissed and the failure to offer her the post was discriminatory

- **Sethi v Greentech International Ltd** ET Case No.1900752/07: S was employed by a family company, having married the owners' son, who was the office manager. While she was on maternity leave, her marriage broke down. Although her employer had no intention of dismissing her, it was assumed that it would be inappropriate for her to return in the circumstances and that she had resigned. However, a tribunal found ample evidence that S did intend to return to work, given her repeated letters asking for the dates and terms of her return to be confirmed. Her claims of unfair dismissal and sex discrimination succeeded

144

- **Wilkinson v RKR Associates Ltd** ET Case No.2407150/07: W, on maternity leave for the second time, suggested to her employer that 'she did not think that she would be [able] to continue working whilst looking after two young children'. The tribunal was 'wholly satisfied' that W had not thereby given notice of her resignation, and found that she was unfairly dismissed and discriminated against when her employer refused to pay her or give her any work to do upon the expiry of her maternity leave

- **Freitas v The Food Atelier Ltd** ET Case No.2302539/11: During F's maternity leave, she visited her workplace believing that she was to collect paperwork necessary to enable her to claim maternity pay. Instead, she was given an envelope containing her P45, which F took to mean that she had been dismissed. TFA Ltd maintained that F had decided not to return to work after her maternity leave ended and had said she wanted her P45. A tribunal found that TFA Ltd's witness was vague and confused when giving evidence and his demeanour suggested that he was not comfortable with the version of facts that he was giving. It did not make sense that F would resign when still trying to pursue her entitlement to SMP and maternity allowance. F was unfairly dismissed and suffered sex discrimination.

Automatically unfair dismissal

4.48

A refusal to allow an employee to return after maternity leave will amount to an automatically unfair dismissal:

- where the reason or principal reason for it related to the fact that she had given birth or taken, sought to take or availed herself of the benefits of, maternity leave (see Chapter 12, 'Detriment and unfair dismissal', under 'Automatically unfair dismissal') – Reg 20(1)(a) MPL Regulations

- where the employee was selected for redundancy where the circumstances constituting the redundancy applied equally to one or more other employees who held similar positions and who were not dismissed and the reason or principal reason for selection was related to the fact that she had given birth or taken, sought to take or availed herself of the benefits of maternity leave (see Chapter 12, 'Detriment and unfair dismissal', under 'Automatically unfair dismissal – automatically unfair redundancy') – Reg 20(2)

- where the reason or principal reason for the dismissal was that her original job was no longer available because of redundancy and the employer had not complied with Reg 10 with regard to offering suitable alternative employment (see 'Redundancy during maternity leave' below) – Reg 20(1)(b).

Exceptions. There are two exceptions to the above rules – see 'Compliance with Reg 10' and 'Job offer from associated employer' below. Where these apply, although the dismissal will not be automatically unfair, the employee will still be able to bring a claim of unfair dismissal under the ordinary rules, **4.49**

145

provided she has the necessary length of service, and it will be for the tribunal to decide whether the dismissal was fair in all the circumstances. She may also be able to claim sex discrimination – see Chapter 12, 'Detriment and unfair dismissal', under '"Ordinary" unfair dismissal', and Chapter 13, 'Discrimination and equal pay'.

4.50 *Compliance with Reg 10.* Where the reason or principal reason for dismissal is that the employee's original job is no longer available because of redundancy (the third of the circumstances outlined above), the employer may avoid a finding of automatically unfair dismissal by complying with the obligations of Reg 10 MPL Regulations (see 'Redundancy during maternity leave' below).

Note that this exception does not apply where the reason or principal reason for the employee's selection for redundancy was a pregnancy, birth or maternity-related reason (the second of the circumstances outlined above). In other words, the employee can still claim automatic unfair dismissal if the reason she was selected for redundancy was that she was absent on maternity leave, even if the employer offered her suitable and appropriate alternative employment on no less favourable terms and conditions in compliance with Reg 10. However, such an offer would be likely to mitigate any compensation she might receive.

4.51 *Job offer from associated employer.* There is a further exception to an employee's right to claim automatically unfair dismissal where:

- she has been dismissed for a pregnancy, birth or maternity-related reason, or because of redundancy in circumstances where the employer has not complied with Reg 10 MPL Regulations (i.e. in either the first or third set of circumstances outlined above)

- it was not reasonably practicable on grounds other than redundancy for the employer (or his successor) to permit her to return to a job which is suitable and appropriate for her to do in the circumstances, and

- an 'associated employer' offered her a suitable and appropriate alternative job which she accepted or unreasonably refused – Reg 20(7) MPL Regulations. (Two employers are 'associated' if one is a company of which the other, directly or indirectly, has control or both are companies of which a third person, directly or indirectly, has control – Reg 2(3).)

This exception would apply, for example, where there is a business reorganisation within a group of companies that does not involve redundancies.

This exception to the right to claim automatic unfair dismissal appears, on the face of it, to qualify both the employee's right to return from maternity leave and the obligations on the employer in redundancy situations imposed by Reg 10. Take, for example, an employee returning from OML. Under Reg 18(1) she has the right to return to the job in which she was employed before her absence. Imagine that her employer reorganises her department while she is on maternity leave and gives her job to someone else on a permanent basis because of her absence. On her return she is offered a suitable and appropriate job in a subsidiary company. The employee has effectively been deprived of her right to return to her own job under Reg 18(1). But she has no automatic right to claim unfair dismissal because of the effect of Reg 20(7) – and, if she does not have one year's service, she cannot claim unfair dismissal at all. Her only option in such circumstances would be to bring a sex discrimination claim – and, if the alternative job was offered on terms and conditions commensurate with her original job, it is likely that the only available remedy would be in respect of injury to her feelings.

Similarly, the effect of Reg 10 is to require employers to offer any suitable **4.52** alternative vacancy to a redundant employee on maternity leave in preference to other redundant employees (as explained under 'Redundancy during maternity leave' below). Such an offer must be of work that is suitable and appropriate for the employee and on 'not substantially less favourable' terms and conditions. Imagine a situation where an employee on maternity leave has been made redundant. The employer has a suitable and appropriate job, but it is not 'reasonably practicable' to offer it to the employee because funding for it is not available. Instead, an associated employer offers her a job that is suitable and appropriate for her, but for substantially less pay. She refuses it.

It seems that the above scenario could fall within the exception in Reg 20(7). This would mean that, despite the fact that the employer has not complied with Reg 10, the employee will have no automatic right to claim unfair dismissal. However, note that the employer would have to show, first, that her refusal of the job with the associated employer was unreasonable – Reg 20(7)(c) and (8). If the employer was contravening Reg 10 in failing to offer her a suitable alternative vacancy on not substantially less favourable terms and conditions, it is likely that it would have an uphill struggle in demonstrating that she was acting unreasonably. So, despite the fact that Reg 20(7) appears to qualify the employer's need to comply with Reg 10, in practice it is unlikely to have much impact.

Has there been a dismissal? There seems to have been an assumption in some **4.53** first instance tribunal decisions (for example, Tighe v Midland Magazine Representation Services Ltd ET Case No.5172/82 and Acteson v Silent Channel Products Ltd ET Case No.15826/79, referred to under 'Returning after ordinary maternity leave – terms and conditions "not less favourable"' above) that where the employer allows the employee to return, but on less favourable terms and conditions, this will amount to a dismissal. The assumption appears to have derived from the old S.96 ERA (and its predecessors), which provided that an employee who had the right to return to work but was not permitted to do so was treated as dismissed. The 'right to return' to work was, and still is, defined as including the right to have the same job on the same terms and

147

conditions, and so, on a strict reading of the statute, a woman who was denied any aspect of the right to return could have been treated as having been 'not permitted to return' and, therefore, dismissed.

The special definition of 'dismissal' in S.96 was needed because a dismissal at common law (and under S.95 ERA for the purposes of unfair dismissal) involves the termination of a contract of employment. Before December 1999 a woman's contract of employment did not automatically subsist beyond the end of what is now known as ordinary maternity leave and this therefore presented a problem for a woman taking extended maternity leave because without a contract she was not an employee and technically could not be dismissed. In December 1999 the law was amended to introduce the concept of additional maternity leave and to provide that the contract of employment continued unbroken throughout. There was thus no longer any need for a special definition of dismissal following maternity leave, since the employee would have a contract and could rely on the ordinary definition of dismissal. S.96 was therefore repealed.

4.54 Where this now leaves us is that for an employee to claim to have been unfairly dismissed she must first of all show that there has been a termination of the employment contract. Clearly, an employer informing an employee that there is no job at all for her after maternity leave would fall squarely within the definition of dismissal. However, it is doubtful that an employer who takes the employee back but unilaterally changes her terms and conditions for the worse – or changes the nature of the work, capacity or place in which she is employed – could automatically be assumed to have 'dismissed' her according to the usual definition of dismissal. This situation is analogous to one where an employer unilaterally changes the terms and conditions of an employee who has not been on maternity leave. The employee in this situation has three options:

- accept the change

- remain in employment under the new terms and conditions 'under protest' and sue for damages or an injunction

- if the breach is sufficiently serious as to go to the root of the contract, resign and claim constructive dismissal, arguing that it is automatically unfair under Reg 20 MPL Regulations (if the reason for the change was related to the fact that the employee took maternity leave) or unfair under S.98 ERA (if the reason was unrelated to that fact).

In Clarke v Lifetime Financial Management Ltd ET Case No.1900103/04 C's employer was bought out by a larger company during her maternity leave. As a result the administration needed to be pruned and those staff at work at the time were consulted about the reorganisation and where appropriate were offered the opportunity to relocate to new premises. C was completely ignored during this process, but heard something of the reorganisation from a colleague.

She was upset and worried, and decided to return to work sooner than she had planned, but when she contacted her employer she discovered that her original job had disappeared and the only option for her involved a demotion. She decided to resign. A tribunal found that she had been unfairly constructively dismissed as a result of her employer's breach of the obligations owed to her and that she had also been discriminated against.

4.55 However, in Bennett v McGinley Recruitment Services ET Case No.3314794/06 an employee failed to demonstrate that she had been constructively dismissed because of a change in her terms and conditions. When B left to go on maternity leave it was agreed that she would return to work on a part-time basis, working 30 hours a week. She returned to work on 2 January 2006, but the next day her employer informed her that she would have to return full time as otherwise there was no job for her to come back to, unless she wanted to take on a part-time receptionist role. She rejected that role (given that she was at the time studying for accountancy qualifications), and matters continued as they were with her working for 30 hours a week until May 2006, when she resigned. A tribunal found that she had not been constructively dismissed. Her employer breached her contract in January by going back on the agreement to allow her to return to her old job for 30 hours a week, but when B rejected the alternative she was allowed to continue doing work that was substantially the same as the work she had previously done, for the agreed number of hours. She had affirmed that contract by the time of her resignation.

The employee may also be able to bring a claim of sex discrimination, detriment, and/or (provided she has not accepted the change and her pay has been affected) unlawful deduction from wages. Detriment claims are discussed in Chapter 12, 'Detriment and unfair dismissal', and sex discrimination is covered in Chapter 13, 'Discrimination and equal pay'. Breach of contract and constructive dismissal claims are dealt with in IDS Employment Law Handbook, 'Contracts of Employment' (2014), in Chapter 10, 'Breach of contract', and Chapter 11, 'Termination by dismissal', under 'Constructive dismissal'. Protection of wages claims are addressed in IDS Employment Law Handbook, 'Wages' (2011), Chapter 3, 'Protection of wages – 1', and Chapter 4, 'Protection of wages – 2'.

Combining different types of leave
4.56

Normally an employee returning from OML is entitled to return to the same job on the same terms and conditions. However, there is an exception where that leave period was the last of two or more consecutive periods of statutory leave which included one of the following:

* any period of unpaid parental leave of more than four weeks – for example, where the employee already has a child under the age of five and has taken a period of unpaid parental leave of more than four weeks to care for that

child immediately before starting maternity, adoption or paternity leave in respect of a newborn child; or

- any period of statutory leave which when added to any other period of statutory leave (excluding unpaid parental leave) taken in relation to the same child means that the total amount of leave taken in relation to that child totals more than 26 weeks – Reg 18(1)(b) MPL Regulations (as amended by Reg 5 of the Maternity and Parental Leave etc (Amendment) Regulations 2014 SI 2014/3221 with effect from 1 December 2014).

'Statutory leave' means leave provided for in Part 8 of the Employment Rights Act 1996 – Reg 2(1). This includes maternity leave, adoption leave, shared parental leave, unpaid parental leave and paternity leave.

4.57 In any of the above situations the employee does not have the right to return to the same job if it is not reasonably practicable for the employer to permit him or her to return to that job, in which case the employee is entitled to return to another job which is both suitable and appropriate for the employee to do in the circumstances. This is the same right to return as that enjoyed by employees returning directly from AML.

4.58 Taking unpaid parental leave after ordinary maternity leave
Special considerations apply where an employee on OML wishes to tack on a period of unpaid parental leave at the end. This situation is unlikely to arise in practice since an employee will usually take a period of AML – which is (at least in part) paid – in preference, and will not need to take unpaid parental leave at the end of OML. However, if (for example) an employee is paid during parental leave under the terms of her contract, it is not inconceivable that the situation might arise. (Note that to avoid confusion with the new right to take shared parental leave – see Chapter 8, 'Shared parental leave and pay' – we refer to parental leave under the MPL Regulations as 'unpaid' parental leave, as there is no statutory right to be paid for such leave. However, as we have made clear, it is always open to an employer to make a payment under the contract.)

Under Reg 18(1)(b) MPL Regulations an employee returning to work after OML followed by a period of unpaid parental leave of four weeks or less enjoys the same right to return as someone who had not taken the unpaid parental leave. An employee who takes a period of unpaid parental leave of more than four weeks is entitled to return to the job in which he or she was employed before the absence unless it is not reasonably practicable to permit the employee to return to that job, in which case he or she is entitled to return to another job which is both suitable and appropriate in the circumstances – Reg 18(2) MPL Regulations. This is the same right to return as that enjoyed by employees returning directly from AML.

Note that an employee taking unpaid parental leave at the end of maternity **4.59** leave must give the requisite 21 days' notice under the default statutory scheme of his or her wish to take such leave in the normal way. In other words, an employee must notify the employer at least 21 days before her maternity leave ends if she wants to take unpaid parental leave immediately after the end of her maternity leave. Furthermore, the employer will be able to postpone the leave if it considers that the leave would unduly disrupt the operation of the business (although it may be hard to argue that the leave would be disruptive when the employee has already been absent for a significant period). The right to take unpaid parental leave is discussed in detail in Chapter 10, 'Unpaid parental leave'.

Sick leave and annual leave

4.60

Taking sick leave or annual leave immediately before or after a period of maternity leave of any length does not affect the employee's rights on returning to work.

Redundancy during maternity leave

4.61

Special provisions apply where, during an employee's maternity leave, it is not practicable by reason of redundancy for her employer to continue to employ her under her existing contract of employment – Reg 10(1) MPL Regulations. In these circumstances, where there is a suitable available vacancy, the employee is entitled to be offered suitable alternative employment with her employer, its successor or an associated employer before the end of her employment under her existing contract – Reg 10(2). The new contract must take effect immediately on the ending of the previous contract and must be such that:

- the work to be done is of a kind which is both suitable in relation to the employee and appropriate for her to do in the circumstances – Reg 10(3)(a), and

- its provisions as to the capacity and place in which she is to be employed, and as to the other terms and conditions of her employment, are not substantially less favourable to her than if she had continued to be employed under the previous contract – Reg 10(3)(b).

The question of whether a redundancy situation has arisen should be answered by reference to the standard definition of 'redundancy' in S.139 ERA – Secretary of State for Justice v Slee EAT 0349/06. In Sefton Borough Council v Wainwright 2015 IRLR 90, EAT, the Council decided to abolish two roles, including that of W, who was on maternity leave, and replace them with one new job. W was not offered the new job and succeeded in a claim of automatically unfair dismissal on the basis that the new role was a suitable available vacancy. On appeal to the EAT, the Council argued that Reg 10 was not engaged until the decision had been taken as to who was the best candidate for the new role – in effect, W was not 'redundant' until the Council had determined who would be slotted into the role, and only at that point would it become obliged to offer a suitable vacancy. The EAT held that this interpretation would undermine the protection offered by Reg 10. Applying the S.139 ERA definition, the tribunal was entitled to conclude that there was a redundancy when the Council decided that two positions would be replaced by one.

4.62 If a suitable alternative vacancy exists (i.e. a vacancy that is suitable, appropriate and not substantially less favourable than the employee's previous job) and the employer fails to offer it to the employee, the dismissal will be automatically unfair under S.99 ERA if the reason or principal reason for the dismissal is redundancy – Reg 20(1)(b). If, however, such a vacancy genuinely does not exist, or the employer does offer her such a vacancy and the employee unreasonably refuses it, her dismissal will almost certainly be fair and she will lose her right to a redundancy payment – see S.141 ERA.

In Simpson v Endsleigh Insurance Services Ltd 2011 ICR 75, EAT, the Appeal Tribunal confirmed that Reg 10(3)(a) and 10(3)(b) MPL Regulations must be read together. In that case S was employed by EIS Ltd as an insurance consultant in London. In May 2008 she went on maternity leave. At around the same time, EIS Ltd announced a proposal to close 119 retail outlets and relocate the business to its call centres in Cheltenham, Burnley and Belfast. It began consulting the workforce about this and sent S regular correspondence, including details of vacancies – although some of this remained unopened until July following S's prolonged stay in hospital due to complications during childbirth. A final consultation document sent to S stated that staff would be automatically offered an insurance consultant position in Cheltenham, Burnley or Belfast if they applied for it. S, however, showed no interest in this position or in any other vacancies, apart from one based in London. She later claimed that this was because she had been very ill following childbirth and her attention was focused on looking after herself and her child.

4.63 Following the closure of the company's retail business and her failure to obtain alternative employment, S was made redundant on 21 August 2008. She subsequently brought an employment tribunal claim for automatically unfair dismissal under S.99 ERA on the basis that EIS Ltd had failed to offer her a suitable vacancy in breach of Reg 10. In the view of the employment tribunal, there were four vacancies that potentially constituted a 'suitable available vacancy' for the purposes of Reg 10(2): assistant broker, cashier, collections adviser and insurance consultant. However, all four positions were based in Cheltenham and the tribunal was not persuaded that S was willing to relocate there. As a result, the tribunal – applying an objective test – found that the employer had been entitled to conclude that the four posts were either not suitable in relation to her or not appropriate for her in the circumstances within the meaning of Reg 10(3)(a) because of the need to relocate. In addition, it held that the new place of employment amounted to a substantially less favourable term for the purpose of Reg 10(3)(b). Accordingly, the obligation under Reg 10(2) was not triggered and the S.99 claim failed.

S appealed to the EAT, contending that the tribunal had been wrong to apply Reg 10(3)(b) when deciding whether or not EIS Ltd had a suitable available vacancy to offer her. The insurance consultant position in Cheltenham had – she argued – met the Reg 10(3)(a) requirements of being both suitable and appropriate and EIS Ltd had therefore been required to offer her that vacancy (as opposed to simply sending her information about it and inviting her to reply) before entering into discussions as to whether the terms were substantially less favourable under Reg 10(3)(b).

The EAT gave short shrift to S's interpretation of Reg 10(3). In its view, the **4.64** requirement to offer a 'suitable available vacancy' under Reg 10(2) can only sensibly be tested if the offer is coupled with a new contract of employment that complies with Reg 10(3)(b). S's suggestion – that a suitable available vacancy had to be offered to the employee when Reg 10(3)(a) is satisfied and that Reg 10(3)(b) need only be looked at afterwards as part of the negotiations – seemed to import a two-stage process into Reg 10(3) that was not apparent from its wording. Both limbs of Reg 10(3) needed to be satisfied before an employee is entitled to be offered alternative employment under Reg 10(2).

Contrary to what S asserted, the tribunal had also been correct to assess the suitability of the available vacancies from the perspective of an objective employer, rather than from an employee's perspective: under Reg 10, it was for the employer to decide whether to offer a suitable available vacancy and there was no requirement for the employee to engage in this process. However, the employer should consider what it knows about the employee's personal circumstances and work experience and decide, on this basis, whether or not a vacancy is suitable. S's appeal was dismissed.

This case makes it clear that the requirement to offer a suitable available **4.65** vacancy under Reg 10(2) is contingent upon the new terms and conditions not being 'substantially less favourable' to the employee. If any of the terms and conditions associated with the vacancy are substantially less favourable, the employee is not then entitled to be offered the position, even if the work is otherwise suitable and appropriate for her. Less favourable terms may, of course, also indicate unsuitability. Indeed, in the above case, the tribunal held that the work in Cheltenham was not, in any event, suitable and appropriate for S because there was no evidence that she was willing to relocate. If an employee is more than happy to move or the new location is not too far away, it would be harder to argue that the post was not suitable or appropriate, or that the term as to place of employment was substantially less favourable.

The EAT also made it clear that it is for the employer to decide whether a vacancy is suitable, 'knowing what it does about the employee', in terms of the employee's work experience and personal circumstances. Although the EAT did not consider that the employee was required to engage in the process of determining suitable vacancies for her, she may well wish to have some involvement. It would, in any event, be wise for the employer to consult with the employee about what might be suitable for her and document what is said, to minimise the potential for future conflict.

4.66 In many cases, the dispute is about whether the employer has to offer the employee a job with *more* favourable terms – such as a more senior position – as a suitable alternative role. In this regard, the EAT in the Simpson case was unwilling to countenance the possibility of suitability being tested by assessment or interview since, in its view, this would negate the special protection provided by Reg 10, under which the employee must be offered any position that satisfies Reg 10(3)(a) and (b), whether or not other employees are better suited to the job. This could put an employee on maternity leave in a more advantageous position than had she been at work, since, if working, she might not have been offered a suitable available vacancy in preference to more highly qualified candidates. That said, if the available role is significantly more senior, it is likely that it will be unsuitable for the employee since she will not have the necessary experience and/or qualifications.

The question may also arise as to whether, if there is a suitable and appropriate vacancy, the employer is obliged to offer it to the employee under Reg 10 even if this involves offering it at a higher salary or on better terms and conditions than it would otherwise have supported. Assuming the content of an available role is suitable and appropriate, we suggest that the wording of Reg 10 implies that it should be offered to the employee even if this means that the terms and conditions need to be bettered in order to ensure that the new contract is 'not substantially less favourable' than the old. But a large salary differential will usually imply that the role itself constitutes a demotion and thus would not be suitable and appropriate. For example, in Sharma v Jato Dynamics Ltd ET Case No.3301996/04 a tribunal accepted that two available roles of help desk coordinator/web developer and help desk administrator – which were 'of the order of £10,000 per annum less' than the claimant's salary as help desk manager – did not constitute suitable alternative employment.

4.67 No suitable alternative vacancy

If there is no suitable alternative vacancy, the employee's employment (and her maternity leave period) will come to an end by reason of redundancy. She will, however, be entitled to her notice period (see Chapter 3, 'Maternity leave', under 'Terms and conditions during maternity leave') and to a written statement of the reasons for her dismissal (S.92(4) ERA). She will also be entitled to a redundancy payment (statutory or contractual), provided she has sufficient qualifying service.

Note that the definition of 'redundancy' for the purposes of Reg 10 is the same as under the ERA. Therefore, following the House of Lords' decision in Murray and anor v Foyle Meats Ltd 1999 ICR 827, HL, an employee may be 'redundant' even if her employer is contractually entitled to move her to work in another area not affected by the redundancy situation – Secretary of State for Justice v Slee EAT 0349/06.

If an employer fails to follow a fair procedure when selecting an employee on **4.68** maternity leave for redundancy, the employee will be able to claim unfair dismissal in the ordinary way (provided she has sufficient qualifying service). She may also be able to claim unlawful sex and/or maternity discrimination. In McGuigan v TG Baynes and Sons EAT 1114/97, for example, the EAT held that a solicitors firm's failure to consult an employee about her impending redundancy amounted to direct sex discrimination, as the effective and predominant cause of the failure was the hope that she would not return to work after her child was born.

Furthermore, if the employee is selected for redundancy on grounds relating to her pregnancy/maternity in preference to other comparable employees, the dismissal will be automatically unfair – Reg 20(2). Whether or not an employee's absence on maternity leave is the reason for her selection for redundancy will be a matter of fact for the tribunal. Two examples:

- **Underwood and Croxson v Johnston** EAT 0026/02: J, a vet, argued that she had been selected for redundancy because she was on maternity leave. However, the EAT found that there was no evidence to justify this conclusion, given that on the facts as found by the tribunal there had been a significant downturn in the employer's business, and that J, unlike the other employees, refused to do emergency out-of-hours work, worked restricted hours and could not work with guinea pigs. Had J been willing to work the required hours, she would not have been made redundant

- **Ivey v Southwark Mediation Centre** ET Case No.2301226/05: I went on maternity leave in July 2004. In June she had been informed that the funding for her post would continue until September and it was hoped that further funding could be obtained thereafter. Another employee was engaged to cover I's maternity leave. I was due to return to work on 10 January but was told that her job would end on 31 December due to lack of funding. A tribunal upheld her sex discrimination claim. It was clear that the funding for the job on which she was engaged had come to an end, but in the past when that happened staff were transferred to other projects. The man who had been engaged to cover her maternity leave was transferred to a different project and the employer could give no satisfactory explanation for retaining him but dismissing I. The tribunal concluded that had I not been on maternity leave at the time she would not have been dismissed.

4.69 An employee selected for redundancy on grounds relating to her maternity leave may also be able to claim unlawful maternity discrimination. For example:

- **Woodall v Cap Gemini Ernst and Young** ET Case No.1301679/04: W's employer reorganised the administrative functions while she was on maternity leave and as a result W's function ceased to exist. The employer overlooked the fact that W would not have a job to return to until shortly before she was due to return to work, and made immediate arrangements to contact her at that point. A tribunal held that W suffered a detriment on the ground of her sex in not being told earlier that her job had disappeared. Had she been at work, she would have been consulted, and though there would have been no difference to the outcome, the tribunal took the view that there must be some detriment in late notification. The tribunal accepted that the failure to consult her was due to carelessness, but did not accept that the same degree of carelessness would have prevailed had W not been on maternity leave

- **Saunders v The Westgate Conference Centre Ltd** ET Case No.2800029/05: S was employed as a general manager. While on maternity leave she had a meeting with her employer to discuss her return to work, only to be told that there had been a number of changes in the business and that she was redundant. The managing director had taken over her duties and her job no longer existed because of financial constraints and a change of emphasis in the business of the conference centre. A tribunal decided that S was redundant and that the dismissal itself was not tainted by sex discrimination. However, she had been unfairly dismissed and had suffered sex discrimination in that she would have been consulted prior to the redundancy had she not been absent on maternity leave.

4.70 An employee who is dismissed during her SML will still be entitled to receive statutory maternity pay for the full 39-week pay period once she has qualified for it.

Unfair dismissal is discussed in Chapter 12, 'Detriment and unfair dismissal'; sex discrimination and pregnancy and maternity discrimination in Chapter 13, 'Discrimination and equal pay'; and statutory maternity pay in Chapter 5, 'Statutory maternity pay'.

4.71 **When does the duty to offer alternative employment arise?**
The first point to note is that employers do not discharge their statutory obligations simply by making an offer of a suitable alternative job. They must first show that it was not practicable to reinstate in the old job. This means that the employer must satisfy the tribunal that it was necessary to implement the redundancy during the period of maternity leave – Calor Gas v Bray EAT 0633/04. An example:

• **Varney v Jaguar Cars Ltd** ET Case No.1304733/04: during V's absence on maternity leave her employer introduced a new method of working into her department, which entailed employees working in teams of four. An employee who was at risk of redundancy in another area was brought into the department to make up such a team. On her return to work, V was not allowed to return to her old job, because of the redeployment into the department of the other employee, and she was moved to a new post. A tribunal upheld V's sex discrimination complaint. The employer had failed to address the question of whether it would have been practicable to return V to her old post. It might have been convenient to replace her with the employee who would otherwise have been redundant, but the cover could have been provided by an employee working on a temporary contract. V suffered a detriment because her post was awarded permanently to another employee while she was on maternity leave, without justification.

Regulation 10 MPL Regulations provides that where it is not practicable by **4.72** reason of redundancy for the employer to continue to employ an employee on maternity leave, she is entitled to be offered alternative employment before the end of her employment under her existing contract. It follows that the right to be offered a suitable vacancy arises when the redundancy situation affecting the employee's job becomes known and extinguishes either when the dismissal takes effect or when maternity leave ends (if sooner). If, during that time, suitable alternative work becomes available, it should be offered as an alternative to dismissal. If it does not, then the woman may be dismissed for redundancy, although she must be given proper notice of dismissal in accordance with her contract (unless there is a provision for payment in lieu) and, since the dismissal itself does not strictly take place until the end of the notice period, she must be offered any suitable vacancy which becomes available during her notice period. However, once the dismissal has taken effect, her maternity leave period automatically comes to an end by virtue of Reg 7(5), so the employer does not need to offer her any vacancy arising after that time because Reg 10 only has effect during the maternity leave period.

Thus, contrary to what some people believe, it is open to an employer to dismiss an employee on the ground of redundancy during her maternity leave, provided a proper procedure is followed. There is no requirement to extend the consultation period during which suitable alternative vacancies should be considered to the end of the maternity leave period – Calor Gas v Bray EAT 0633/04.

Precedence over other employees   **4.73**
What is surprising about the employer's duty under Reg 10 MPL Regulations to offer any suitable vacancy to a woman whose job becomes redundant while she is on maternity leave is that it appears to be absolute. This means that if suitable alternative employment is available it *must* be offered to that woman in preference to any other employee who is similarly affected by the redundancy

157

situation but who is not absent on maternity leave. A failure to do so will make the woman's dismissal automatically unfair. To a large extent, this puts a woman on maternity leave in a far more advantageous position than if she were at work, since it may be that, had she been at work, she would not have been offered one of the available alternative jobs in preference to other more highly qualified candidates.

Normally speaking, an employer who fails to offer a suitable alternative vacancy to a redundant employee may be found to have unfairly dismissed that employee under the ERA, which does not explicitly state that employees on maternity leave must have first refusal on job offers. However, the difference is that where the dismissed employee is on maternity leave at the time of the redundancy the dismissal will be automatically unfair if the vacancy is not offered, whereas with other employees the failure to offer a suitable vacancy is just one of the factors to be considered by the tribunal when assessing whether the employer acted reasonably or not. Presumably, where an employee not on maternity leave is made redundant simply because the only suitable available vacancy has been offered to a woman on maternity leave, the employer's need to comply with Reg 10 in relation to the employee on maternity leave will be taken into account by a tribunal deciding whether the employer acted reasonably in making the other employee redundant.

4.74 Note that the duty is to offer suitable alternative employment, not simply to offer the opportunity to apply for it, as the following cases demonstrate:

- **Jones-Fraser v First Rung Ltd** ET Case No.3302366/02: J-F went on maternity leave in April 2002. Although she intended to return to work, a full-time replacement was employed on a permanent basis. J-F was then told that due to lack of work, she could be offered only 1.5 days' work a week. Later, the employer wrote to her saying that there was a possibility of an alternative full-time post and if she was interested in applying she should come for an interview. J-F refused to apply, pointing out that her right was to return to her old job on her old conditions. Her employer maintained that she should apply for the job as it was the only possible alternative to redundancy. A tribunal upheld J-F's unfair dismissal and sex discrimination claims. J-F would not have been redundant had she not taken maternity leave, but even if she was genuinely redundant, Reg 10 requires employees to be offered alternative work when it is available, not simply to be offered the opportunity to apply for it

- **Perli v St Mungo's Community Housing Association Ltd** ET Case No.2204235/04: P was employed on a fixed-term contract for one year from July 2003. She went on maternity leave in February 2004 and was told before she went that failing any communication to the contrary, she should expect to be made permanent in her post. However, during her leave, the HR Director offered someone else a temporary contract to perform P's job on the assumption that P would not return. When she visited the office to discuss her return to work, the Director was surprised and two days later he informed her that her post would end on the termination of her fixed-term contract and that a new permanent post of Recruitment Manager was to be established, for which she could apply. However, membership of CIPD was said to be a requirement of the job when it was advertised and P was not a member. P did not apply for that post, believing the recruitment process to be a sham, and a tribunal held that P had been discriminated against on the ground of her sex and automatically unfairly dismissed. The 'new' post was essentially the job that P had been employed to do, at the same grade and salary. Had she not gone on maternity leave she would have continued in post and her employment would have been made permanent.

The mandatory nature of the duty under Reg 10 was highlighted in Community Task Force v Rimmer 1986 ICR 491, EAT. There, R was employed by CTF in a post funded by the Manpower Services Commission. Due to a reorganisation while she was on maternity leave, her post became redundant, but a vacancy became available in another division. However, the Commission's funding rules prohibited her from being transferred to this job and so CTF refused to offer her the vacancy since this would have resulted in a cut in funding from the Commission. The EAT held that the employer was obliged to offer R the job since it was 'available' and the test of availability is not qualified by considerations of what is economic or reasonable. The consequences, however unpleasant, of the employer giving the applicant the job are not relevant to the question of whether the job is 'available'. (There can be little doubt that under the general law of unfair dismissal, an employee who was not on maternity leave could have been dismissed fairly for redundancy in circumstances similar to those in the Rimmer case, since the tribunal would be able to consider the reasonableness – from the employer's perspective – of refusing to offer the job to the employee.)

4.75 Given the mandatory nature of the requirement to offer a suitable available vacancy, ignorance of the existence of such a vacancy does not excuse an employer. Reg 10 applies 'where there is' such a vacancy, not just where the employer knows of it. This means that an employer will need to check across the whole organisation, including any associated employers (i.e. other businesses owned by the same person, or other companies in the same group), to ensure that no suitable vacancy exists.

Note that if a redundancy situation arises and the employer is considering dismissing an employee who is on maternity leave but the employee returns to work before dismissal takes place, she loses her right under Reg 10 to be offered a vacancy in preference to other employees. However, she still has the right, under the general law relating to redundancy, to be considered for any suitable vacancies along with the other employees. For a detailed analysis of the law governing redundancy, see IDS Employment Law Handbook, 'Redundancy' (2011).

4.76 Meaning of 'suitable available vacancy'

As we have seen above, the offer of a suitable available vacancy must be on terms such that:

- the work to be done is suitable in relation to the employee and appropriate for her to do in the circumstances, and

- the provisions of the contract as to the capacity and place in which she is to be employed and the other terms and conditions are not substantially less favourable than they would have been if the employee had continued to be employed under the previous contract – Reg 10(3) MPL Regulations.

Note that the terms and conditions attaching to the alternative job need only be not 'substantially' less favourable. Contrast this to the usual position on returning from maternity leave, where terms and conditions must be no less favourable at all. What is or is not substantial will be a question of fact for a tribunal to decide.

4.77 The alternative employment may be with the employer, its successor or an associated employer. Any two employers are treated as associated if one is a company of which the other (directly or indirectly) has control or both are companies of which a third person (directly or indirectly) has control – Reg 2(3).

The suitability of a job is a question of fact to be decided in the light of the individual employee's circumstances. The MPL Regulations refer to work that is suitable in relation to the employee and appropriate for her to do in the circumstances. This means that a tribunal can take into account any additional domestic problems caused by having a young baby – e.g. if there is an issue over increased travelling time to get to a job in a different location. However, suitability should be judged from the perspective of an objective employer, not from the employee's perspective – Simpson v Endsleigh Insurance Services Ltd 2011 ICR 75, EAT. According to the EAT in that case, it is up to the employer at the end of the day, knowing what it does about the employee's personal circumstances and work experience, to decide whether or not a vacancy is suitable and there was no requirement for the employee to engage in this process.

4.78 Three cases on the question of suitability:

- **Gillespie v Stamping Alliance Co Ltd** ET Case No.4554/81: G was a comptometer operator whose job became redundant during her maternity leave. She was offered a job as a clerk in the plant department but turned it down because she was not a clerk and the new job was in the middle of the factory and in noisy surroundings. The tribunal held that the job was suitable and G was unreasonable not to give it a try. G was not entitled to a redundancy payment

- **Brown-Williams v Microgen Ltd** ET Case No.31782/82: B-W was one of two regional production managers. She was paid a higher salary than the other manager and handled a much larger share of the company's workload. During her maternity leave the company reorganised and replaced the two regional production managers with a single national production manager. B-W was not offered this job but instead was offered jobs as 'client services representative' and 'enquiry service manager', which she refused. The tribunal held that while the two jobs offered were on the same grade and salary as her old job, they were not suitable because they were of lower status. But there was a suitable available vacancy – that for a national production manager. Failure to offer this to B-W made the dismissal automatically unfair

- **Hill v Supasnaps Ltd** ET Case No.13110/87: H was a branch manager of a photography shop before she went on maternity leave. While she was absent the company passed to new owners. This resulted in a reorganisation and changes were made to the branch managers' jobs. H was informed that there was no vacancy at her old branch and she was given the option of a similar job at one of two other branches. However, H argued that an increase in travelling time and additional childcare costs made these offers unsuitable. The tribunal agreed that H had been unfairly dismissed. It held that the employer had not established that H's old job had ceased to exist and had no contractual right to move her to a different branch. The tribunal also added that, even if her job had disappeared, the offers of alternative employment were not suitable because of the increase in travelling time and the cost of extra childcare.

An employer cannot rely on the fact that there is no identical job available as **4.79** an excuse for not offering an alternative. In Winterton v Tony's Pharmacy ET Case No.29186/78 the employer relied on the disappearance of W's morning job through redundancy. But there was a job available on the afternoon shift which would have been suitable and failure to offer this made the dismissal automatically unfair. The tribunal made a re-engagement order.

Under Reg 10 the only relevant question for the tribunal to ask itself is 'was there a suitable available vacancy?' If there is such a vacancy, then any unfavourable consequences for the employer are irrelevant. This was the view of the EAT in Community Task Force v Rimmer 1986 ICR 491, EAT, where it was held that R was automatically unfairly dismissed when her employer refused to offer her a new job that was available even though to have made such an offer would have led to a third party cutting funding for the post in question.

5 Statutory maternity pay

Qualifying for statutory maternity pay

Continuous employment

Normal weekly earnings

Notice of absence or childbirth

Medical evidence

Stopping work

Disentitlement to statutory maternity pay

Rates of statutory maternity pay

Manner of payment

Liability for SMP

The maternity pay period

Statutory maternity pay examples

Maternity Allowance

There are two types of statutory benefit available to women taking maternity **5.1** leave: statutory maternity pay (SMP) and Maternity Allowance. Claimants may be entitled to one or other of the benefits (but not both) depending on their employment status, their service record with present or past employers and the level of their earnings. SMP is paid by employers to those employees who satisfy the conditions of eligibility. Employers are, depending on their size, entitled to recover most if not all of their SMP bill from HM Revenue and Customs (HMRC) – see Chapter 9, 'Administering statutory payments', under 'Statutory maternity pay – recovery of payments', for details. Maternity Allowance is a social security benefit payable to the self-employed, women who do not satisfy the service requirement for SMP, and to women who are not employed or self-employed, but who work for their self-employed spouse or civil partner. It is payable not by the employer but through Jobcentre Plus, an executive agency of the Department for Work and Pensions (DWP). (Note that a woman who is not entitled to either SMP or Maternity Allowance may be able to claim Employment and Support Allowance (ESA), depending on her national insurance (NI) contributions in recent years.)

This chapter considers the qualifying conditions for SMP (which are quite independent of the qualifying conditions for statutory maternity leave

163

(SML) – see Chapter 3, 'Maternity leave', under 'Entitlement to maternity leave') and the circumstances in which women may become disentitled to SMP. We also deal with the payment of SMP. In particular, we outline the current rates of maternity pay, the manner in which both SMP and Maternity Allowance are paid, the period during which these payments are payable and the circumstances in which employees in receipt of SMP are disentitled to statutory sick pay.

5.2 SMP claims are dealt with by the Inland Revenue NI contributions office, which is now part of HMRC. Employees may appeal to the HMRC Statutory Payments Disputes Team against an employer's refusal to pay SMP or if the employer cannot pay because it has become insolvent. For further details on the administration and enforcement of the SMP scheme, see Chapter 9, 'Administering statutory payments'.

Most of the statutory provisions governing SMP are contained in Part XII (Ss.164–171) of the Social Security Contributions and Benefits Act 1992 (SSCBA). Ss.35–35B of Part II SSCBA set out the main provisions relating to Maternity Allowance. In addition, a number of different sets of Regulations set out the details of the statutory schemes. These include the Statutory Maternity Pay (General) Regulations 1986 SI 1986/1960 ('the SMP Regulations') and the Social Security (Maternity Allowance) Regulations 1987 SI 1987/416. Both these sets of Regulations and the SSCBA have been subject to numerous amendments over the years, most recently by the Social Security (Miscellaneous Amendments) Regulations 2015 SI 2015/67 and the Social Security (Maternity Allowance) (Miscellaneous Amendments) Regulations 2014 SI 2014/884. (Note that the SMP Regulations themselves still make a number of references to the Social Security (Contributions) Regulations 1979 SI 1979/591, even though these were revoked and replaced by the Social Security (Contributions) Regulations 2001 SI 2001/1004, which consolidated all the previous amendments to the 1979 Regulations. In this chapter we refer to the 2001 Regulations where relevant.) The SMP Regulations also make a number of references to Part V of the Social Security Act 1986, which has been repealed. Instead, those references should be read as referring to Part XII SSCBA.

5.3 Section references in this chapter are to the SSCBA and not, as elsewhere in this Handbook, to the Employment Rights Act 1996 (ERA). References to regulations are to the SMP Regulations unless otherwise stated.

The SMP scheme as described in this Handbook applies to England, Scotland and Wales. Similar, but not identical, provisions have been introduced for Northern Ireland by Orders in Council. The differences are ones of detail, reflecting the different institutions in Northern Ireland.

5.4 To explain the complex scheme of maternity benefits, a guide entitled 'Maternity benefits: technical guidance' (2014), which covers both SMP and Maternity

Allowance, has been published by the DWP. HMRC also publishes a booklet entitled 'Maternity pay and leave'. This explains the basic facts about the calculation and payment of SMP. Although these booklets are very useful, they are not legally binding and in cases of doubt reference should always be made to the statutory provisions and regulations.

Qualifying for statutory maternity pay 5.5

SMP is payable to a woman who is or has been an employee and who satisfies conditions of eligibility based on her length of service and her average earnings – S.164(1) SSCBA (see 'Continuous employment' and 'Normal weekly earnings' below). Women who do not qualify for SMP may still qualify for Maternity Allowance from Jobcentre Plus – see 'Maternity Allowance' below.

Definition of 'employee' 5.6
The usual definition of 'employee' for most statutory employment law rights is someone who works under a contract of service or apprenticeship. Indeed, this is the definition of employee for the purposes of entitlement to maternity leave – see Chapter 3, 'Maternity leave', under 'Entitlement to maternity leave'. However, the definition of 'employee' for SMP purposes is slightly wider. Under S.171(1) SSCBA an 'employee' is 'a woman who is gainfully employed in Great Britain [(England, Wales or Scotland)] either under a contract of service or in an office (including elective office) with earnings (within the meaning of Parts 1 to 5 [SSCBA])'. This is subject to any regulations that provide for cases where any such woman is not to be treated as an employee for the purposes of SMP and for cases where a woman who would not otherwise be an employee for those purposes is to be treated as an employee. For instance, Reg 17(1) SMP Regulations provides that a woman who is treated as an 'employed earner' by virtue of the Social Security (Categorisation of Earners) Regulations 1978 SI 1978/1689 will be treated as an employee for the purposes of SMP. It also states that where such a woman is treated otherwise than as an employed earner by virtue of those regulations, she shall not be treated as an employee for SMP purposes – see 'Employed earners' below.

For further discussion on whether someone is employed under a contract of service, see IDS Employment Law Handbook, 'Contracts of Employment' (2014), Chapter 2, 'Employment status'.

Earnings within the meaning of Parts 1–5 SSCBA. Under Parts 1–5 SSCBA, 5.7 earnings includes 'any remuneration or profit derived from an employment' – S.3(1)(a). S.4 goes on to provide that the following payments are to be treated as remuneration and earnings:

- any sum paid to or for the benefit of a person in satisfaction (whether in whole or in part) of any entitlement of that person to statutory sick pay,

165

statutory maternity pay, statutory paternity pay, statutory adoption pay, or statutory shared parental pay – S.4(1)(a)

- any sickness payment made to or for the benefit of the employed earner in accordance with arrangements under which the person who is the secondary contributor in relation to the employment concerned has made, or remains liable to make, payments towards the provision of that sickness payment – S.4(1)(b)

- the amount of any gain calculated under S.479 of the Income Tax (Earnings and Pensions) Act 2003 (ITEPA) in respect of which an amount counts as employment income of the earner under S.476 ITEPA (charge on acquisition of employment-related securities pursuant to option etc), reduced by any amounts deducted under S.480(1)–(6) ITEPA in arriving at the amount counting as such employment income – S.4(4)(a)

- any sum paid (or treated as paid) to or for the benefit of the earner which is chargeable to tax by virtue of S.225 or S.226 ITEPA (taxation of consideration for certain restrictive undertakings) – S.4(4)(b)

- any payment made by a body corporate to or for the benefit of any of its directors where that payment would, when made, not be earnings – S.4(5) SSCBA and Reg 22(2) Social Security (Contributions) Regulations 2001

- any amount on which an employed earner is chargeable to income tax under the employment income parts of ITEPA as remuneration derived from the earner's employment – Reg 4(6)(a) SSCBA and Reg 22 Social Security (Contributions) Regulations 2001, and

- any amount which in accordance with Social Security (Contributions) Regulations 2001 constitutes remuneration as an amount of remuneration paid, at such time as may be determined in accordance with those regulations, to or for the benefit of the earner in respect of his employment – Reg 4(6)(b) SSCBA and the Social Security (Contributions) Regulations 2001.

5.8 **Office holders.** Section 171 applies to office holders as well as those employed under a contract of service. A company director, for example, is an office holder but may or may not be employed under a contract of service. She is nonetheless likely to qualify for SMP, given the wide definition of 'earnings' (see above). (An office holder who is not employed under a contract of service will not be entitled to SML, however. This is because she is not an employee for the purposes of the SML scheme, although she may have a contractual right to maternity leave.)

5.9 **Employed earners.** There are special cases where someone will be treated as an employee, despite not falling within the definition set out above. S.171(1) makes it clear that its definition of 'employee' is subject to any regulations which may provide that a woman is or (as the case may be) is not to be 'treated as an employee' for SMP purposes. Under the Social Security (Categorisation of Earners) Regulations 1978 SI 1978/1689 ('the Categorisation of Earners Regulations') certain categories of persons who do not have a contract of service or hold an office with earnings are nonetheless treated as 'employed earners' for NI purposes. Conversely, certain categories of persons are treated as 'self-employed earners' notwithstanding that they are employed under a contract of service or are in an office with earnings. By virtue of Reg 17(1) SMP Regulations, the same categories apply for SMP purposes. So those falling into the category of 'employed earners' under the Categorisation of Earners Regulations are 'treated as employees' for SMP purposes. These include office cleaners, ministers of religion, persons employed by their spouse or civil partner; and certain agency workers – Part 1, Sch 1 Categorisation of Earners Regulations. And those falling into the category of 'self-employed earners' are 'not treated as employees' for SMP purposes. This is a smaller category comprising examiners, moderators and invigilators – Part 2, Sch 1 Categorisation of Earners Regulations.

The overall effect is that anyone whose earnings attract Class 1 NI contributions (or would do so if their earnings were high enough) qualifies for SMP. Therefore, as with office holders above, SMP may be available in some cases where SML is not available on account of the fact that the woman is not an 'employee' for the purposes of the SML scheme. A woman who notionally qualifies for SMP but does not have a statutory right to maternity leave would have to rely upon a contractual right to such leave in order to take advantage of her SMP rights. (Note that there may also be cases where a woman is entitled to SML, but not SMP – see 'Normal weekly earnings' below.)

Agency workers. As stated under 'Employed earners' above, Part 1 of Schedule **5.10** 1 to the Categorisation of Earners Regulations provides for certain categories of persons who do not have a contract of service or hold an office with earnings to nonetheless be treated as 'employed earners' and, by virtue of Reg 17(1) SMP Regulations, women falling within those categories will be treated as 'employees' for SMP purposes. Agency workers will be treated as employees for SMP purposes where the following conditions are met:

- the worker personally provides (or is under an obligation personally to provide) services to the end client

- the services are supplied by or through the agency under the terms of an agency contract

- the worker is subject to (or to the right of) supervision, direction or control as to the manner in which the services are provided, and

- remuneration is receivable by the worker (from any person) in consequence of providing the services.

167

Certain agency workers are excluded, however – namely, those who work for the end client as an actor, singer, musician or other entertainer, or as a fashion, photographic or artist's model. Also excluded are those agency workers who provide services wholly:

- in the worker's own home, or
- at other premises which are neither controlled or managed by the client nor prescribed by the nature of the services.

5.11 The effect of these provisions seems to be that agency workers (except home-workers, entertainers and models) who render personal service under supervision, direction or control qualify for SMP regardless of whether they are treated as employees for other purposes, but only where the worker is paid. If this condition is satisfied, the agency is treated as being the employer and is liable for NI contributions and any SMP that is due. This would appear to be the case regardless of whether the worker is under the supervision, direction or control of the agency or the end-user.

However, the agency will not be liable where the end-user and worker have entered into a separate contract whereby the end-user pays the worker directly and the agency does not retain an ongoing financial interest. This is often the case where someone has been recruited through a headhunter or other recruitment-only agency.

5.12 Note that the Agency Workers Regulations 2010 SI 2010/93 (AWR) exclude 'any payment in respect of maternity, paternity or adoption leave' from an agency worker's entitlement to the same basic and working conditions as an employee following a 12-week qualifying period – see Reg 6(3)(c) AWR. In other words, an agency worker will not be entitled to SMP purely on the basis that under Reg 5 AWR she should be treated – in terms of pay – as if she had been recruited directly by the end-user. For more information about the rights of agency workers, see IDS Employment Law Handbook, 'Atypical and Flexible Working' (2014), Chapter 1, 'Agency workers'.

5.13 **Crown servants.** Crown servants are treated as employees for SMP purposes – S.169 SSCBA.

5.14 **Foreign employers.** A woman will not qualify for SMP, despite falling within the definition of employee, if she is employed by a foreign organisation and the employer is not resident or present in the UK or does not have a place of business in the UK at the point in time when the employer's NI contributions become payable – Reg 17(3) SMP Regulations and Reg 145(1)(b) Social Security (Contributions) Regulations 2001. (Note that Reg 17(3) refers to Reg 119(1)(b) of the Social Security (Contributions) Regulations 1979 SI 1979/591. However, the 1979 Regulations were repealed and replaced by the Social Security (Contributions) Regulations 2001.)

Employees working abroad for British employers. A woman who is 'absent **5.15** from Great Britain for any purpose' will be treated as an employee if she is 'gainfully employed' by an employer who is liable to pay secondary Class 1 NI contributions in respect of her – Reg 2A Statutory Maternity Pay (Persons Abroad and Mariners) Regulations 1987 SI 1987/418. There is a further provision in Reg 2 whereby a person working in an EU Member State other than the UK who would have been treated as an employee had she been working in Great Britain will be so treated if she is deemed to be subject to UK social security legislation by virtue of EU Council Regulation No.1408/71 (which is a measure designed to secure the social security rights of workers moving within the European Union).

Note that there is a general restriction under Reg 3 of the 1987 Regulations to the effect that a woman will only be treated as an employee under those Regulations if she would have qualified had her employment been in Great Britain.

Since the repeal of Reg 9 of the 1987 Regulations on 6 April 1996, women who travel abroad during maternity leave will continue to be eligible for SMP.

Mariners and continental shelf workers. A mariner employed on a 'home- **5.16** trade ship' is treated as an employee for SMP purposes unless the employer does not have a place of business in the UK – Reg 7 Statutory Maternity Pay (Persons Abroad and Mariners) Regulations. A mariner employed on a 'foreign-going ship' is not treated as an employee. 'Home-trade ship' has the same, rather complicated, meaning as in S.115 of the Social Security (Contributions) Regulations 2001 and includes every ship or vessel employed in trading or going within the UK, the Channel Islands, the Isle of Man and Europe. 'Foreign-going ship' is any ship which is not a 'home-trade ship'.

Similarly, women employed in certain designated areas of the continental shelf are treated as employees – Reg 8 Statutory Maternity Pay (Persons Abroad and Mariners) Regulations. As with employees working abroad for British employers (see 'Employees working abroad for British employers' above), a woman will only be treated as an employee under the 1987 Regulations if she would have qualified had her employment been in Great Britain – Reg 3.

Abolition of minimum age requirement. Note that the requirement that an **5.17** employee had to be over the age of 16 to qualify for SMP was repealed in January 2007 by the Employment Equality (Age) Regulations 2006 SI 2006/1031. In addition, para (1A) was inserted into Reg 17 SMP Regulations by the Employment Equality (Age) (Consequential Amendments) Regulations 2007 SI 2007/825 to clarify that the categories of 'employed earners' and 'self-employed earners' under the Categorisation of Earners Regulations do not exclude people under the age of 16 for the purposes of SMP. See 'Employed earners' above for further details of Reg 17.

5.18 Qualifying conditions

There are two vitally important weeks that will determine entitlement to SMP:

- *the expected week of confinement* (EWC). This is the week in which the child is expected to be born (see below for definition of 'confinement'). The phrase 'expected week of childbirth', used in relation to maternity leave, has the same meaning – see Chapter 3, 'Maternity leave'

- *the qualifying week*. This is the week immediately preceding the 14th week before the EWC. Put more simply, it is the 15th week before the EWC. (This week is also significant as the week in or by which the employee must give her employer notice of her pregnancy in order to qualify for SML – see Chapter 3, 'Maternity leave', under 'Entitlement to maternity leave – notice provisions'). Note that 'qualifying week' is not a statutory term but it is convenient shorthand to describe this particular week.

'Week' in this context means a period of seven days beginning with Sunday and ending on Saturday – S.171(1) SSCBA. It is irrelevant that the employee's pay week may span a different seven-day period.

5.19 'Confinement' effectively means the same as 'childbirth' in Reg 2 of the Maternity and Parental Leave etc Regulations 1999 SI 1999/3312 (see Chapter 3, 'Maternity leave', under 'Entitlement to maternity leave'). It is defined as 'labour resulting in the issue of a living child, or... labour after 24 weeks of pregnancy resulting in the issue of a child whether alive or dead' – S.171(1) SSCBA. Therefore a stillbirth occurring after 24 weeks' pregnancy will attract SMP entitlement. However, if a woman's pregnancy results in a stillbirth before the end of the 24th week of pregnancy she is disqualified from receiving SMP (although she may be entitled to statutory sick pay if she satisfies the qualifying conditions). It should be noted that even if the child survives only for an instant, this constitutes a live birth. In such a case, the birth would attract SMP entitlement even if the child was born (and died) before 24 weeks of pregnancy. Where the woman's labour continues into another day, she is deemed to be 'confined' on the day the child is born or, where twins (or more) are born, on the day the last of them is born – S.171(1). No extra SMP is payable for multiple births.

There are six conditions an employee must satisfy to be entitled to SMP – S.164(2), (4) and (5) SSCBA and Reg 22 SMP Regulations. She must:

- have 26 weeks' continuous service up to and including the qualifying week. (Note that this contrasts with maternity leave where there is no minimum qualifying service – see Chapter 3, 'Maternity leave', under 'Entitlement to maternity leave')

- have become pregnant and have reached, or been confined before reaching, the start of the 11th week before the EWC

- have ceased working for the employer (in the majority of cases this will be by reason of maternity leave)

- have normal weekly earnings for the eight weeks up to and including the qualifying week equal to at least the lower earnings limit for the payment of primary Class 1 NI contributions (£111 a week for the tax year 2014/15; £112 for the tax year 2015/16). The limit in force at the end of the qualifying week should be used for these purposes

- have given 28 days' notice to her employer (in writing if the employer so requests) of the date when she expects its liability for SMP to begin or, if 28 days' notice was not reasonably practicable, such lesser notice as was reasonably practicable (note that in certain circumstances there may be additional notice requirements – see 'Notice of absence or childbirth – further notices' below), and

- have produced evidence of the EWC and (where her entitlement to SMP depends upon this) the actual week of confinement.

These preconditions for entitlement to SMP are considered in more detail in the next five sections of this chapter. **5.20**

Note that S.63(3)(a) of the Welfare Reform Act 2012 introduced a new condition that, at the end of the week immediately preceding the qualifying week, the woman must be 'entitled to be in employment' under UK immigration law. However, this provision has not yet been brought into force.

Continuous employment
5.21

As stated under 'Qualifying for statutory maternity pay – qualifying conditions' above, to qualify for SMP an employee must have been employed for a continuous period of at least 26 weeks including the qualifying week as at the end of the 15th week before the EWC – S.164(2)(a) SSCBA. This means that the first week of the requisite minimum 26-week period will be the 40th week before the EWC. (Note that the employee does not need to show continuity of employment after the qualifying week during the remaining 14 weeks before the EWC.)

The SSCBA and the SMP Regulations refer to continuous 'employment', rather than 'work'. A woman will be taken to be in 'employment' for these purposes so long as her contract of employment continues in existence: she does not need to attend her workplace and do her work in order for a contract of employment to be in existence – Satchwell Sunvic Ltd v Secretary of State for Employment 1979 IRLR 455, EAT. Nor is there any need to show that the contract involved any minimum number of hours a week – a 'zero-hours' contract would suffice – but women who work very few hours may not satisfy the lower earnings limit (see 'Normal weekly earnings' below).

171

5.22 The provisions relating to the calculation of continuous employment for the purposes of claiming SMP are based on employment by the same employer without a break. However, the SMP Regulations also provide for continuity to be preserved in some cases where there have been breaks in a woman's employment and where there is a change of employer. The details are discussed under 'Breaks in employment' below.

5.23 Dismissal to avoid maternity pay

The SMP Regulations state that where an employer has terminated an employee's contract of employment solely or mainly for the purpose of avoiding SMP liabilities, she will still be entitled to SMP from the former employer provided she has been employed continuously for at least eight weeks at the time of the dismissal – Reg 3. She is deemed to have been employed up to the end of the qualifying week (regardless of her dismissal), and her normal weekly earnings are calculated on the basis of the last eight weeks in respect of which she has been paid – Reg 3(2). Note that the dismissal would also be automatically unfair and would constitute an act of pregnancy discrimination – see Chapter 12, 'Detriment and unfair dismissal', under 'Automatically unfair dismissal', and Chapter 13, 'Discrimination and equal pay', under 'Direct discrimination – pregnancy and maternity discrimination'.

5.24 Weeks that count

The SMP Regulations deal with a number of special situations in which it might not otherwise be clear that a particular week counts towards a woman's period of continuous employment.

5.25 Start of employment. Regulation 16A SMP Regulations makes special provision in respect of employees who commenced employment during the first week of the 26-week period of continuous employment required by S.164(2)(a), i.e. the 40th week before the EWC ('the first week'). Although 'week' is normally defined as seven days running from Sunday to Saturday, Reg 16A provides that it is sufficient for the woman to have commenced employment at some point *during* the first week, even if it is the last day (i.e. Saturday), in order to accumulate the 26 weeks' service required to qualify for SMP. In other words, the woman does not have to have been employed for the whole of the first week in order for that week to count.

5.26 Employment ending in qualifying week. Continuous employment must extend into the qualifying week but it is not necessary for a woman to be employed for the whole of that week. Reg 11(4) SMP Regulations provides that where a women is employed for only part of the qualifying week, the whole of that week shall count in computing any period of continuous employment for the purposes of Part V of the Social Security Act 1986 (SSA). Therefore, if a woman is employed for only part of the week (even just a day) then the whole week counts towards her period of continuous employment. This means that a woman who resigns or is dismissed for any reason in the qualifying week could still qualify for SMP. (Note that Part V SSA was repealed by the Social Security (Consequential Provisions) Act 1992 (SS(CP)A) following the enactment of the SSCBA and the Social Security Administration Act 1992 ('the consolidating Acts'). However, S.2 SS(CP)A, which deals with the continuity of the law, provides that any reference in any enactment to a repealed provision is construed, so far as is required for continuing its effect, as including a reference to the corresponding provision of the consolidating Acts. Thus Reg 11(4) SMP Regulations should be read as if it refers to Part XII of the SSCBA.)

Employment ending before qualifying week. Normally a woman who is not **5.27** employed at all during the qualifying week will not be entitled to SMP. But there are two exceptional circumstances:

- where the woman is confined before the qualifying week. In such a case the employer must work out if the woman would but for her confinement have been continuously employed for 26 weeks ending with the qualifying week and if her normal weekly earnings for the eight weeks immediately preceding the week of confinement were equal to, or in excess of, the lower earnings limit. If both these conditions are met, the requirement of continuous employment is treated as having been satisfied – Reg 4(2) SMP Regulations. Normally, of course, the woman would remain employed while on maternity leave. However, if for some reason her employment comes to an end after a birth in these circumstances, but before the qualifying week, then she still has the right to SMP

- where the woman is dismissed by her employer before the qualifying week solely or mainly in order to avoid liability for SMP. As noted under 'Dismissal to avoid maternity pay' above, in such a case a woman who was continuously employed for at least eight weeks is entitled to be paid maternity pay by her former employer – Reg 3(1) SMP Regulations. Her normal weekly earnings are calculated by reference to the eight weeks ending with the last day for which she was paid – Reg 3(2).

Breaks in employment   5.28

The general rules for computing continuity of employment contained in Ss.210–219 ERA – for which see IDS Employment Law Handbook, 'Continuity of Employment' (2012), Chapter 1, 'The general framework' – are incorporated with some variations into the SMP scheme by Part III of the SMP Regulations. As stated previously, the continuity provisions by and large contemplate employment by the same employer without a break. There are circumstances, however, where employment will be deemed to be continuous notwithstanding that a woman has left work and then returned to work for the same employer after a break. Clearly, if the contract of employment is not terminated but rather continues throughout the period of the break, then continuity will not be

173

broken notwithstanding that no work is done. But Reg 11 sets out the circumstances in which a period when there is *no contract of service* in existence nevertheless counts as a period of continuous employment. These are:

- weeks during the whole or part of which a woman is incapable of work because of sickness or injury – Reg 11(1)(a) SMP Regulations. Not more than 26 consecutive weeks can count under this paragraph: if the period of absence because of sickness or injury is longer, continuity will be broken – Reg 11(2)

- weeks during the whole or part of which a woman is absent from work on account of a temporary cessation of work – Reg 11(1)(b)

- weeks during the whole or part of which a woman is absent from work in circumstances such that, by arrangement or custom, she is regarded as continuing in her employment for any purpose – Reg 11(1)(c)

- weeks during the whole or part of which a woman is absent from work because of pregnancy or confinement – Reg 11(1)(d). Only 26 weeks' absence can count under this paragraph, unless the woman has returned to work after additional maternity leave or has returned in pursuance of an offer of alternative work (in which case, there is no limit to the number of weeks) – Reg 11(3)

- weeks during which the woman was absent in consequence of taking paternity leave (which is possible where a child is adopted), adoption leave, shared parental leave or unpaid parental leave – Reg 11(3)(e).

(Note that the first three circumstances parallel those set out in S.212 ERA.)

5.29 If a woman is absent during any week for one of the reasons outlined above, she must return to work after her absence in order to preserve continuous employment – Reg 11(1) (and in the case of absence through sickness or injury, or because of pregnancy or confinement, she must return after 26 weeks – Reg 11(2) and Reg 11(3)). This means that if, just before the qualifying week, a woman's contract is terminated for one of the reasons set out above, and the reason for the absence continues beyond the qualifying week, then the break in employment will only be bridged for the purposes of showing continuity if she is re-employed by the employer before commencing maternity leave. If, for example, a woman was dismissed because of illness or injury prior to the qualifying week, and she was not re-engaged before the time she would have commenced maternity leave, then she will have failed to preserve continuity and will not qualify for SMP. Alternatively, she may be working on a series of short-term contracts and the reason for her absence is that she is between contracts (which might count as a temporary cessation of work). There is no need for the new contract to be offered before the previous one comes to an end. So long as she returns to work for the same employer, continuity is preserved despite her absence.

It is important to reiterate that in the vast majority of cases, an employee's contract will not be brought to an end simply by reason of absence on grounds of illness, injury, temporary cessation of work, etc, in which case continuity will not be broken. The provisions discussed above apply only where there are breaks in employment during which the contract of employment does not subsist. So, for example, a period of incapacity lasting longer than 26 weeks will not break continuity if the contract is still continuing (as will normally be the case). Likewise, continuity of employment is preserved during a maternity leave period because the contract is deemed to continue during the employee's absence – Reg 11(3)(e) SMP Regulations and Reg 9 Maternity and Parental Leave etc Regulations 1999 SI 1999/3312 (see Chapter 3, 'Maternity leave', under 'Terms and conditions during maternity leave', for further details).

Early confinement. As stated under 'Weeks that count – employment ending **5.30** before qualifying week' above, where an employee's child is born before the qualifying week, the 26 weeks' continuous employment rule is deemed to be satisfied if she would have satisfied the requirement but for the early confinement – Reg 4(2). Her normal weekly earnings are calculated by reference to the eight weeks before the week in which the child is born – S.165(7) SSCBA and Reg 4(2) SMP Regulations. Similarly, if she is confined during the qualifying week, the requirement for her to be employed during that week will still be satisfied, as she need not be employed for the whole of the qualifying week – Reg 11(4).

Agency workers. As stated in the section 'Qualifying for statutory maternity **5.31** pay', under 'Definition of "employee" – agency workers' above, agency workers (except home-workers, entertainers and models) can qualify for SMP as 'employed earners' regardless of whether they are treated as employees for other purposes, provided the agency (which is treated as the employer for SMP purposes) retains an ongoing role in paying the worker. Thus, agency workers qualify for SMP from their employing agency if they have 26 weeks' continuous service inclusive of the qualifying week.

Continuity is preserved if a contract subsists between the worker and agency, even if the worker is doing no work. Even with no ongoing agency contract, there can still be continuity. A week in which a woman does some work, even for part of the week, counts as a whole week. There may, however, be weeks when an employee with no ongoing contract is not working for the agency. Applying the general principles in Reg 11(1) and (2), continuity is not broken (and the weeks will still count towards continuity) where:

- the agency had no work for the pregnant agency worker in any particular week (which could, for example, constitute a temporary cessation of work), or

- the agency did offer work but the worker was unable to work because of sickness or injury lasting no more than 26 weeks, or because of paternity leave, adoption leave, shared parental leave or unpaid parental leave, pregnancy or confinement, and

in either of the above cases, she returned to work for the agency after the absence.

5.32 A worker who has stopped looking for work through a particular agency before the qualifying week is not entitled to SMP from that agency but may be entitled to claim Maternity Allowance – see 'Maternity Allowance' below.

5.33 **Working in the EEA.** HMRC's guidance, 'Statutory Maternity Pay: how different employment types affect what you pay', states that if a woman works for a UK employer outside the UK but within the European Economic Area (EEA) she may still qualify for SMP if:

- her employer was liable to pay Class 1 NI contributions on her earnings throughout the requisite 26 weeks of continuous employment, or would have been if her earnings had been high enough

- her employer was not liable to pay Class 1 NI contributions throughout that period but the woman worked for her employer in the UK in the qualifying week and her employer was liable to pay Class 1 NI contributions on her earnings for that week, or would have been if her earnings had been high enough.

In these circumstances her employment in the EEA counts towards the requisite 26 weeks' continuous employment.

5.34 The countries forming the EEA are the 28 Member States of the European Union (i.e. Austria, Belgium, Bulgaria, Croatia, Republic of Cyprus, the Czech Republic, Denmark, Estonia, Finland, France, Germany, Greece, Hungary, Ireland, Italy, Latvia, Lithuania, Luxembourg, Malta, the Netherlands, Poland, Portugal, Romania, Slovakia, Slovenia, Spain, Sweden and the UK (including England, Wales, Scotland and Northern Ireland but not the Channel Islands or the Isle of Man)); Gibraltar (which is part of the EU under Art 355(3) of the Treaty on the Functioning of the European Union, by virtue of the United Kingdom's membership); and three non-EU Member States within the European Free Trade Association (EFTA) (namely, Iceland, Liechtenstein and Norway). In addition, Switzerland is treated as an EEA country for certain benefits, including SMP, even though it is not a member of the EEA.

5.35 **Working in non-EEA countries.** If a woman works in another country that is not part of the EEA, her employment in that country may still count towards her continuous employment for SMP purposes provided her employer pays UK NI contributions for her during that time – see HMRC's guidance, 'Claiming benefits if you live, move or travel abroad'.

5.36 **Spasmodic employment and seasonal workers.** Employees who work at certain times of the year only or on an 'as-and-when' basis, such as seasonal workers or regular temporary workers, do not necessarily lose their continuity of employment even though their relationship is not governed by an employment contract during the periods of inactivity. During such periods a woman may, depending on the circumstances, be viewed as absent 'on account of a temporary cessation of work' or absent 'in circumstances such that, by arrangement or custom, she is regarded as continuing in the employment of her employer for all or any purpose' – Reg 11(1)(b) or (c) SMP Regulations. We note above that, generally speaking, a period of absence during which a contract of employment does not subsist will only be counted as continuous employment under Reg 11 once the woman returns to work after that absence and then only if the absence is for one of the five specified reasons set out in Reg 11(1). There is an exception to this general rule, however, in the case of spasmodic employment. Under Reg 11(3A), the exception applies if it is customary for the pregnant woman's employer to offer work for a fixed period of not more than 26 consecutive weeks:

- on two or more occasions in a year for periods that do not overlap, and

- to persons who have worked for the employer during the last or a recent such period.

5.37 If these conditions apply and the pregnant woman is employed on such spasmodic work then if she is absent in any week

- wholly or partly because of pregnancy or confinement, or

- because of disease or disablement,

continuity of service is preserved for SMP purposes even though she does not in fact return to the original employer's employment before starting her maternity absence.

5.38 **Reinstatement after service with reserve forces.** Continuity is also preserved if a woman re-enters her employment after not more than six months' reserve service in the armed forces – Reg 15 SMP Regulations. Although continuity is not broken, the period of absence does not count towards her total period of continuous employment unless the contract of employment is preserved during that time.

Re-employment after complaint of unfair dismissal
5.39
Regulation 12 SMP Regulations covers the situation where a woman is dismissed and then re-employed in consequence of:

- her presenting an unfair dismissal complaint under S.111 ERA – Reg 12(1)(a)

- her making a claim in accordance with a dismissals procedure agreement under S.110 ERA. (A dismissals procedure agreement is a procedure for collective contracting out of the ERA's unfair dismissal provisions which has been approved by the Secretary of State) – Reg 12(1)(b), or

- any action taken by an Acas conciliator under S.18A or S.18B of the Employment Tribunals Act 1996 before any complaint has been presented to an employment tribunal – Reg 12(1)(c).

(Regulation 12(1) also refers to a dismissal and re-employment in consequence of a decision arising out of the use of a statutory dispute resolution procedure contained in Schedule 2 to the Employment Act 2002 – see Reg 12(1)(d). However, this procedure has now been repealed.)

5.40 If any of the above applies, the interval between dismissal and re-employment counts as a period of continuous employment.

The re-employment must be with the employee's employer, a successor or associated employer to qualify. A 'successor' is a person who, in consequence of a change occurring in the ownership of the undertaking, or part of the undertaking for the purposes of which the employee was employed, has become the owner of the undertaking or part – Reg 12(3) and S.235 ERA. Two employers are associated if one is a company directly or indirectly controlled by the other or both are companies over which a third person has direct or indirect control – Reg 12(3)/S.231 ERA.

5.41 Stoppage because of trade dispute

If there is a week or part of a week during which a woman does not work because of a stoppage of work due to a trade dispute at her place of employment, there is no break in her continuity of employment but the whole week is discounted in computing her total period of continuous employment – Reg 13(1) SMP Regulations. A 'trade dispute' is any dispute between employers and employees, or between employees and employees, which is connected with the employment or non-employment or the terms and conditions of employment of any persons, whether or not they are employees employed by the employer with whom the dispute arises – S.35(1) Jobseekers Act 1995. This is a wide definition which will cover most workplace disputes but not 'lock-outs' or disputes of a purely political nature.

The above rules mean that if, for example, a woman who takes part in a trade dispute works for 27 weeks ending with the qualifying week, she would normally qualify for SMP provided that her participation in the dispute occurred in only one of those 27 weeks. The trade dispute will not break her continuity of employment and, discounting that week, she will still have 26 weeks' continuous employment. But if she did not work on the Friday of one week and the Monday of the following week because of a stoppage of work caused by a trade dispute, she will lose two whole weeks' continuity of employment. She will then have only 25 weeks' service, which is not sufficient to qualify for SMP.

However, periods during which the employee is 'locked out' by the employer **5.42** are not deducted (since Reg 13(1) does not apply to lock-outs). Nor will any time be deducted from the calculation of a woman's period of continuous employment where she can prove – and the onus is on her to do so – that at no time did she have a direct interest in the trade dispute causing the stoppage of her work – Reg 13(3).

If a woman is dismissed during a stoppage of work caused by a trade dispute, her continuity of employment is to be treated as ending on the first day on which she stopped work – Reg 13(2). This does not apply if she can prove that at no time did she have a direct interest in the trade dispute in question – Reg 13(3). So if the woman is subsequently re-employed, continuity of employment will only be restored if she can show that she was not involved in any way in the dispute.

Employees who are dismissed during a trade dispute are frequently re-employed **5.43** when the dispute has been settled. In cases dealing with continuity of employment under S.216 ERA (which governs preservation of continuity for ERA purposes when there is a strike or lock-out) it has been held that continuity is not necessarily broken by dismissal followed by subsequent re-employment – see Bloomfield and ors v Springfield Hosiery Finishing Co Ltd 1972 ICR 91, NIRC. However, it seems that this is not the case under the SMP Regulations, since Reg 13(2) expressly states that 'where during the stoppage of work a woman is dismissed from her employment, the continuity of her employment shall not be treated... as continuing beyond the commencement of the day she stopped work'. Continuity seems to be broken by a dismissal with nothing to restore it when re-employment takes place (unless the woman can prove that she had no direct interest in the trade dispute or the re-employment occurs in circumstances covered by Reg 12 – for example, where the employee has presented a complaint of unfair dismissal to an employment tribunal – see 'Re-employment after complaint of unfair dismissal' above).

Change of employer **5.44**

Regulation 14 SMP Regulations sets out the circumstances in which employment is treated as continuous even though the identity of the employer changes. The circumstances correspond precisely (with some simplification of wording) with those set out in S.218 ERA and are explained fully in IDS Employment Law Handbook, 'Continuity of Employment' (2012), Chapter 4, 'Changes of employer'. Briefly, the circumstances in which continuity is preserved are where:

* the employer's trade or business or an undertaking is transferred to another person – Reg 14(a)

* one employer is substituted by another under an Act of Parliament – Reg 14(b)

* the woman, following the death of her employer, is re-employed by the deceased's personal representatives or trustees – Reg 14(c)

179

- there is a change in the employing partners, personal representatives or trustees – Reg 14(d)

- employment is transferred to an associated employer. 'Associated employer' has the meaning given in S.231 ERA – i.e. two or more employers are associated if one is a company directly or indirectly controlled by the other or both are companies over which a third person has direct or indirect control – Reg 14(e)

- the woman is transferred from employment by a local education authority to employment by the governors of a school maintained by that authority (or vice versa) – Reg 14(f).

5.45 Where a trade or business is transferred from one employer to another or where there has been a 'service provision change', continuity may also be preserved by virtue of Reg 4 of the Transfer of Undertakings (Protection of Employment) Regulations 2006 SI 2006/246 (TUPE). For further information, see IDS Employment Law Handbook, 'Transfer of Undertakings' (2011), Chapter 2, 'Who transfers?'.

Where there has been a transfer of an undertaking under TUPE, the new employer is liable to pay SMP provided that the woman in question has satisfied all the conditions necessary for entitlement to SMP. If there is no TUPE transfer and the change of employer does not fall within one of the circumstances listed in Reg 14 SMP Regulations, then continuity of employment is broken, and previous service is not taken into account.

5.46 Normal weekly earnings

A woman is entitled to SMP if her normal weekly earnings for the eight weeks ending with the qualifying week are at least the lower earnings limit for paying primary Class 1 NI contributions – S.164(2)(b) SSCBA. (For the definition of 'qualifying week', see 'Qualifying for statutory maternity pay – qualifying conditions' above.) The lower earnings limit for the tax year 2015/16 is £112 a week (£111 a week for the tax year 2014/15). (The figure is normally adjusted upwards annually in line with the Consumer Price Index.) It is the limit in force at the end of the qualifying week that should be used.

Note that the lower earnings limit requirement does not apply to SML. Therefore, employees earning less than the national insurance lower earnings limit may be entitled to SML but not SMP. However, while low-paid mothers on maternity leave may not be entitled to SMP, they may be entitled to Maternity Allowance (see 'Maternity Allowance' below).

'Earnings' for the purposes of 'normal weekly earnings' means gross earnings and includes any remuneration or profit derived from a woman's employment – Reg 20(2) SMP Regulations. In effect, the test is whether the payment is treated as earnings for the purpose of NI contributions.

'Earnings' also includes certain additional payments or benefits that an employee may receive, including:

- any amount retrospectively treated as earnings by regulations made by virtue of S.4B(2) SSCBA – Reg 20(4)(za). Under this provision, the Social Security (Contributions) (Amendment No.2) Regulations 2007 SI 2007/1057 retrospectively amended Reg 22 of the Social Security (Contributions) Regulations 2001, which sets out various payments and benefits to be treated as earnings (such as payments to directors, interest on shares, etc)

- any amount payable by way of arrears of pay under an employment tribunal's reinstatement or re-engagement order following a successful unfair dismissal claim – Reg 20(4)(a) SMP Regulations

- any amount payable under an employment tribunal's continuation of contract order following a successful interim relief claim – Reg 20(4)(b)

- any amount payable under a protective award – Reg 20(4)(c)

- statutory sick pay – Reg 20(4)(d)

- statutory maternity, paternity, adoption, or shared parental pay – Reg 20(4)(e)–(h).

Bonuses and overtime
5.47

Bonuses and overtime payments, whether contractual or not, count as earnings and normal weekly earnings may be considerably inflated if an annual bonus, say, falls within the relevant eight weeks.

Statutory sick pay
5.48

Although statutory sick pay (SSP) counts as earnings for the purposes of calculating normal weekly earnings, a woman who is sick during the relevant eight-week calculation period (see 'Calculation of earnings' below) may nonetheless fail to qualify for SMP. This is because the standard rate for SSP of £88.45 a week for the tax year 2015/16 is below the lower earnings limit of £112 a week. (For the tax year 2014/15 the standard rate for SSP was £87.55 and the lower earnings limit was £111.) Therefore, a woman whose weekly pay would normally have been more than the lower earnings limit might nonetheless be disqualified from receiving SMP if her earnings during the eight weeks before the end of the qualifying week are limited to SSP, or if she receives SSP for a sufficient number of weeks to bring her average below the lower earnings limit.

181

5.49 Pay rises

Any pay rise awarded after the beginning of the eight-week calculation period and before the end of the maternity leave period must be taken into account when calculating normal weekly earnings – Reg 21(7). This provision is not limited to backdated pay rises and provides that in any case where:

- a woman is awarded a pay increase (or would have been awarded such an increase had she not been absent on SML), and

- that pay increase applies to the whole or any part of the period between the beginning of the calculation period and the end of her SML

her normal weekly earnings shall be calculated as if such an increase applied in each week of the calculation period.

Regulation 21(7) initially covered only backdated rises. It was introduced as a result of the European Court of Justice's decision in Gillespie and ors v Northern Health and Social Services Board and ors 1996 ICR 498, ECJ, where it was held that the principle of non-discrimination enshrined in what is now Article 157 of the Treaty on the Functioning of the European Union requires that the amount of benefit payable to a woman on maternity leave must take into account any pay rises backdated to the period used for calculating the earnings-related element of her SMP (see 'Calculation of earnings' below).

5.50 However, Reg 21(7) was subsequently amended to cover *all* pay rises awarded in the relevant period following the ECJ's decision in Alabaster v Woolwich plc 2005 ICR 695, ECJ. In that case the employee received a pay rise after the qualifying week but before she started her maternity leave. Under Reg 21(7) (as then drafted) her normal weekly earnings did not have to be recalculated because the pay rise came into effect after the calculation period (and was not backdated to this period). However, she argued that the ECJ's decision in Gillespie should apply to all pay rises awarded between the beginning of the calculation period right up to the end of maternity leave. The employment tribunal and the EAT upheld her claim but the Court of Appeal referred the issue to the ECJ. First, the Court of Appeal wanted to know whether Article 157 and the ECJ's judgment in Gillespie should be interpreted as meaning that a woman is entitled to have her SMP calculated to include a pay rise that takes effect after the period used for calculating SMP but before the end of her maternity leave. Secondly, the Court of Appeal asked how, if a woman is so entitled, the pay rise is to be taken into account in calculating or recalculating the pay due to her during maternity leave.

On the first question, the ECJ noted that in Gillespie and ors v Northern Health and Social Services Board and ors (above) the Court held that Article 157 required that a woman on maternity leave must benefit from any pay rise made between the beginning of the calculation period and the end of maternity leave, even if backdated. Denying a woman on maternity leave such an increase would amount to discrimination since, had she not been pregnant, she would have received the pay rise. In the ECJ's view, Gillespie must be interpreted as requiring that where the maternity pay guaranteed to a worker by national law is calculated at least partly on the basis of the pay she earned before her maternity leave began, any pay rise awarded after the beginning of the calculation period but before the end of maternity leave must be included. Furthermore, contrary to the contention put forward by the UK Government, this entitlement was not limited to cases where the employer agrees to backdate the pay rise to a date falling within the calculation period.

The ECJ then considered the Court of Appeal's second question; namely, how such a pay rise should be taken into account in calculating (or recalculating) the pay due to a worker during maternity leave. The ECJ thought that, provided national authorities acted in accordance with the general principles of EU law, it was for those authorities to determine how a pay rise should be taken into account when calculating maternity pay. **5.51**

Finally, the ECJ declined to give guidance on whether a decrease in pay after the calculation period but before the end of maternity leave should also be taken into account in calculating SMP and, if so, how that decrease should be calculated. Since the facts of the instant case related only to the refusal of the employer to take a pay rise into account in calculating SMP, the Court of Appeal's hypothetical question on pay decreases was inadmissible.

(Note that the ECJ also held that Article 157 did not require that a woman should receive full pay during maternity leave, but that the amount of benefit payable during maternity leave must not be 'so low as to undermine the purpose of maternity leave, namely, the protection of women before and after giving birth' – this aspect of the judgment is discussed under 'Is the lower earnings limit unlawful?' below.) **5.52**

Where the recalculation of normal weekly earnings takes effect after SMP has been refused by the employer on the ground that the woman did not satisfy the earnings requirement at the relevant time, and she claimed Maternity Allowance instead, the employer must pay the woman the difference between the SMP she has become entitled to and the amount received by way of Maternity Allowance (to the extent that SMP exceeds Maternity Allowance) – Reg 21B.

Payments excluded from earnings

5.53

Certain payments are expressly excluded from the normal weekly earnings that may be taken into account for SMP purposes – Reg 20(2) SMP Regulations. These mirror the payments that are excluded from earnings for NI purposes. The specific details are lengthy, complex and subject to frequent change, and are not set out in detail here. For further information, see Reg 25, Reg 27 and Schedule 3 to the Social Security (Contributions) Regulations 2001 and the HMRC guide, 'Employer Further Guide to PAYE and NICs' (CWG2).

183

5.54 The excluded payments fall into the following broad categories:

- certain payments by a company to its directors, where the director is liable to account to another company or firm for that payment – Reg 27

- payments in kind or by way of the provision of services, board and lodging or other facilities (Part II, Sch 3), but excluding:

  - payments by way of readily convertible assets (Part III, Sch 3)

  - payments by way of specific assets, such as securities, options to acquire assets, currency, precious metals or other options, alcoholic liquor (on which duty has not been paid), gemstones, certificates or other instruments which confer rights in respect of assets and vouchers (Part IV, Sch 3); and

  - any contract of long-term insurance that falls within paragraph I, III or VI of Part II of Schedule 1 to the Financial Services and Markets Act 2000 (Regulated Activities) Order 2001

- certain non-cash vouchers, including qualifying childcare vouchers (Part V, Sch 3)

- pensions and employers' pension contributions (Part VI, Sch 3)

- certain payments in respect of training and similar courses (Part VII, Sch 3)

- certain travelling, relocation and other expenses and allowances of employment, including council tax on accommodation and overseas medical expenses (Part VIII, Sch 3)

- certain payments under share incentive schemes (Part IX, Sch 3)

- payments on account of sums already included in the computation of earnings (Part X, Sch 3)

- redundancy payments (Part X, Sch 3)

- contractual sick pay which is attributable to payments made by an employee into a sick pay fund (Part X, Sch 3)

- any VAT payable in respect of goods or services supplied by the employee (Part X, Sch 3)

- payments towards an employee's indemnity insurance (Part X, Sch 3)

- contributions to membership fees of a professional body (Part X, Sch 3)

- fees paid to a minister of religion which do not form part of a stipend or salary (Part X, Sch 3)

- payments to a miner in lieu of coal (Part X, Sch 3)

- fees relating to the Disclosure and Barring Service (Part X, Sch 3)

- any payment, or reimbursement, for obtaining relevant advice relating to a proposed employee shareholder agreement (Part X, Sch 3).

Calculation of earnings   5.55

The method of calculating normal weekly earnings for SMP purposes is very different to that used for calculating a 'week's pay' under the ERA. In a normal case – i.e. one in which neither confinement nor dismissal because of pregnancy occurs before the qualifying period – the method used depends on whether a woman is paid weekly, monthly or at other (perhaps irregular) intervals – Reg 21 SMP Regulations.

Remember that when calculating earnings the qualifying week is the 15th week before the EWC. Furthermore, it is a woman's actual earnings during the relevant eight-week period that apply for the purposes of calculating normal weekly earnings. Thus, a woman who is paid on an hourly basis may find that her entitlement to SMP has been lost because, before going on maternity leave, she worked reduced hours and therefore earned less. A woman's level of earnings may also be affected by other situations; for example, she may have been on stand-by or have been locked out during the calculation period.

Below we give some examples of how normal weekly earnings are calculated **5.56** according to different methods of payment. For the purposes of Reg 21, which sets out the formulas for calculating normal weekly earnings, a woman's 'normal pay day' is defined as 'a day on which the terms of [her] contract of service require her to be paid, or the practice in her employment is for her to be paid, if any payment is due to her' – Reg 21(2). If a woman has no identifiable normal pay day, then the relevant day is her actual day of payment – Reg 21(4). This is the date the employer makes the payment rather than the date when employee receives it – Dahal v Commissioners for HM Revenue and Customs and anor 2012 UKFTT 311, First Tier Tribunal (Tax Chamber).

The 'relevant period' (over which normal weekly earnings is calculated) is defined in Reg 21(3) as the period between:

- the last normal day to fall before the 'appropriate date' (which generally is the first day of the 14th week before the EWC, i.e. the week after the qualifying week – Reg 21(2)), and

- the last normal pay day to fall at least eight weeks earlier than this.

(The last normal day before the appropriate date is included in the relevant period, but the last normal pay day to fall at least eight weeks earlier is not.)

Weekly paid employees. Add together the gross earnings for the last eight **5.57** normal pay days falling on or before the end of the qualifying week and divide by eight. The resulting figure is the woman's normal weekly earnings. Note that every pay day during the calculation period must be included in this process

185

even if the employee had already received monies for a particular week in advance and so was not actually paid that week. For example, she may have been paid in advance for a holiday.

5.58 **Monthly paid employees.** Take the gross payment for the last normal pay day falling before the end of the qualifying week and add to it any other payments made after (but not including) the last pay day which fell at least eight weeks before that date. If the woman is paid at regular monthly intervals, there will be only two pay days to take into account. Then divide the earnings for the period by the number of calendar months involved, or, if it is not a whole number, the nearest whole number (which should be two), multiply the answer by 12 and then divide by 52. This gives the normal weekly earnings. Except in a very exceptional case where monthly payments are made at different times in the month, there will never be more than two pay days to take into account: this means that the same result can be reached more quickly by multiplying the total sum paid to the employee on those two pay days by six and dividing by 52.

5.59 *Example.* An employee is paid monthly on the 15th of the month. Her EWC (Sunday to Saturday) is 20–26 September 2015. The qualifying week (Sunday to Saturday) is, therefore, 7–13 June 2015. Her last normal pay day before the end of the qualifying week will be 15 May. The last normal pay day falling at least eight weeks before that is 15 March. Her earnings between these two dates (i.e. from 16 March up to and including 15 May) are the ones that count. Her pay packets on 15 April and 15 May should therefore be added together, along with any bonus or other earnings received during the relevant period. This sum should then be multiplied by six and divided by 52 to ascertain the average weekly pay.

5.60 **Employees paid monthly but in multiples of a week.** Take the gross payment for the last normal pay day falling on or before the end of the qualifying week and add to it any other payments made after (but not including) the last pay day which fell at least eight weeks before that date. The total is then divided by the number of weeks covered by the payments. An example of this situation is where an employee is paid on the last Friday of every month.

5.61 **Employees paid at other intervals.** Earnings may need to be looked at over a longer period than eight weeks. Take the payment made on the last pay day on or before the end of the qualifying week and add to it all other payments made after (but not including) the last pay day that fell at least eight weeks earlier than that day. Count the number of days in that period. If the number of days is divisible by seven, do this to give the number of whole weeks within that period and then divide the sum of the payments by that number to give the normal weekly earnings. If the total number of days is not divisible by seven, then divide the total sum of payments by the number of days and then multiply by seven to give a figure for normal weekly earnings.

Example. An employee is paid on a commission basis at irregular intervals. **5.62** Her qualifying week is 24–30 May 2012 and her last commission payment before that was 19 May. The last payment at least eight weeks before that date was 13 March. Add together all her earnings for the period 14 March to 19 May inclusive. Divide the total by 67 (the number of calendar days in that period) to get the daily average and multiply that by seven to get the average weekly figure.

Child born early. The above methods of calculation cover the normal cases. **5.63** There is one exception: where confinement takes place before the qualifying week. The relevant period for calculating normal weekly earnings is that ending with the last pay day before the actual week of confinement. Normal weekly earnings are then calculated using the appropriate method but with the substitution of this pay day as the base date instead of the last pay day before the end of the qualifying week – Reg 21(2) and (3) SMP Regulations. Note, however, that a woman in this situation will only be entitled to SMP if she would have been so entitled had she continued in employment until the qualifying week – see the section 'Continuous employment' above, under 'Weeks that count – employment ending before qualifying week'.

Aggregation of earnings under different contracts/employers   5.64

If an employee works under more than one contract for the same employer, then the employer must treat the different contracts as one for the purposes of Part XII SSCBA, and the employee is entitled to aggregate her earnings for the purposes of calculating normal weekly earnings – Reg 5 SMP Regulations. However, an employer is not required to aggregate earnings under different contracts for the purposes of calculating the employee's normal weekly earnings if the earnings from those contracts are not aggregated for NI purposes because the earnings under the respective contracts are separately calculated and it is not reasonably practicable to do so – Reg 14 Social Security (Contributions) Regulations 2001. The provisions on aggregation obviously help part-time workers, for example, who may work under different contracts for the same employer in circumstances where the gross wages from the individual contracts fall below the specified lower earnings limit for qualification for SMP. HMRC's 'Employer Further Guide to PAYE and NICs' (CWG2 (2014)) sets out guidelines for applying the rules on aggregation of earnings.

Similar provisions apply where a woman is employed under separate and concurrent contracts with two associated employers, i.e. different employers who 'carry on business in association with each other' – Reg 15(1)(a) Social Security (Contributions) Regulations 2001 and Reg 18(1) SMP Regulations. As with employment under different contracts with the same employer, a woman who is employed concurrently by associated employers will not be entitled to have her earnings aggregated if 'it is not reasonably practicable to do so' for NI purposes. It is more likely in the case of employment by associated employers

187

that a woman's pay, tax and national insurance are handled under wholly separate pay administration systems run by the different employers. As a result, it may be slightly easier for such employers to show that it was 'not reasonably practicable' to aggregate earnings and treat their separate payments of wages/salary as a single payment. This will mean that it may be correspondingly harder for a woman to meet the earnings thresholds needed to qualify for SMP if she is on relatively low pay with two separate, albeit associated, employers. Where, however, a woman is able to aggregate her earnings with the two employers and thereby meets the earnings threshold for SMP, liability to pay SMP is apportioned between the employers – Reg 18(2) SMP Regulations.

5.65 If an employee works under more than one contract but for different employers who are not associated, she is not entitled to aggregate her earnings because liability for paying NI contributions lies separately with each individual employer. Accordingly, SMP liabilities are entirely separate and the woman is entitled to SMP from each employer, provided she meets the qualifying conditions in respect of each employment and has stopped work under each contract by reason of maternity or confinement – S.164(3) SSCBA. She can, of course, stop work under each contract at different times and have a different maternity pay period with each employer.

In some rare cases where two employers are not 'associated', the earnings paid to an employee under each contract are nonetheless aggregated and treated as a single payment of earnings for NI purposes – see Reg 15(1) Social Security (Contributions) Regulations 2001 and Schedule 3 to the Social Security (Categorisation of Earners) Regulations 1978 SI 1978/1689. In these situations, liability for SMP is apportioned between the employers – Reg 18(2) SMP Regulations.

5.66 *Example one.* W works for two different subsidiaries of a parent company (which are therefore associated employers). At X Ltd she does ten hours a week and earns £120 a week gross. With Y Ltd she has a similar part-time job for which she receives £80 a week. Although she is paid separately, the employers are required to aggregate her earnings with them and pay secondary Class 1 NI contributions on the aggregated sum. Her qualifying week ends in the tax year 2015/16. Since the aggregated sum exceeds the lower earnings limit of £112 a week for that tax year, she qualifies for SMP, payment of which is apportioned between X Ltd and Y Ltd in a ratio of 6:4 (unless the employers agree otherwise).

5.67 *Example two.* W works for two entirely separate employers. At A Ltd she does 15 hours a week and earns £115 a week gross. She also has a part-time job with B Ltd for eight hours a week for which she receives a weekly wage of £50. She is not entitled to aggregate her earnings and SMP is assessed separately for each employer. With A Ltd she earns more than the lower earnings limit of £112 (for the tax year 2015/16) and is entitled to SMP. At B Ltd she is not entitled to SMP because her earnings are below the lower earnings limit.

Is lower earnings limit unlawful?

In Banks v Tesco Stores Ltd and anor 1999 ICR 1141, EAT, the complainant, a part-time cashier at Tesco, failed to qualify for SMP because her average weekly earnings were below the lower earnings limit. She brought an action before an employment tribunal to challenge the validity of S.164(2)(b) SSCBA, which, as previously noted, prevents women from claiming SMP if they are paid less than the lower earnings limit. The complainant argued that the refusal to pay her during maternity leave was contrary to what is now Article 157 of the Treaty on the Functioning of the European Union, which sets out the principle of equal pay for equal work. She cited the case of Gillespie and ors v Northern Health and Social Services Board and ors 1996 ICR 498, ECJ (discussed under 'Pay rises' above), in which the ECJ held that Article 157 did not require that a woman should receive full pay during maternity leave, but that the amount of benefit payable during maternity leave must not be 'so low as to undermine the purpose of maternity leave, namely, the protection of women before and after giving birth'. Relying on this reasoning, the complainant argued that to deprive her of any entitlement to SMP simply because she earned less than the lower earnings limit would defeat the purpose of maternity leave. The EAT pointed out that the EU Pregnant Workers Directive (No.92/85) ('the Pregnant Workers Directive') envisages that in certain circumstances a woman may receive no payment during maternity leave. The Directive was not relevant to the Gillespie case, however, because it had been adopted after the date when the women in Gillespie took maternity leave. Article 8(1) of the Pregnant Workers Directive requires Member States to ensure that female workers are entitled to at least 14 weeks' maternity leave. Article 11(2)(b) states that Member States must ensure that workers are entitled to a payment and/or an 'adequate allowance' during this period. By virtue of Article 11(3), the allowance referred to in Article 11(2)(b) is deemed to be adequate if it guarantees income 'at least equivalent to that which the worker concerned would receive in the event of a break in her activities on grounds connected with her state of health, subject to any ceiling laid down under national legislation'. Article 11(4) goes on to provide that the payment or allowance may be made subject to certain conditions of eligibility by the Member State, provided that any qualifying service requirement must not exceed 12 months. The EAT pointed out that if the complainant had been absent on sick leave, as opposed to maternity leave, she would not have qualified for statutory sick pay (SSP), because SSP is also subject to the lower earnings limit. In the EAT's view, therefore, there was no breach of Article 11(3). The EAT also thought that the application of the lower earnings limit as a qualifying condition for SMP was permitted by virtue of Article 11(4).

The case therefore turned on the ECJ's decision in Gillespie. If the proper interpretation of the ECJ's judgment was that Article 157 required every woman on maternity leave to receive some payment, then there would be an apparent conflict between that Article and the Pregnant Workers Directive. If such a conflict existed, the EAT would be obliged to make a reference to the ECJ. The Appeal Tribunal accepted that SMP was 'pay' for the purposes of Article 157. If a woman's maternity pay was based on her earnings, it would be unlawful not to give her the benefit of any increases in pay that she would have received had she remained at work. Absence on maternity leave must not deprive a woman of all the rights and benefits she would have received had she not been on leave. However, this did not mean that she was entitled to be paid what she would have received had she been at work. The EAT said that, subject to the exceptions contemplated by Article 11, the Pregnant Workers Directive is designed to ensure that women receive both maternity leave and maternity pay, which must not be set at a level that defeats the objective of the Directive. However, the EAT thought it inherently unlikely that the ECJ in Gillespie had intended to say that Article 157 required Member States to set maternity pay at such a level in cases where a woman fell within an exception contemplated by Article 11 of the Directive. In the EAT's view, the judgment in Gillespie was to be interpreted as meaning that, where a woman otherwise qualifies for maternity pay, the level at which the pay is set must be sufficient to satisfy the overriding requirement that maternity leave should not be undermined. If SMP had been payable in the instant case, the complainant would have received no less than if she had been off work sick. Article 11(3) of the Pregnant Workers Directive provides a minimum level for maternity pay and it was this provision, in the EAT's view, which prompted the ECJ's observation in Gillespie that the payment must not be pitched so low as to defeat the purpose of maternity leave. If, however, a woman falls within an exception contemplated by Article 11, she cannot rely on Article 157 to claim a right to maternity pay. The EAT concluded that the complainant could not rely on Article 157 to found a claim that she could not bring under UK law and that would not have been available to her under the Pregnant Workers Directive. In the EAT's view, there was no need to make a reference to the ECJ. The appeal was therefore dismissed.

5.69 **National Minimum Wage Act 1998**
The right to receive the national minimum wage (NMW) came into effect on 1 April 1999. From October 2014 the rates are £6.50 an hour for those aged 21 and over, £5.13 for those aged 18–20, and £3.79 for workers aged 16 and 17. There is no mention in the legislation of whether, if a woman is being paid less than the minimum wage, her 'earnings' for SMP means her actual earnings or the amount she should have received under the National Minimum Wage Act 1998 (NMWA). Although there does not appear to be any reported case on this point, a case did arise under prior legislation (since repealed) – the Wages Councils Act 1979 – which set a statutory minimum wage. In that case the EAT decided that the woman's weekly pay should be calculated by reference to the amount she should have been paid rather than what she actually received – Cooner v PS Doal and Sons 1988 ICR 495, EAT. There seems to be no reason why the same principle should not apply under the NMWA, since that Act, like

the earlier legislation, operates by varying the contract of employment to make the minimum rate a contractual right. If we are correct, then the NMW should be treated as contractual remuneration, thus creating a floor on earnings for the purposes of SMP even if the employer is in fact paying less than the required minimum wage.

Reduction of normal working hours

5.70

In Harris v Evans t/a Richmond Court ET Case No.18688/95 H informed her employer in July 1994 that she was pregnant. At the beginning of September her hours were significantly reduced for no valid reason, which meant that she no longer earned a sufficient amount to qualify for payment of Class 1 NI contributions. An employment tribunal found that the employer had reduced H's hours in an attempt to avoid having to pay SMP. This amounted to a detriment and to unlawful sex discrimination.

Notice of absence or childbirth

5.71

To qualify for SMP, a woman must give 28 days' notice to her employer of the date on which she expects its liability to pay SMP to begin – S.164(4) SSCBA. The notice must be in writing if the employer so requests – S.164(5). The notice which she must give under Reg 4(1) of the Maternity and Parental Leave etc Regulations 1999 SI 1999/3312 in order to qualify for maternity leave (see Chapter 3, 'Maternity leave', under 'Entitlement to maternity leave – notice provisions') will normally suffice for these purposes, since liability for SMP will be triggered by the employee starting leave. (However, to ensure that she fully complies with S.164(4), the employee should specifically state the date she expects SMP liability to begin.) Note, however, that if the woman wants to start her maternity leave in the 11th week before the EWC then she will need to ensure that notice is given earlier than the deadline in Reg 4(1) for giving notice to take maternity leave (this deadline being the end of the 15th week before the expected week of childbirth) as, otherwise, she will not have given the required 28 days' notice to qualify for SMP under S.164(4) SSCBA.

If 28 days' notice is not reasonably practicable, the woman must give notice as soon as is reasonably practicable – S.164(4)(b) SSCBA. If the employee does not give 28 days' notice, it is essentially up to the employer to decide whether it was reasonably practicable for her to have done so and whether or not to pay her SMP. If an employer refuses to pay SMP on account of a failure to give notice within the proper time limit, then a woman loses her entire right to SMP. There is no provision for paying a pro rata portion of the SMP in circumstances where inadequate notice is given. An employee who is aggrieved about her employer's decision may ask for a written statement of the reasons for refusing to pay, and if she is dissatisfied with the employer's response, she may refer the matter to an HMRC officer for a formal decision – see further

191

Chapter 9, 'Administering statutory payments', under 'Statutory maternity pay – rejecting claims for SMP' and 'Statutory maternity pay – disputes over entitlement to SMP'.

5.72 Varying the leaving date

Where a woman has given notice of her intended leave date she can vary it in accordance with the provisions for varying the start of maternity leave under Reg 4(1A) MPL Regulations. She must give notice 28 days before whichever is the earlier of the new date and the old date. There is an exception if 28 days' notice is not reasonably practicable. For further details, see Chapter 3, 'Maternity leave', under 'Entitlement to maternity leave – notice provisions'. There are no additional requirements for SMP purposes – the notice given under Reg 4(1A) will almost certainly also comply with the requirements of S.164(4) SSCBA. However, to be on the safe side, the woman should also specifically state the date on which she now expects the employer's SMP liability to begin.

5.73 Leaving employment

There is one special case where a woman is exempt from the normal requirement to give 28 days' notice before she leaves work. This applies where she leaves her employment (i.e. her employment is terminated) after the start of the qualifying week – Reg 23(4) SMP Regulations (for the definition of 'qualifying week', see 'Qualifying for statutory maternity pay – qualifying conditions' above). Under the regulations applicable before 6 April 2003, this provision would only have applied where the employee had been dismissed or her employment otherwise terminated without her consent. However, this condition was removed, and a voluntary resignation effective after the start of the qualifying week will suffice.

Although, in these circumstances, the employee is exempt from giving her employer 28 days' notice of the date on which she intends SMP to start, she is nonetheless required to give her employer notice of the actual date of birth if it occurs before the 11th week before the EWC – Reg 23(5). This is because the maternity pay period would normally start with the 11th week. But if a woman is confined earlier it begins with the week following the week of confinement – and, in order for the employer to know precisely when to start paying her, it needs the information as to the actual date of the birth.

5.74 In cases where a woman leaves her employment after the qualifying week and her child is not born before the 11th week before the EWC, she does not have to give notice of the confinement when it happens. Having qualified for SMP, she is entitled to start receiving SMP at the start of the 11th week before the EWC, or (if later) the start of the first week after she leaves her employment – see 'The maternity pay period – termination of employment after qualifying week starts' below.

Further notices   5.75

There are two special cases where a woman who may have given the proper 28 days' notice of her absence (and the employer's liability) under S.164(4) SSCBA must then give additional notice to the employer:

- where she is confined (i.e. gives birth) before or during the qualifying week, she must give notice to the employer of the date of confinement. The notice must be given within 28 days of the actual date of confinement or, if that is not practicable in the circumstances, as soon as is reasonably practicable, and it must be in writing if the employer so requests – Reg 23(1) SMP Regulations

- where she has given due notice of her intended date of absence but is then confined before that date, she must give a further notice to her employer specifying both the date of confinement and the date her absence from work began. This notice must be given within 28 days of the actual confinement, subject to the usual proviso about practicability, and it must be in writing if the employer so requests – Reg 23(2).

A woman who fails to comply with these additional notice requirements risks losing her entitlement to SMP altogether. If, having given the appropriate notice later than the 28-day time limit, the employer does not accept her reasons for the lateness and refuses to pay SMP, she is entitled to a written statement from her employer setting out the decision and the reasons for it – Reg 25A(2). If dissatisfied by the employer's response, she can then apply for a formal decision by an HMRC officer – see Chapter 9, 'Administering statutory payments', under 'Statutory maternity pay – rejecting claims for SMP'.

For these purposes, a written notice posted in a properly stamped and addressed   5.76
envelope is deemed to have been given on the date of posting – Reg 23(3). Note that this provision does not apply to the initial 28 days' notice of impending absence under S.164(4) SSCBA, presumably because at the time such notice is given the woman will still be at work and can simply tell her employer or, if the employer requests it in writing, hand in a written notice in person.

Medical evidence   5.77

As well as giving notification of her intention to be absent from work, a woman must also provide her employer with evidence of the expected week of confinement (EWC) or of the actual date of confinement if that is what her entitlement to SMP depends on (e.g. where she is confined before the qualifying week or before the date she intended to start her maternity leave) – Reg 22(1) SMP Regulations (for the definition of 'qualifying week' see 'Qualifying for statutory maternity pay – qualifying conditions' above). This evidence must be submitted to the employer no later than the end of the third week of the maternity pay period (for details of which, see 'The maternity pay period' below), although the employer may accept it later if the woman has 'good cause'. Even then, the notice has to be given no later than the end of the 13th week of the maternity pay period – Reg 22(3). A certificate that is posted in a properly stamped and addressed envelope is deemed to have been given on the day it is posted – Reg 22(4) (mirroring Reg 23(3) – see 'Notice of absence or childbirth – further notices' above). No SMP should be paid until the employer receives the medical evidence.

Section 15(1) of the Social Security Administration Act 1992 states that a woman must provide her employer with evidence as to her pregnancy and the expected date of confinement 'in such form and at such time as may be prescribed'. The format and timing are prescribed by the Statutory Maternity Pay (Medical Evidence) Regulations 1987 SI 1987/235, which state that the evidence of pregnancy or EWC must take the form of a 'maternity certificate' – MAT B1 – that must not be dated earlier than the beginning of the 20th week before the week in which the child is due to be born – Reg 2. The certificate must be given by a doctor or registered midwife who has attended the woman (the woman cannot give herself a certificate even if she is a doctor or midwife) and must contain the following information:

- the woman's name

- the EWC or, if the certificate is issued after confinement, the actual date of confinement and the date on which confinement was expected

- the date of the examination on which the certificate is based

- the date on which the certificate is signed

- the address of the doctor signing the certificate or, if the certificate is signed by a registered midwife, his or her registered number and the expiry date of that registration; and

- opposite the word 'signature', the signature of the person giving the maternity certificate (written after the other information has been entered) – para 4, Sch 1.

5.78 No further certificates may be issued in respect of the same medical examination other than a replacement for the original, which must be clearly marked 'duplicate' – para 5, Sch 1.

Failure to produce a proper certificate, or no certificate at all, will almost certainly result in a woman losing her entitlement to SMP. Arguably, however, the necessity to produce a certificate is simply an administrative requirement, as opposed to a statutory prerequisite for the receipt of SMP, given that it is not set out in S.164 SSCBA – see 'Qualifying for statutory maternity pay – qualifying conditions' above. However, the DWP guide, 'Maternity benefits: technical guidance' (2014), states that if a woman does not provide the medical evidence of her expected week of childbirth within the time prescribed, SMP might not be payable. Given this real possibility, women would be well advised to provide the evidence in the form and manner prescribed by the above Regulations as a matter of course.

Note that in cases of early confinement, a birth certificate would be sufficient **5.79** evidence of the woman's confinement in the week in which the child was born – Reg 22(2) SMP Regulations. Therefore, it is not strictly necessary for the woman to produce a MAT B1 form in these circumstances.

Stopping work **5.80**

The final condition for qualifying for SMP is that the employee must have stopped work for the employer who is liable to pay her SMP. This condition is tucked at the end of S.164(2)(a) SSCBA. Apart from work carried out on 'keeping-in-touch' days, any work done for that employer during the maternity pay period (currently 39 weeks) will mean that no SMP will be payable for the week(s) in which it is done. This is explained in the section on 'Disentitlement to statutory maternity pay' below.

A woman who ceases work for any reason after the start of the qualifying week, and who satisfies the other conditions, will be entitled to SMP. The reason does not have to be related to her pregnancy. Normally, of course, the reason for stopping work will be that the woman has started her maternity leave. However, it could be because of a dismissal (e.g. redundancy) or resignation.

Once the employee stops work, then provided she does not do anything to lose **5.81** her right to SMP (see 'Disentitlement to statutory maternity pay' below), her right to continue receiving it is 'absolute' and 'indefeasible', even if she does not intend to return to work after the child is born, or if the employer goes out of business – Secretary of State for Employment v Cox 1984 ICR 867, EAT. That case was decided under a differently worded provision in the Employment Protection (Consolidation) Act 1978 (since repealed) but the principle remains good law.

Although an employer is not entitled to seek to recover SMP from an employee who decides not to return to work at the end of her maternity leave, there is nothing to prevent the exercise of an express contractual right to recoup the difference between the SMP paid and any contractual maternity pay should the employee decide not to return. This was made clear by the European Court of Justice in Boyle and ors v Equal Opportunities Commission 1999 ICR 360, ECJ. In that case the ECJ ruled that nothing in EU equality law precluded a clause in a contract of employment whereby a woman who does not return from maternity leave is required to repay the contractual maternity pay she has received. This case is discussed further under 'Rates of statutory maternity pay – sex discrimination and equal pay claims' below.

195

5.82 Although the woman must normally have 'reached' the 11th week before the EWC for SMP to be payable (see S.164(2)(c) SSCBA), it is worth clarifying that it is not necessary for her to have worked, or even been employed, up to that time, provided she remained employed during the qualifying week. She cannot, of course, take maternity leave any earlier than the 11th week unless the child has already been born (see Chapter 3, 'Maternity leave', under 'Commencement of ordinary maternity leave'). However, once she has worked into the qualifying week, she could resign or be dismissed and still qualify for SMP once she reaches the 11th week or (if earlier) once the child is born.

5.83 Disentitlement to statutory maternity pay

There are various events during the maternity pay period (MPP) that can terminate or suspend entitlement to SMP.

If a woman is detained in legal custody or sentenced to imprisonment (except a suspended sentence) during any week within the MPP, she loses her right to SMP for that week and all subsequent weeks – Reg 9 SMP Regulations. She may, however, be entitled to Maternity Allowance after she is released. Note that entitlement to SMP is not lost if a woman is voluntarily helping the police with their enquiries – see the DWP's 'Maternity benefits: technical guidance' (2014).

5.84 The death of an employee during her MPP terminates an employer's liability to pay SMP at the end of the week in which the employee's death occurs – Reg 10 SMP Regulations. There is no provision for claims on behalf of a deceased employee's estate.

5.85 Working during the maternity pay period

If in any week during the MPP a woman carries out any work under a contract of service for an employer who is paying her SMP, she loses a whole week's SMP, even if she only worked for one day in that week – S.165(4) SSCBA. It does not matter whether the contract under which she works is the same as the contract under which she worked before the MPP or a different contract – S.165(5). 'Week' in this context means a period of seven days beginning with the day of the week on which the maternity pay period begins – S.165(8). Note that the MPP can begin on any day of the week and, therefore, a 'week' for these purposes does not have to start on a Sunday.

5.86 **Exception.** There is one important exception to the above rule. Provided the employer and employee agree, an employee can work for up to ten 'keeping-in-touch' ('KIT') days without losing her SMP for the weeks in which that work is done (see Chapter 3, 'Maternity leave', under 'Work during maternity leave', for further discussion of KIT days). The amount of pay the employee receives for work done is subject to agreement but the minimum the employer must pay is the SMP rate the employee is entitled to.

Therefore, if a week during the MPP contains only KIT days, SMP should be paid. However, if a week during SML contains the last of the KIT days plus an additional day or days of work (or if the employee is working in that week having already used up all her KIT days) the employer must stop SMP for that week (and for any additional week in which work is done). However, SMP will resume in respect of the next week of the MPP that the employee does not work, and continue until the end of the MPP, assuming no other disentitling event occurs.

Note that KIT days can be used at any time during the statutory leave period, **5.87** except during the two-week compulsory leave period immediately following the date of childbirth – Reg 12A(5) MPL Regulations. Compulsory maternity leave is discussed in Chapter 3, 'Maternity leave', under 'Compulsory maternity leave'.

Rate at which SMP is lost. As set out under 'Rates of statutory maternity pay' **5.88** below, SMP is paid at the 'earnings-related rate' (currently 90 per cent of salary) during the first six weeks of leave, and at whichever is the lower of the earnings-related rate and the 'prescribed rate' (£139.58 from 5 April 2015) during the last 33 weeks of the MPP. Since the earnings-related rate is paid for 'the first six weeks in respect of which [SMP] is payable' – S.166(1) SSCBA – this means that if SMP is not payable for part of the first six weeks (because the woman has continued working) then the right to receive the earnings-related rate is carried over to the subsequent week or weeks until her full six weeks at the earnings-related rate has been used up. She then goes onto the prescribed rate (if lower) for the remainder of the MPP. However, the MPP is not extended. Therefore, by working during the MPP, a woman loses SMP at the lowest rate payable, even if the work was done during the first six weeks.

Working for other employers. The rules regarding working for another **5.89** employer – i.e. one who is not liable to pay SMP to the employee – are more complicated. In this section, for ease of reference, we will refer to the other employer (i.e. the one who is not liable to pay SMP) as Employer B. We will refer to the original employer (i.e. the one from whom the woman is claiming SMP) as Employer A.

Before the child is born. Working for Employer B before the child is born **5.90** does not affect entitlement to SMP. A woman can theoretically draw SMP from Employer A while working for Employer B right up to the date of the confinement.

After the child is born. If a woman works for Employer B after the child is **5.91** born, Employer A's liability for SMP ceases for the rest of the maternity pay period, including the week in which she starts such work – S.165(6) SSCBA and Reg 8(2) SMP Regulations. Note that Employer A's liability for SMP will not resume even if she should stop working for Employer B during what would

197

have been the rest of her period of SMP entitlement. It is the woman's duty to inform Employer A within seven days that she has started work for another employer – Reg 24 SMP Regulations. Unlike the equivalent adoption pay provisions, there is no statutory requirement for this notice to be in writing if Employer A so requests – see Chapter 6, 'Adoption leave and pay', under 'Statutory adoption pay – disentitlement to SAP', for further details.

There is an exception under Reg 8(1) that preserves an employee's entitlement to SMP from Employer A when she works for Employer B after the week of confinement and during the maternity pay period if:

- she was employed by both Employer A and Employer B during the qualifying week, but

- Employer B is a 'non-liable employer', i.e. is not liable to pay her SMP (for example, because her earnings were below the lower earnings limit).

5.92 The effect of this provision is that a woman who has a second, low-paid job during the qualifying week is not obliged to give up that job during maternity leave in order to preserve entitlement to SMP from the main employer: if she was in employment with Employer B during the qualifying week, she can work for that employer – both before and after the child is born – while continuing to draw SMP from Employer A.

The wording of Reg 8(1) suggests that under this exception there is no limit to the number of non-liable employers who may employ the woman. So long as she was employed by them during the qualifying week, she can continue to work for them throughout the whole of her maternity pay period without losing her entitlement to SMP from the main employer.

5.93 It appears that the woman only has to show that she was employed by Employer B at some point during the qualifying week for Reg 8(1) to apply – so one day's employment would suffice. The wording of that provision also suggests that, as long as the woman is employed by Employer B during the qualifying week, she does not actually have to be working for it. This contrasts with the equivalent provision regulating adoption pay (Reg 25 of the Statutory Paternity Pay and Statutory Adoption Pay (General) Regulations 2002 SI 2002/2788), which appears to suggest that the employee does actually have to be working for Employer B in the relevant week – see Chapter 6, 'Adoption leave and pay', under 'Statutory adoption pay – disentitlement to SAP', for further details.

Note that where this exception applies (i.e. where Employer A's SMP liability is unaffected), there is no obligation on the woman to inform Employer A that she has started work for another employer – Reg 24 SMP Regulations.

Rates of statutory maternity pay 5.94

SMP is currently payable by employers for a continuous period of 39 weeks (see 'The maternity pay period' below) to all women who satisfy the qualifying conditions outlined earlier in this chapter. There are two rates of SMP, as follows:

- the first six weeks are payable at the 'earnings-related rate', which is 90 per cent of the employee's 'normal weekly earnings' – S.166(1)(a) SSCBA (see 'Normal weekly earnings – calculation of earnings' above for an explanation of how to calculate normal weekly earnings)

- the remaining 33 weeks are paid at the 'prescribed rate', which is £139.58 from 5 April 2015, or at the earnings-related rate if that is lower – S.166(1)(b) SSCBA and Reg 6 SMP Regulations).

'Week' for these purposes means 'any period of seven days' – S.166(1A). Therefore, unlike, for example, the qualifying week (which must run from Sunday to Saturday), the woman can choose to start her maternity pay period ('MPP') on any day of the week. If the woman chooses to start her MPP on Friday, then each week for the purposes of S.166 will run from Friday to Thursday.

SMP is subject to tax and Class 1 NI contributions (provided it reaches the **5.95** required thresholds) as if it were pay. It is also subject to any other deductions which can lawfully be made from pay under the employee's contract, such as pension contributions and trade union subscriptions. (See Chapter 3, 'Maternity leave', under 'Terms and conditions during maternity leave – pensions', for the treatment of pension contributions during maternity leave.) However, as stated in the DWP's guidance booklet, 'Direct Earnings Attachment: A Guide for Employers', Attachment of Earnings Orders and Deductions from Earnings Orders made by the Child Support Agency (in Scotland, Arrestment of Earnings Orders) cannot be deducted from SMP.

Offsetting contractual remuneration 5.96
Certain contractual payments to an employee can be offset against SMP (or vice versa) – para 3(2), Sch 13 SSCBA. If any of the following is payable for any week during which SMP is due, it can be treated as reducing or extinguishing the liability to SMP for that week:

- any contractual remuneration if the employer continues to pay a woman when she is no longer at work – Reg 19(a) SMP Regulations

- contractual sick pay – Reg 19(b)

- contractual maternity pay – Reg 19(c).

199

'Week' in this context means a period of seven days beginning with the day of the week on which the maternity pay period begins – para 3(2A), Sch 13 SSCBA.

5.97 Alternatively, the employer can pay SMP in the normal way and withhold a corresponding sum from any contractual payment of the above types. In effect, this means that a woman can never claim SMP in addition to her full contractual pay.

Payments under jointly funded or employee-funded schemes (such as holiday payments funds) cannot be offset against SMP. However, if maternity, sick or holiday pay is paid from a jointly funded scheme and counts as earnings for NI contributions purposes, that proportion of the payment which is funded by the employer can be offset against SMP. So, for example, if an employer makes a 50 per cent contribution towards an occupational maternity scheme (the other 50 per cent being paid by the employee), and this pays out £50 per week, £25 of that amount can be offset against the SMP due to be paid each week.

5.98 Note that the employer cannot offset contractual remuneration paid in the first part of the maternity pay period against SMP due in the remaining part of the pay period. This is because para 3(2) of Schedule 13 to the SSCBA states that 'any contractual remuneration paid to a woman by an employer of hers in respect of a week in the maternity pay period shall go towards discharging any liability of that employer to pay [SMP] to her *in respect of that week*' (our stress). In other words, contractual pay can be offset against SMP but only on a week-by-week basis. For example, it would be unlawful for an employer to pay enhanced contractual maternity pay for the first 26 weeks of the pay period and then pay nothing for the remaining 13 weeks, even if the amount paid for the first 26 weeks exceeds the total amount of SMP due for the full 39 weeks.

5.99 **Salary sacrifice.** As explained in Chapter 3, 'Maternity leave', under 'Terms and conditions during maternity leave', an employee should continue to receive any non-cash benefits throughout her SML that she would have received had she not been absent, even if these benefits were provided as part of a salary sacrifice arrangement. The SMP payable will be calculated on the basis of the reduced salary but the non-cash benefit cannot be offset against the SMP (because it does not constitute 'remuneration') – see the HMRC guide, 'Statutory maternity leave – salary sacrifice and non-cash benefits' (now only available on the Government's national archive site) for further details.

5.100 **Childcare vouchers.** The HMRC guidance lists the provision of childcare vouchers as an example of a non-cash benefit that must be provided throughout SML. However, this raises potential problems for employers. While an employee is earning, she sacrifices part of her salary in return for the receipt of tax-efficient childcare vouchers – thus there is no loss to the employer. But where an employee is receiving only SMP, or is on unpaid leave, the employer must continue to provide the vouchers, but cannot deduct the value of the vouchers against SMP. The cost to the employer could therefore be significant.

It is suggested that one way round the problem could be for employers to agree with employees that childcare vouchers will not be provided while they are on maternity leave, and that their salary will revert to normal for this period. It may well be in employees' interests to agree to this arrangement; partly because they are less likely to use childcare while they are on maternity leave, and partly because the earnings-related part of their SMP will then be based on their full salary, without deduction for childcare vouchers. (Note that this problem does not arise in respect of contractual maternity pay, which the employer and employee can agree to offset against any salary sacrifice arrangement.)

Sex discrimination and equal pay claims 5.101

In Gillespie and ors v Northern Health and Social Services Board and ors 1996 ICR 498, ECJ, it was argued that European equality law required that women receive full pay during maternity leave. The claimants were all employees in the National Health Service in Northern Ireland and had taken maternity leave during 1988. Under the terms of the relevant collective agreement they were entitled to full weekly pay for the first four weeks of their maternity leave, 90 per cent of weekly pay for two weeks thereafter, and half of full weekly pay for 12 weeks. This was more favourable than the levels of SMP then in force, which provided for 90 per cent of full weekly pay for six weeks and a flat rate allowance of £47.95 per week for 12 weeks thereafter. The women commenced proceedings before an employment tribunal arguing that they had been discriminated against on the ground of sex because, during their maternity leave, they had suffered a reduction in pay compared with their normal weekly wage. The tribunal dismissed the women's applications and they appealed to the Northern Ireland Court of Appeal, which referred the case to the ECJ.

The basic question posed by the Northern Ireland Court of Appeal was whether a woman on maternity leave must continue to receive full pay. If there were no such requirement, the Court asked whether EU law nonetheless laid down specific criteria – and, if so, what criteria – for determining the amount of any benefit payable during maternity leave.

The European Court held that nothing in relation to Article 141 of the EC 5.102 Treaty (now Article 157 of the Treaty on the Functioning of the European Union (TFEU)) or the EC Equal Pay Directive (No.75/117) (now recast in the EU Equal Treatment Directive (No.2006/54)) requires that a woman should continue to be paid full pay during maternity leave. The Court noted that the Pregnant Workers Directive requires Member States to introduce various measures to protect the health and safety of female workers, including a right to a payment or 'adequate' allowance during maternity leave. However, the provisions of that Directive were not in force at the time and the Court held

201

that it therefore fell to the national legislature to set the amount of maternity pay, provided that the amount payable was not 'so low as to undermine the purpose of maternity leave, namely, the protection of women before and after giving birth'. When assessing the adequacy of the amount that is payable from this perspective, the national court must take into account not only the duration of maternity leave but also the other forms of social protection afforded by national law in the case of justified absence from work.

The case was subsequently returned to the Northern Ireland Court of Appeal – Gillespie and ors v Northern Health and Social Services Board and ors (No.2) 1997 IRLR 410, NICA – before which it was agreed that the only remaining question was whether the level of maternity pay paid to the claimants was so low as to undermine the purpose of maternity leave. The Court took the ECJ's reference to 'social protection afforded by national law' to be a reference to statutory rather than contractual benefits and noted that, on the particular facts, all the applicants had received maternity pay at a rate that exceeded the statutory levels of maternity pay and sickness benefit. Furthermore, Article 11(3) of the Pregnant Workers Directive stipulated that maternity pay 'shall be deemed adequate if it guarantees income at least equivalent to that which the worker concerned would receive in the event of a break in her activities on grounds connected with her state of health, subject to any ceiling laid down under national legislation'. The Court accepted that this provision was also intended to refer to statutory sickness benefit and not contractual sick pay. On the basis of these observations, the Court concluded that maternity pay that was higher than statutory sickness benefit could not be said to be inadequate.

5.103 The Court's reasoning leads to the inevitable conclusion that provided a woman is paid SMP at a rate no lower than the statutory sick pay rate (£88.45 for the tax year 2015/16), there will be no discrimination under EU law. SMP is only payable to women whose normal weekly earnings are at least the lower earnings limit (£112 for the tax year 2015/16) and it therefore will never be less than 90 per cent of that amount. And the prescribed rate will never fall below the rate of SSP – S.166(3) SSCBA. For further discussion of the impact of sex discrimination and equal pay law on maternity rights, see Chapter 13, 'Discrimination and equal pay'.

5.104 **Recoupment of contractual maternity pay.** In Boyle and ors v Equal Opportunities Commission 1999 ICR 360, ECJ, the complainants argued that a term of their employer's contractual maternity leave scheme requiring them to repay the difference between their SMP and their contractual maternity pay if they did not return to work after maternity leave was contrary to what is now Article 157 TFEU because a man who did not return to work after a period of sick leave would not have been required to repay his contractual sick pay. In rejecting this argument, the ECJ explicitly stated that the position of a woman on maternity leave is not comparable to that of a man or a woman on sick leave. The Court also ruled that a clause requiring repayment of contractual maternity pay did not breach the Pregnant Workers Directive. Article 11(2)(b) and (3) of that Directive was intended to ensure that, during the minimum period of at least 14 weeks' maternity leave referred to in Article 8, a woman receives an income at least equivalent to the sickness allowance provided for by national social security legislation. As the decision of the Court in Gillespie and ors v Northern Health and Social Services Board and ors (above) made clear, it was not intended to guarantee a woman a higher income equivalent to contractual sick pay.

Manner of payment

5.105

Payment of SMP may be 'made in a like manner to payments of remuneration' – Reg 27 SMP Regulations. This means that although SMP is a weekly payment due on the last day of each week of the maternity pay period, it can nevertheless be paid to the employee on the next usual pay day after that time. Therefore if the employee is normally paid monthly, her SMP can be paid on her normal pay day in any one month, in which case she will be entitled to receive the total sum of SMP payments that have fallen due since her last pay day.

Section 166(4) SSCBA provides that 'the amount payable by way of statutory maternity pay for any day shall be taken as one seventh of the weekly rate'. This allows a weekly payment of SMP to be divided by seven to give a daily amount. This means that SMP can be paid as part weeks to help employers align the payments to their employees' normal pay period. The weekly rate may be split into two and, if it is, the calculation is done on the basis of dividing the weekly rate by seven. For example, if the pay period covers the end of one month and the beginning of the next (e.g. two days in April and five days in May) the employer can pay two sevenths in one month and five sevenths the next month. There is nothing to prevent employers from paying SMP as a lump sum, although this can cause problems. In particular, if a woman who was paid in a lump sum loses her entitlement to SMP for some reason, the employer is likely to suffer administrative inconvenience trying to recover the overpayment. Furthermore, if an employer has already recovered the lump sum from HMRC and the woman subsequently becomes disentitled to it, the employer will be required to repay to HMRC the amount wrongly recovered. Also, both the employer and the employee will pay more in NI contributions on a lump-sum payment than if the employee is paid SMP weekly or monthly, since NI contributions must be calculated on the lump-sum payment and cannot be spread out over the period the lump sum is intended to cover.

SMP can be paid through an agent – for example, an insurance company, friendly society or payroll service. The employer, however, remains responsible for ensuring that SMP is only paid to women who satisfy all the qualifying

5.106

conditions for SMP and that SMP is paid subject to deductions of PAYE income tax and NI contributions.

Note that SMP cannot be made up of payments in kind or the provision of board or lodgings, services or other facilities – Reg 27.

5.107 Employees unable to act for themselves

Where SMP is payable to a person who is unable for the time being to act and no receiver has been appointed by the Court of Protection with power to receive SMP on her behalf (or, in Scotland, the person's estate is not being administered by any tutor, curator or other guardian acting or appointed in terms of law) HMRC may, upon written application by a person over 18, appoint that person to exercise any right to payment on behalf of the person unable to act – Reg 31(1) SMP Regulations. SMP is then payable to that person and he or she will take on the employee's rights and obligations in respect of SMP.

Any appointment of an agent for these purposes will end if a court order is made appointing another person to handle the employee's affairs – Reg 31(2).

5.108 Liability for SMP

Generally, liability to pay SMP rests with the employer who employs the woman claiming SMP. The 'employer' for the purposes of SMP is any person who is liable to pay secondary Class 1 NI contributions in relation to any of the employee's earnings or would be so liable but for the fact that the woman is:

- earning below the secondary threshold in S.5(1)(b) SSCBA, or
- under the age of 16 – S.171(1).

However, there may be situations in which liability to pay rests elsewhere. These cover the following:

- former employers
- where an employee is employed by more than one employer
- where the employer is insolvent or in default.

5.109 Former employers

A former employer will be liable to make payments of SMP to a woman who had been employed by it for a continuous period of at least eight weeks and her contract was brought to an end by the former employer solely, or mainly, for the purpose of avoiding liability for SMP – Reg 3(1) SMP Regulations (see 'Continuous employment – dismissal to avoid maternity pay' and 'Continuous employment – weeks that count' above).

More than one employer   5.110

Where a woman has two (or more) jobs and she satisfies the SMP qualifying conditions in respect of each of them, she is entitled to SMP from each of the employers – S.164(3) SSCBA. If, however, the woman's employers are 'associated' and her earnings from each job have to be aggregated to satisfy the requirement as to NI contributions, then the SMP to which she is entitled is apportioned between the employers in proportion to the woman's earnings from each unless the employers agree some other proportion – Reg 18 SMP Regulations. Maternity leave does not have to be taken from both jobs at the same time but, of course, SMP is only payable in respect of each job at the point when the employee stops working in that job – see 'Normal weekly earnings – aggregation of earnings under different contracts/employers' above for further details.

The rules regarding working for another employer who is not liable to pay SMP are more complicated and are discussed in the section 'Disentitlement to statutory maternity pay' above, under 'Working during the maternity pay period – working for other employers'.

Where a woman is self-employed in one job (and does not fall into the category   5.111 of 'employed earner' – see 'Qualifying for statutory maternity pay – definition of "employee"' above) and employed in another, SMP is payable in respect of the job in which she is employed. Where she receives SMP from her employment, she is not entitled to Maternity Allowance in respect of her self-employed status as well.

Insolvent and defaulting employers   5.112

If the employer becomes insolvent, liability for SMP passes to HMRC with effect from the week in which the employer became insolvent – Reg 7(3) SMP Regulations. In England and Wales, an individual employer is insolvent if he or she is adjudged bankrupt, has made a composition or arrangement with his or her creditors, or if he or she has died and his or her estate falls to be administered according to an order under S.421 of the Insolvency Act 1986 – Reg 7(4)(a)(i)–(ii). A company is insolvent if a winding up or administration order is made, a resolution for voluntary winding up is passed, a receiver or manager is appointed, debenture holders take possession of any property under a floating charge, or a voluntary arrangement is approved under the Insolvency Act – Reg 7(4)(a)(iii). Similar provisions apply in Scotland, although different terminology is used – Reg 7(4)(b). An employer who is merely having problems with cash flow is not insolvent.

The first payment that HMRC is liable to make will be made as soon as practicable after becoming liable and subsequent payments will be made at weekly intervals. Any SMP due for the period before the week of insolvency remains the responsibility of the employer. However, if this is not paid, HMRC

205

will take responsibility for making this payment – see 'Default not due to insolvency' immediately below.

5.113 **Default not due to insolvency.** HMRC will also take responsibility for paying SMP where the Revenue has made a decision that SMP is payable and the employer fails to make the payment, if the time for appealing against the decision has expired and the employer has made no appeal or leave to appeal has been refused – Reg 7(1) SMP Regulations. Failure to pay SMP by an employer following an HMRC decision is an offence.

5.114 **Contracting out**

There is no getting round an employer's liability for SMP. Any agreement will be void to the extent that it purports:

- to exclude, limit or modify any provision of the SMP scheme; or

- to require an employee to contribute (directly or indirectly) to any costs incurred by the employer under the SMP scheme – S.164(6) SSCBA.

Note that this does not prevent the employer from requiring the employee to contribute towards any costs incurred under a contractual maternity scheme. However, the employer should be cautious in doing so as the contractual and statutory maternity schemes may be interlinked.

5.115 ## The maternity pay period

The maternity pay period (MPP) is the period during which SMP is payable to an eligible employee – currently 39 weeks (see Reg 2(2) SMP Regulations). The relevant statutory provisions on the MPP are contained in S.165 SSCBA and Reg 2 SMP Regulations.

In most cases a woman may choose, within limits, when she wants to start her maternity leave and therefore when she wants the MPP to start running. The earliest date on which the MPP may start is the beginning of the 11th week before the EWC, unless the child is born earlier, in which case the MPP starts on the day after the birth – S.165(2) and Reg 2(3).

5.116 ### MPP starting in accordance with employee's notice

In the normal course of events, the employee will have given 28 days' notice of her intention to stop working (see 'Notice of absence or childbirth' above). Reg 2(1) provides that the MPP will start on the day set out in the notice (i.e. the date on which the employee expects her employer's liability to begin), which can be any day of the week. This means that her MPP can start on the same day as her maternity leave. So, for example, if the woman stops work on Friday (this being the day specified in her notice), her MPP will start on that Friday and each week in the MPP will run from Friday to Thursday. This ties in with

S.166(1A), which provides that for the purposes of S.166(1), 'week' means 'any period of seven days' – see 'Rates of statutory maternity pay' above; and S.166(4), which is designed to give flexibility to employers regarding the payment of SMP, allowing them to align SMP payments to the woman's normal pay day – see 'Manner of payment' above.

Nominating a date for SMP to commence. Although Reg 2(1) allows a **5.117** woman to nominate a date for payment of SMP to commence, she must have notified the employer of the date and 'in conformity with that notice' have ceased to work for it in a week which is later than the 12th week before the EWC'. So, what of the situation where a woman has started a period of contractual maternity leave prior to the 12th week before the EWC, but wants her MPP to start at a later date? This matter was addressed in Wade v North Yorkshire Police Authority and anor 2011 IRLR 393, Upper Tribunal (Tax and Chancery), where W had already commenced police maternity leave but sought to delay the start of her MPP until the 4th week before her EWC. The Police Authority contended that since W had already stopped work, she could not cease to work 'in conformity with' her notice, with the result that Reg 2(1) did not apply and the start of her MPP was governed by the default position in S.165(2) SSCBA (which provides that the MPP will begin with the 11th week before the EWC). However, the Upper Tribunal disapproved of this literal construction of Reg 2(1), noting that it would have undesirable consequences. In addition to preventing a woman in W's position from nominating a later start date for her MPP, the literal construction would also mean that Reg 2(1) could not apply to a woman who took a period of outstanding annual leave or time off in lieu prior to commencing maternity leave, or a woman who had been off sick prior to her maternity leave beginning. The Upper Tribunal's preferred construction of Reg 2(1) was that a woman may cease to work 'in conformity with' a notice even if she has previously ceased to work on some other basis.

Events which trigger MPP early **5.118**

Sometimes a woman's MPP will start earlier than the date she had intended when she gave notice of her intention to stop working:

- where the woman is confined before the start of the 11th week before the EWC, her MPP starts the day after the day on which she is confined – Reg 2(3)(a)

- where she is confined after the 12th week before the EWC but on a day which precedes the date specified in the notice given to her employer, her MPP starts the day after the day on which she is confined – Reg 2(3)(b)

- where she is absent from work wholly or partly because of pregnancy or confinement on any day after the beginning of the fourth week before the

207

EWC (but no later than the day after she is confined), then the MPP starts on the day after she is so absent – Reg 2(4)

- where the woman's employment ends after the start of the 11th week before the EWC but before the MPP has started (and not later than the week after the actual day of confinement), the MPP starts on the day after her employment ended – Reg 2(5).

(Note that these provisions do not appear to cover confinement that actually takes place in the 11th or 12th week before the EWC but presumably the MPP will start on the day after the day on which she is confined in accordance with Reg 2(3).)

5.119 **Pregnancy-related absence.** As noted above, the SMP Regulations state that the MPP is triggered if 'a woman is absent from work wholly or partly because of pregnancy or confinement on any day which falls on or after the beginning of the fourth week before the expected week of confinement' – Reg 2(4). The Regulations do not specifically state that a woman has to be absent on account of a pregnancy-related illness. The wording is wide enough to cover a variety of situations which do not amount to an illness – for example, swollen ankles or a bad back on account of pregnancy. For further discussion of similar problems of interpretation in circumstances where the maternity leave period is triggered by a pregnancy-related absence, see Chapter 3, 'Maternity leave', under 'Commencement of ordinary maternity leave – pregnancy-related absence'. Note that absence on sick leave during the four-week period before the EWC for a reason that is not pregnancy-related will not trigger the MPP.

The MPP will start on the day after the first day of the pregnancy-related absence and the weeks of the MPP will run from that day. Two examples:

- W is sick with a pregnancy-related illness on Sunday 5 April 2015, which is the start of the fourth week before her EWC. She is still sick on Monday 6 April, which is a bank holiday. She recovers and goes into work on Tuesday 7 April as normal. Although she was ill with a pregnancy-related illness during the fourth week before her EWC, the MPP was not triggered because she does not normally work on Sundays and her place of work was closed for the bank holiday. She was therefore not 'absent from work' for a reason related to pregnancy

- W is off work with an illness unrelated to her pregnancy in the fifth week before the EWC. This illness continues into the fourth and third weeks before the EWC. She is still entitled to receive SSP for this period. She then recovers and returns to work on the Wednesday of the third week, only to find that she is sick again on the Thursday for a pregnancy-related reason. Her MPP automatically starts on the Friday, and the weeks of her MPP run from Fridays to Thursdays.

Waiving days of pregnancy-related absence. As stated in Chapter 3, 'Maternity **5.120** leave', under 'Contractual and composite maternity rights', where an employee has a statutory right to maternity leave and also a 'right which corresponds to that right and which arises under the employee's contract of employment or otherwise', the employee can take advantage of whichever right is more favourable to her – Reg 21 Maternity and Parental Leave etc Regulations 1999 SI 1999/3312 ('the MPL Regulations'). This is known as a composite right and it means that, where an employee's ordinary maternity leave (OML) would normally have been triggered by a pregnancy-related absence, the employer can offer her the opportunity to delay the start of maternity leave without any loss in the overall period of leave.

Unfortunately, where an employer and employee agree to ignore a period of pregnancy-related absence so as to defer the start of OML, a problem arises in relation to the payment of SMP. The statutory provisions that cause the triggering of the SMP period apply in precisely the same way to trigger the maternity leave period. But, whereas SML entitlement is governed by the ERA and the MPL Regulations, SMP entitlement is governed by the SSCBA and the SMP Regulations. The 'composite right' provisions in Reg 21 MPL Regulations do not apply to SMP, and any agreement between the parties to exclude or modify the operation of the SSCBA is void – S.164(6) SSCBA. It follows that, while any agreement by the parties to ignore short periods of maternity absence may validly delay the start of maternity leave, it will not be effective to prevent the automatic triggering of the SMP period. As maternity pay is not payable during any week in which the employee works for the employer after the start of the MPP, the employee could lose out financially – S.165(4) SSCBA. She will still have her full six weeks' payment at the 'earnings-related rate' of 90 per cent of her salary, since payment at this rate will simply be deferred to the next week in which she does no work – S.166(1) SSCBA. However, she will lose one week of her 33 weeks' entitlement to SMP at the prescribed rate of £139.58 (from 5 April 2015) – or at the earnings-related rate, if lower – for each week she works after the MPP has been triggered (subject to her KIT day entitlement) – see 'Disentitlement to statutory maternity pay – working during the maternity pay period' above. For details of the 'prescribed rate' and 'earnings-related rate', see 'Rates of statutory maternity pay' above.

Although this lacuna is regrettable, in practice employers often disregard the **5.121** trigger date for SMP, start paying it from the date maternity leave actually starts, and claim reimbursement in the normal way from HMRC, which will be unaware of any irregularity. Indeed, most if not all employers in this situation will themselves not have been aware that there is a problem.

Premature and late births
5.122
If a child is born unexpectedly early, the timing of the MPP may be affected. Reg 2(3) SMP Regulations provides that, if the baby is born before the MPP is

209

due to start in accordance with the woman's notice of her intended date to stop working (see 'Notice of absence or childbirth' above), the MPP begins the day after the baby is born. The employee must, if reasonably practicable, inform the employer of the birth within 28 days (see 'Notice of absence or childbirth' above).

If the child is born early but the MPP has already started (for example, because of a pregnancy-related illness or because the employee's chosen start date has passed) then neither the MPP nor the payment of SMP is affected.

5.123   If a child is born after the EWC – i.e. it is late – the MPP is unaffected if it has already started. If a woman has chosen to work right up to the birth and the child is born late, the MPP is unaffected and starts on the day following the birth.

5.124 Termination of employment after qualifying week starts

A woman whose employment is terminated before the qualifying week will not qualify for SMP (unless Reg 3 – 'Contract of service ended for the purpose of avoiding liability for statutory maternity pay' – applies (see 'Continuous employment – dismissal to avoid maternity pay' above)). However, once she has worked any part of that week then, provided the other conditions are satisfied, her right to SMP will be preserved if she subsequently leaves employment. This could be as a result of dismissal for redundancy or misconduct, for example, or simply resignation. The start date of her MPP will depend on whether her employment terminated before or after the beginning of the 11th week before the EWC.

5.125   **Termination during or after the 11th week before EWC.** Regulation 2(5) provides that where the woman's employment is terminated after the beginning of the 11th week before the EWC but before the MPP has started, the MPP is triggered the day after her employment ends.

5.126   **Termination before the 11th week before EWC.** The Regulations unfortunately do not specifically provide a date for the MPP to start where the woman's employment has ended between the start of the qualifying week and the start of the 11th week before the EWC.

The MPP cannot start before the 11th week (unless she gives birth) as that would offend S.164(2)(c) SSCBA. If she had previously given 28 days' notice of the date she had intended to stop work, then one might expect that the MPP would start on the date set out in the notice. However, under Reg 2(1), this date only applies where the woman ceases to work 'in conformity with that notice', whereas if her employment has ended prematurely for some other reason then she has not left 'in conformity' with the notice. HMRC takes the view that in this situation the MPP begins on the Sunday at the beginning of the 11th week before the EWC, unless the woman gives birth earlier (in which case see 'Premature and late births' above) – see 'Maternity benefits: technical guidance' (2014).

Note that if an employee becomes unemployed before the qualifying week, as **5.127** a result of either resigning or being dismissed (and Reg 3 does not apply), even though she loses her right to SMP she may be entitled to claim Maternity Allowance – see 'Maternity Allowance' below.

Statutory sick pay **5.128**
Statutory sick pay (SSP) cannot be paid to a woman during the 39-week period in which SMP (or Maternity Allowance) is payable – S.153(2)(d) and (12) SSCBA. This is called the 'disqualifying period'. The disqualifying period starts at the beginning of the week in which the woman is first entitled to SMP (or Maternity Allowance).

A woman who is not entitled to SMP (or Maternity Allowance) will also be barred from claiming SSP for 18 weeks – Reg 3(4) and (5) Statutory Sick Pay (General) Regulations 1982 SI 1982/894. (Note that this has not been changed to 39 weeks to mirror the notional maternity pay (or Maternity Allowance) period.) The 18-week period starts on:

- the day of confinement, or
- the start of the week in which the woman becomes incapable of work for a pregnancy-related reason (on or after the start of the fourth week before the EWC).

If the woman is already receiving SSP, her entitlement will end on the day of **5.129** confinement or on the day she is first off sick, either wholly or partly because of her pregnancy, if this is on or after the fourth week before the EWC.

Note that a woman who is off work with a non-pregnancy-related illness or injury at the start of the fourth week before the EWC does not lose her right to SSP.

Women who are barred from claiming SSP have to fall back either on sickness **5.130** benefit (if they have made sufficient NI contributions) or on income support if their income is below a certain level.

For further details, see HMRC's 'Maternity benefits: technical guidance' (2014).

No extension of MPP **5.131**
As noted in Chapter 3, 'Maternity leave', under 'General considerations', the Work and Families Act 2006 introduced a framework for various amendments to maternity, adoption and other parental rights. S.2 of that Act amended S.165(1) SSCBA to provide that the MPP shall be 'of a duration not exceeding 52 weeks'. This paved the way for Reg 2(2) (which, as noted above, sets out

the actual duration of the MPP – currently 39 weeks) to be amended to extend the MPP to cover the whole of the employee's SML period. However, this change was postponed indefinitely. The European Parliament proposed an extension of the minimum period of maternity leave to 20 weeks on full pay but that proposal was rejected by the Council of the European Union in December 2010.

5.132 **Curtailing MPP to create right to statutory shared parental pay**
On 1 December 2014 a new statutory system of shared parental leave and pay came into force under powers introduced by the Children and Families Act 2014. The scheme allows a woman who is eligible for SML and SMP to choose to bring both an early end and share the balance with the father of her child (or her spouse, civil partner or partner). The scheme is designed to give parents more flexibility in how to share the care of their child in the first year of its life. They will be able to share the pot of leave and pay, and can decide to be off work at the same time and/or take it in turns to have periods of leave to look after the child.

In order to create a right to statutory shared parental pay the woman must bring her entitlement to SMP to an end by curtailing her MPP. She will then be able to share the balance of her pay with her partner. The procedure for curtailing the MPP is set out in the Statutory Maternity Pay and Statutory Adoption Pay (Curtailment) Regulations 2014 SI 2014/3054. Reg 7 provides that the woman must submit a 'maternity pay period curtailment notice' in writing to the person who is liable to pay her SMP, specifying the date on which she wants her MPP to end. This will usually be her current employer, although there may be cases where liability rests elsewhere.

5.133 For more information about the curtailment requirements and the statutory shared parental leave and pay scheme in general, see Chapter 8, 'Shared parental leave and pay'.

5.134 ## Statutory maternity pay examples

Below are two examples that give practical guidance on how to work out whether a woman is entitled to SMP and the amount that should be paid. These examples assume that the woman concerned has complied with the relevant notice requirements and provided the necessary medical evidence.

5.135 **Example one**
Y is paid on a commission basis at irregular intervals and has worked for the same company for five years. She is pregnant and the baby is due on 24 November 2015. The EWC is Sunday 22 – Saturday 28 November and the qualifying week (being 15 weeks before the EWC) is Sunday 9 – Saturday

15 August. Y's last pay day before the end of the qualifying week fell on 21 July and the last pay day to fall at least eight weeks earlier than that was 11 May. The relevant pay period therefore runs from 12 May – 21 July inclusive, a period of 71 calendar days. During that period, W's gross earnings were as follows:

2 June   £2,700

19 June   £2,400

21 July   £5,200

Total   £10,300

- thus her normal weekly earnings are calculated by adding together her earnings over the period and dividing that total by the number of days in that period (71) and multiplying by 7: (10,300/71) x 7 = £1015.4929577 per week. (Note that the figure is not rounded up or down to a whole number of pence at this stage)

- Y clearly earns well over the current lower earnings limit of £112 per week and is therefore entitled to SMP

- Y's earnings-related rate SMP is paid at 90 per cent of £1015.4929577 per week for the first six weeks of the MPP period: i.e. £913.95 per week. Always round up fractions of a penny at this stage – Reg 28 SMP Regulations. Thereafter, she would be paid for the remaining 33 weeks at the prescribed rate (currently £139.58 per week).

Example two   5.136

W is expecting a child on 22 September 2015. The EWC begins on Sunday 20 September and the qualifying week is Sunday 7 – Saturday 13 June 2015. She earns £24,000 per annum, is paid monthly on the 26th of each calendar month, and receives a £600 bonus with her May pay cheque. The last normal pay day before the end of the qualifying week is 26 May. The last normal pay day falling at least eight weeks before that is 26 March:

- her normal weekly earnings are calculated by taking into account all gross payments made on 26 April and 26 May plus the bonus of £600: £2,000 + £2,000 + £600 = £4,600. Divided by the number of months (2) = £2,300 per month. Multiplied by 12 and divided by 52 = £530.7692 per week

- she earns more than the lower earnings limit and is entitled to SMP

- higher rate SMP paid for the first six weeks is calculated as 90 per cent of £530.7692 = £477.70 (rounded up to a whole number of pence). She is thereafter entitled to 33 weeks at the prescribed rate.

213

5.137 Maternity Allowance

Maternity Allowance is a social security benefit payable to employed women whose service with their current employer does not qualify them for SMP, but who satisfy conditions relating to NI contributions on the basis of previous employment or self-employment. Thus it may be paid to women who gave up work or changed job before the qualifying week, or who are self-employed. A lower rate of allowance is also payable to women who are not employed or self-employed but who have worked for the business of their self-employed spouse or civil partner.

Maternity Allowance is a weekly benefit paid by the Department for Work and Pensions (DWP) through Jobcentre Plus for a maximum period of 39 weeks (or 14 weeks at the lower rate). Unlike SMP, Maternity Allowance is not liable to income tax and NI contributions. A detailed examination of Maternity Allowance is beyond the scope of this Handbook but we highlight the main points below. Details of the Maternity Allowance scheme are set out in the DWP guide, 'Maternity benefits: technical guidance' (2014) ('the DWP guide').

5.138 Qualifying conditions for employed or self-employed earners

A woman qualifies for Maternity Allowance if all the conditions in S.35(1) SSCBA are satisfied, namely that:

- she is pregnant and has reached, or has been confined before reaching, the start of the 11th week before the EWC

- she has been an employed or self-employed earner (and, if self-employed, registered with HMRC for this purpose) for at least 26 weeks in the 66 weeks preceding the EWC. Unlike SMP, the 26 weeks do not have to be continuous and do not have to be with the same employer. Furthermore, she does not have to work a full week for it to count towards the 26 weeks

- her average weekly earnings are not less than the Maternity Allowance threshold for the tax year in which the beginning of the 66-week period falls (currently £30 per week, a figure that has not changed since 2000). Her earnings can be averaged over any 13 weeks in that period and those weeks do not have to be consecutive

- she is not entitled to SMP for the same week in respect of the same pregnancy.

(Note that the Welfare Reform Act 2012 has introduced a new condition that, at the commencement of the 11th week before the EWC, the woman must be 'entitled to be in employment' under UK immigration law. However, this provision is not yet in force.)

5.139 Maternity Allowance is payable for 39 weeks – the Maternity Allowance period (MAP). The earliest the MAP can start is the beginning of the 11th week before the week in which the child is due. The woman can choose to start receiving Maternity Allowance later but the latest it can start is the day following the birth. Maternity Allowance is generally payable for the period that would have been the maternity pay period (MPP) had the woman been entitled to SMP – see S.35(2) SSCBA. The rules for computing the MAP are therefore generally the same as for the MPP – see 'The maternity pay period' above. Like the MPP, the MAP is triggered by a premature birth or by a pregnancy-related absence in the last four weeks before the EWC.

Qualifying conditions for spouses/civil partners of self-employed   5.140

In 2010 the European Union issued a 'Directive on the application of the principle of equal treatment between men and women engaged in an activity in a self-employed capacity' (No.2010/41). Article 8 of that Directive requires that women who are the spouses or civil partners of self-employed earners 'be granted a sufficient maternity allowance enabling interruptions in their occupational activity owing to pregnancy or motherhood for at least 14 weeks'.

This obligation has been implemented into UK law by the Social Security (Maternity Allowance) (Participating Wife or Civil Partner of Self-employed Earner) Regulations 2014 SI 2014/606, which inserted a new S.35B into the SSCBA. This provides that if a woman is not, or has not been, employed or self-employed but she takes part in the business of her self-employed spouse or civil partner she may be entitled to Maternity Allowance for 14 continuous weeks if she satisfies certain qualifying conditions. The qualifying conditions are that for at least 26 weeks in the 66 weeks preceding the EWC she:

- has regularly taken part in activities relating to the business of her self-employed spouse or civil partner
- is not an employee or partner in the business
- is not an employed or self-employed earner, and
- is not receiving SMP or the higher rate of Maternity Allowance for the same pregnancy.

During that same 26-week period, the woman's self-employed spouse or civil   5.141
partner must be:

- registered as self-employed with HMRC
- liable for payment of Class 2 NI contributions, and
- working as a self-employed earner.

If the woman ceases to work for her spouse or civil partner before the commencement of the 11th week before the EWC, the 14-week MAP begins with the commencement of the 11th week before the EWC. If she ceases to work on a day that falls within the period beginning with the commencement

215

of the 11th week before the EWC and ending with the end of the fifth week before the EWC, the 14-week MAP begins immediately after that day. If she ceases work, or refrains from working wholly or partly because of her pregnancy or confinement, on any day falling within the four weeks before the EWC, the 14-week MAP begins immediately after the day on which she ceases, or refrains from, work. In any other circumstances, the 14-week period begins immediately after the date of confinement – S35B(5)–(8) SSCBA.

5.142 Excluded groups

Maternity Allowance is not payable in the following circumstances:

- where the woman is in prison or in legal custody

- where the woman is absent from Great Britain – S.113(1) SSCBA.

The DWP guide states that the UK has special arrangements with certain other countries (including countries within the EEA) that may help a woman to get Maternity Allowance if she is going abroad or if she has recently been abroad and returned to the UK.

5.143 Special rules apply to women who are ordinarily resident in Great Britain but who worked abroad during the 12 months before the qualifying week for Maternity Allowance. The rules are contained in the Social Security (Maternity Allowance) (Work Abroad) Regulations 1987 SI 1987/417.

5.144 Claiming Maternity Allowance

A claim for Maternity Allowance may not be made before the end of the qualifying week – Reg 14 Social Security (Claims and Payments) Regulations 1987 SI 1987/1968, but it should be made as soon as possible after that. (For the definition of 'qualifying week' see 'Qualifying for statutory maternity pay – qualifying conditions' above.) The DWP guide states that if the woman claims more than three months after the date her Maternity Allowance period is due to start, she will lose money.

The DWP guide sets out the procedure that should be followed when a woman claims Maternity Allowance. She should submit the following to her local Jobcentre Plus:

- claim form MA1

- form MAT B1 (the medical evidence of when the child is due)

- proof of her income (e.g. original payslips, or a Certificate of Small Earnings Exemption (if applicable))

- form SMP1, completed by her employer, stating that the employee is not entitled to SMP (if she was refused SMP by her employer).

She may also need to give more information about her partner's self-employed business and what she does if she is applying for lower-rate Maternity Allowance.

Rate of Maternity Allowance

There are effectively two rates of Maternity Allowance: a higher rate paid to women who were employed or self-employed, and a lower rate paid to women who are not employed or self-employed but who participate in the business of their self-employed spouse or civil partner.

The higher rate of Maternity Allowance is payable at whichever is the lowest of:

- 90 per cent of the woman's average weekly earnings

- the prescribed rate of SMP under S.166(1)(b) SSCBA – £139.58. (Note that for the purposes of calculating Maternity Allowance this rate applies from 6 April 2015. For SMP purposes, the increased rate applies from 5 April 2015 – see 'Rates of statutory maternity pay' above).

If a woman is entitled to the lower rate of Maternity Allowance she will be treated as having earnings equal to the Maternity Allowance threshold, which is currently £30 a week, and she will receive 90 per cent of that amount (i.e. £27). Maternity Allowance is paid every 2 or 4 weeks.

Curtailing MAP to create right to statutory shared parental pay

A woman who is entitled to Maternity Allowance but not SMP is not entitled to shared parental leave (SPL) or statutory shared parental pay (SSPP). However, she may still enable the father of her child (or her spouse, civil partner or partner) to take SPL and SSPP by curtailing her MAP. To do this, she must notify the Secretary of State of the date it will come to an end in accordance with Reg 5(1) of the Maternity Allowance (Curtailment) Regulations 2014 SI 2014/3053. There is no express requirement for this notice to be in writing.

For more information about the curtailment provisions (for instance, the restrictions that apply as to the date a woman can choose to end her MAP) and the shared parental leave and pay scheme in general, see Chapter 8, 'Shared parental leave and pay'.

5.145

5.146

5.147

6 Adoption leave and pay

Time off for adoption appointments

Ordinary adoption leave

Additional adoption leave

Terms and conditions during adoption leave

Keeping in touch during adoption leave

Disrupted placement during adoption leave

Returning to work after adoption leave

Contractual and composite adoption rights

Detriment and unfair dismissal rights

Redundancy and adoption leave

Statutory adoption pay

The Employment Act 2002 introduced a statutory right to adoption leave and **6.1** adoption pay for employees who are newly matched with a child for adoption in order for them to build a relationship with the child when he or she starts living with them. In essence, such employees have a right to:

- 52 weeks' statutory adoption leave (SAL) (comprising 26 weeks' ordinary adoption leave and 26 weeks' additional adoption leave); and

- 39 weeks' statutory adoption pay (SAP). Since 5 April 2015, SAP is paid at 90 per cent of the employee's normal weekly earnings for the first six weeks and at the 'prescribed rate' for the remaining 33 weeks, which brings it into line with statutory maternity pay. (Previously, the rate of SAP was the lesser of the prescribed rate or 90 per cent of the employee's normal weekly earnings for the full 39 weeks.) The prescribed rate for the tax year 2015/16 is £139.58.

In order to assist with the adoption process, would-be adoptive parents also have the right to take time off work to attend adoption appointments prior to the placement of the child. This right, which was introduced by the Children and Families Act 2014 and came into effect on 5 April 2015, may be paid or unpaid, depending on whether it is requested by the child's primary or secondary adopter.

The rights to adoption leave and pay and to time off are in addition to the right **6.2** for adoptive parents to take unpaid parental leave (see Chapter 10, 'Unpaid parental leave') and the right for the adopter's partner to take two weeks' paid paternity leave around the time of the placement (see Chapter 7, 'Paternity leave and pay'). Adoptive parents may also make use of the new shared parental leave scheme, which allows an adopter who is eligible for statutory adoption leave and pay to bring the leave and pay to an early end and share the balance with his or her partner. The scheme, which applies in respect of children who are placed for adoption on or after 5 April 2015, is designed to give parents more flexibility over how to share the care of their child. Shared parental leave replaced the (more limited) additional paternity leave scheme, under which the adopter's partner was allowed to take up to 26 weeks of any unused adoption leave and pay to care for the child when the primary adopter returned to work. The shared parental leave scheme is discussed in detail in Chapter 8, 'Shared parental leave and pay'.

The majority of employees who are entitled to SAP will also be entitled to SAL and there is a considerable amount of overlap between the two. However, it should be noted that the two rights are separate, being governed by two different statutes: Chapter IA of the Employment Rights Act 1996 (ERA) in the case of adoption leave, and Part XIIZB of the Social Security Contributions and Benefits Act 1992 (SSCBA) in the case of adoption pay. Both Chapter IA and Part XIIZB were, however, inserted into their respective Acts by the Employment Act 2002.

6.3 There are also separate regulations governing how the rights to adoption leave and adoption pay operate in practice. The Paternity and Adoption Leave Regulations 2002 SI 2002/2788 ('the PAL Regulations') are the main provisions governing the operation of the adoption leave scheme and the Statutory Paternity Pay and Statutory Adoption Pay (General) Regulations 2002 SI 2002/2822 ('the General Regulations') are the principal provisions governing the operation of the statutory adoption pay scheme. Both sets of Regulations cover England, Wales and Scotland. The corresponding provisions for Northern Ireland are the Paternity and Adoption Leave Regulations (Northern Ireland) 2002 SR 2002/377 and the Statutory Paternity Pay and Statutory Adoption Pay (General) Regulations (Northern Ireland) 2002 SR 2002/378.

Although the overall structure of the adoption leave scheme has remained the same, numerous changes have been made since it was first introduced in 2002. Notable amendments were made by the Work and Families Act 2006 and the Maternity and Parental Leave etc and the Paternity and Adoption Leave (Amendment) Regulations 2006 SI 2006/2014 issued under it, and by the Maternity and Parental Leave etc and the Paternity and Adoption Leave (Amendment) Regulations 2008 SI 2008/1966, which saw the removal of the distinction between ordinary and additional adoption leave in respect of the preservation of the employee's employment terms and conditions, the introduction of 'keeping-in-touch' days during the adoption leave period and an increase in the amount of notice the employee is required to give when intending to return to work early. Recent changes have further aligned the rights available to adoptive parents more closely with those of birth parents. In summary, the key changes to the rights of adoptive parents with effect from 5 April 2015 were:

- the introduction of new rights to time off work to attend pre-adoption appointments (see 'Time off for adoption appointments' below)

- the extension of the right to adoption leave and pay to local authority foster parents in the 'fostering for adoption' scheme and to intended parents in a surrogacy arrangement (see 'Ordinary adoption leave – who has the right?' and 'Statutory adoption pay – eligible persons' below)

- the removal of the 26 weeks' continuous service requirement for the right to SAL, making SAL a 'day one' right (see 'Ordinary adoption leave – conditions of entitlement' below)

- the enhancement of the rate of SAP to 90 per cent of the employee's normal weekly earnings for the first six weeks, followed by 33 weeks at the prescribed rate of £139.58 (for the tax year 2015/16). This brings SAP into line with the rate for statutory maternity pay (see 'Statutory adoption pay – rate of SAP' below)

- the introduction of the shared parental leave scheme, allowing adopters to convert any unused adoption leave and pay into shared parental leave and pay. Shared parental leave is discussed in Chapter 8, 'Shared parental leave and pay'.

These changes were implemented in England, Wales and Scotland by the **6.4** Children and Families Act 2014 and various statutory instruments issued under it, and by the Paternity and Adoption Leave (Amendment) Regulations 2014 SI 2014/2112. In Northern Ireland, the bulk of the changes were brought in by the Work and Families Act (Northern Ireland) 2015.

The first part of this chapter explains the new right to take time off work to attend appointments prior to the finalisation of an adoption. The next part (covering the sections from 'Ordinary adoption leave' to 'Redundancy and adoption leave') deals with adoption leave. Statutory references in this part are to the provisions of the ERA, and references to regulation numbers are to the PAL Regulations, unless otherwise stated. The remainder of the chapter deals with adoption pay. Statutory references in this part are to the provisions of the SSCBA, and references to regulations are to the General Regulations, unless otherwise stated.

Note that the statutory adoption provisions have significant similarities to the **6.5** statutory maternity provisions dealt with in Chapter 1, 'Time off for ante-natal care'; Chapter 3, 'Maternity leave'; Chapter 4, 'Returning to work after maternity leave'; and Chapter 5, 'Statutory maternity pay'.

221

6.6 Time off for adoption appointments

The Children and Families Act 2014, which received Royal Assent on 13 March 2014, introduced new rights for employees and qualifying agency workers to take time off work to attend appointments in advance of a child being placed with them for adoption or for 'fostering for adoption'. The purpose of pre-adoption appointments is to make the adoption process easier for both the child and his or her would-be adoptive parents. According to the Act's Explanatory Notes, the appointments are intended to enable the adopters and the child to bond prior to the child going to live with the adopters, and for the adopters to meet the professionals who are involved in the child's care. It is hoped that this new right, which came into effect on 5 April 2015, will increase the chances of a successful adoption.

The details of the rights to time off for adoption appointments are set out in Ss.57ZJ– ZS ERA, which were inserted by S.128 of the Children and Families Act 2014. In essence, a person who has been notified that a child is to be placed with him or her for adoption, either alone or jointly with another person, is entitled to take time off work in order to attend pre-adoption appointments. For employees, this right to time off is a 'day one' right; i.e. no minimum period of qualifying service is required. However, agency workers must have completed at least 12 weeks' service with the same hirer and in the same role in order to qualify. The amount of time off available, and any payment for the time off, depends on whether the employee or agency worker is the child's sole or primary adopter, or whether he or she has elected to be the child's secondary adopter.

6.7 In summary, the child's sole or primary adopter has the right under the ERA:

- not to be unreasonably refused time off to attend up to five pre-adoption appointments during working hours – Ss.57ZJ/57ZN; and

- to be paid for each period of absence – Ss.57ZK/57ZO.

The child's secondary adopter has the right under the ERA:

- not to be unreasonably refused unpaid time off to attend up to two pre-adoption appointments during working hours – Ss.57ZL/57ZP.

An unreasonable refusal to allow paid or unpaid time off, or a failure to pay the employee or agency worker for time off, may result in a claim to an employment tribunal.

6.8 Employees and agency workers are also protected from being subjected to a detriment as a result of exercising their right to time off work in connection with an adoption, and employees further benefit from protection against dismissal in relation to the right to time off – see further 'Remedies' below.

These provisions apply to England, Wales and Scotland. Equivalent provisions covering Northern Ireland were introduced by the Work and Families Act (Northern Ireland) 2015.

Note that the rights to time off for adoption appointments are similar to a pregnant woman's right to time off to attend ante-natal appointments and her partner's right to accompany her to such appointments. For a full discussion of these rights, see Chapter 1, 'Time off for ante-natal care'.

Who has the right?

6.9

In this section we consider the various categories of employee and worker who are entitled to time off under Ss.57ZJ–ZS ERA. We also identify those employees and workers who are excluded from their scope.

Employees. The new right to (paid or unpaid) time off to attend adoption appointments is available to all employees (unless they are specifically excluded – see 'Excluded employees and workers' below). An 'employee' is an individual who works under a contract of service, as opposed to a contract for services – S.230 ERA (see IDS Employment Law Handbook, 'Contracts of Employment' (2014), Chapter 2, 'Employment status', for further details). No minimum period of qualifying service is necessary. An employee has the right to time off for adoption appointments from the day he or she starts the job, whether he or she is full time or part time and whether he or she is engaged on a permanent or temporary basis.

6.10

Agency Workers. With effect from 1 October 2011, the Agency Workers Regulations 2010 SI 2010/93 (AWR) introduced new employment protections for agency workers, including a right to be permitted, by both the temporary work agency and the hirer, to take paid time off for ante-natal care in the same way as employees – see Chapter 1, 'Time off for ante-natal care', under 'Right to time off for ante-natal care – who has the right?'. On 5 April 2015, agency workers also became entitled to take time off to attend pre-adoption meetings. The Children and Families Act 2014 inserted a new set of provisions – Ss.57ZN–ZR – into the ERA to that effect. An 'agency worker' is defined for the purposes of the Regulations and by extension the ERA (see S.57ZR(4)) as a worker who has either a contract of employment with the temporary work agency, or any other contract to perform work and services personally for the agency – Reg 3.

6.11

The relevant statutory provisions afford agency workers the right to paid time off for adoption appointments (Ss.57ZN and 57ZO) and the right to unpaid time off for adoption appointments (S.57ZP), and enable them to enforce these rights by way of a complaint to an employment tribunal (S.57ZQ). However, by virtue of S.57ZR(1)(a), in order to qualify for these rights, the worker must first satisfy the relevant 'qualifying period'. In this regard, Reg 7(2) AWR provides that 'the agency worker must work in the same role with the same hirer for 12 continuous calendar weeks, during one or more assignments'.

6.12 Seafarers and Crown employees. Seafarers employed on ships registered under S.8 of the Merchant Shipping Act 1995 are covered provided that the ship is registered as belonging to a port in Great Britain, that under his or her contract of employment the employee does not work wholly outside Great Britain, and that he or she is ordinarily resident in Great Britain – S.199(7) and (8) ERA. Crown employees and parliamentary staff are also covered – Ss.191, 194 and 195 ERA.

6.13 Foster parents. The right to time off to attend adoption appointments is also available where a local authority in England notifies foster parents that a child is to be, or is expected to be, placed with them in a 'fostering for adoption' placement. A 'fostering for adoption' placement is a placement with local authority foster parents who are also approved prospective adopters. Under S.22C of the Children Act 1989, a local authority is under a duty to consider a 'fostering for adoption' placement where it is considering adoption as an option for the child's long-term care (whether as the only option or as one of several) but it does not yet have authorisation to place the child for adoption. S.57ZS(1) and (2) ERA provides that 'fostering for adoption' placements should be treated in the same way as adoption placements in terms of the right to time off work to attend adoption appointments. However, once the child is in a 'fostering for adoption' placement and the foster parents then receive notification from the adoption agency that the child is to be, or is expected to be, placed with them for adoption, no new entitlement to the right to time off for adoption appointments arises – S.57ZS(3).

6.14 Intended parents in a surrogacy arrangement. Intended parents of a child born through a surrogacy arrangement are now entitled to adoption leave and pay in respect of that child if they meet specified conditions. For obvious reasons, they are not covered by the provisions allowing time off for pre-adoption meetings, but instead fall under the provisions for time off for ante-natal appointments. In other words, they may be entitled to take unpaid time off work to accompany the surrogate mother to ante-natal appointments. This right is fully discussed in Chapter 1, 'Time off for ante-natal care', under 'Right to time off for ante-natal care – who has the right?'.

6.15 Excluded employees and workers. Employees excluded from the right to time off under Ss.57ZJ–ZL ERA are those employed in:

- the armed forces – S.192 (read with para 16, Sch 2)
- share fishing – S.199(2)
- the police service – S.200.

Under S.126 of the Criminal Justice and Public Order Act 1994 prison officers are covered by the employment protection legislation and so will qualify for the right to time off for adoption appointments.

Apart from agency workers (as discussed above), all other workers who are not **6.16** 'employees' within the meaning of S.230 ERA are not entitled to time off for pre-adoption meetings. So, for example, casual workers, homeworkers and labour-only subcontractors – unless they are employees or otherwise satisfy the definition of 'agency worker' in Reg 3 AWR – will not qualify for time off rights for adoption appointments.

Scope of right   **6.17**

As mentioned above, would-be adopters have a right to paid or unpaid time off to attend appointments prior to a child being placed with them for adoption. It is worth noting at the outset that the right is 'to be permitted' the time off. Permission must therefore be sought from the employer (or, in the case of an agency worker, the temporary work agency and the hirer) prior to attending any adoption appointment during working hours. That said, the employer must allow any reasonable requests for time off (see 'Remedies' below).

Conditions. There are a number of prerequisites before the employee or agency **6.18** worker is entitled to take time off from work in order to attend adoption appointments. They are that:

- the employee/agency worker must have been notified by an adoption agency that a child is to be, or is expected to be, placed for adoption with him or her, either alone or jointly – Ss.57ZJ(1), (2)(a) and 57ZL(1)(a)/Ss.57ZN(1), (2)(a) and 57ZP(1)(a) ERA. For these purposes, 'adoption agency' means an adoption agency within the meaning of S.2 of the Adoption and Children Act 2002 or S.119(1)(a) of the Adoption and Children (Scotland) Act 2007 – Ss.57ZJ(13) and 57ZL(11)/Ss.57ZN(13) and 57ZP(11)

- the appointment has been arranged by or at the request of the adoption agency – Ss.57ZJ(7) and 57ZL(6)/Ss.57ZN(7) and 57ZP(6)

- the appointment must be for the purpose of having contact with the child or for any other purpose connected with the adoption – Ss.57ZJ(1), (2) and 57ZL(1)/Ss.57ZN(1), (2) and 57ZP(1)

- if the employer/temporary work agency/hirer requests it, the employee/agency worker must produce a document showing the date and time of the appointment and that it has been arranged by or at the request of the adoption agency – Ss.57ZJ(8), (9)(b) and 57ZL(7)(b)/Ss.57ZN(8), (9)(b) and 57ZP(7)(b). This document may be given in electronic form – Ss.57ZJ(10) and 57ZL(8)/Ss.57ZN(10) and 57ZP(8).

Where the employee or agency worker intends to adopt a child jointly with another person as part of a couple, there is an additional requirement in that he or she must *elect* to exercise either the right to paid time off or to the right to unpaid time off in connection with the adoption; it is not possible for one person to take both types of time off. In other words, one person must choose

225

to take paid time off under S.57ZJ or S.57ZN, and the other person must choose to take unpaid time off under S.57ZL or S.57ZP.

6.19 If the employer/temporary work agency/hirer requests it, the employee/agency worker must produce evidence as to which right has been chosen in the form of a declaration, signed by him or her and stating that he or she has elected to take either paid or unpaid time off in connection with the adoption – Ss.57ZJ(9)(a) and 57ZL(7)(a)/Ss.57ZN(9)(a) and 57ZP(7)(a). The declaration may be given in electronic form – Ss.57ZJ(10) and 57ZL(8)/Ss.57ZN(10) and 57ZP(8).

The legislation makes it clear that the two rights to time off are mutually exclusive. S.57ZJ(3) states that an employee cannot take advantage of the right to paid time off under that section where he or she has already elected to take unpaid time off in connection with the adoption under S.57ZL. Nor can he or she elect to take paid time off where the other person with whom the child is expected to be placed is an agency worker who has elected to take paid time off under S.57ZN in connection with the adoption. Conversely, S.57ZL(2) provides that the employee cannot elect to take unpaid time off under that section if he or she has already chosen to take paid time off in connection with the adoption under S.57ZJ. Nor can he or she elect to take unpaid time off where the other person with whom the child is expected to be placed is an agency worker who has elected to take unpaid time off under S.57ZP in connection with the adoption. Similar restrictions for agency workers who adopt jointly with another person are set out in Ss.57ZN(3) and 57ZP(2).

6.20 Importantly, the right to take time off to attend adoption appointments is only available until such time as the child is placed with the employee or agency worker – Ss.57ZJ(4) and 57ZL(3)/Ss.57ZN(4) and 57ZP(3). Where more than one child is to be, or is expected to be, placed for adoption as part of the same arrangement, the right to time off applies until the date the first child is placed with the employee or agency worker – Ss.57ZJ(11)(d) and 57ZL(9)(d)/Ss.57ZN(11)(d) and 57ZP(9)(d).

6.21 **Relationship with paternity leave.** Note that where the employee has exercised the right to paid time off under S.57ZJ to attend adoption appointments, he or she is then no longer entitled to take one or two weeks' paternity leave in respect of the same child when the child is placed for adoption. This is the effect of Reg 8(1A)(b) of the Paternity and Adoption Leave Regulations 2002 SI 2002/2788 – see Chapter 7, 'Paternity leave and pay', under 'Entitlement to paternity leave – (adoption)'.

6.22 **Amount of time off.** The number of adoption appointments that the employee or agency worker is entitled to attend depends on whether he or she is making a request for paid or unpaid time off. That number is unaffected where more than one child is to be, or is expected to be, placed for adoption as part of the same arrangement – Ss.57ZJ(11)(e) and 57ZL(9)(e)/Ss.57ZN(11)(e) and

57ZP(9)(e). In other words, the amount of time off does not increase simply because more than one child is to be placed for adoption.

Right to paid time off. An employee or agency worker who requests paid time off is entitled to attend up to *five* adoption appointments during working hours – S.57ZJ(5)/S.57ZN(5). A maximum of six and a half hours can be taken during working hours in respect of each adoption appointment – S.57ZJ(6)/S.57ZN(6). It would seem that in most cases this would cover not only the time needed to attend the appointment itself but also any travelling and waiting time. **6.23**

Right to unpaid time off. In respect of unpaid time off, the employee or agency worker is entitled to attend up to *two* adoption appointments during working hours in relation to any particular adoption – S.57ZL(4)/S.57ZP(4). Again, the maximum time allowed on each occasion is six and a half hours of working time – S.57ZL(5)/S.57ZP(5). **6.24**

When is a refusal reasonable? It is important to stress that the statutory right is not to be *unreasonably* refused time off (see 'Remedies' below). It can be deduced from this that there may be circumstances where it is reasonable for the employer or the temporary work agency/hirer to refuse a request for time off for adoption appointments. The ERA does not give any guidance on how to determine reasonableness in these circumstances and it is likely to depend on the individual facts of each case. Consider the following scenario. A female employee who works for the employer two days a week has received notification that a child is to be placed with her for adoption and is planning to take advantage of the right to time off for pre-adoption appointments. As the employee works part time, the employer may consider it reasonable to refuse her request where the adoption appointment falls on a working day. However, the employee may take the view that such a refusal is unreasonable because she had no influence over the timing of the appointment, which is arranged by the adoption agency. The tribunal would have to decide on the particular facts of the case, and on circumstances of the individual employee, whether the employer was acting reasonably. **6.25**

Time off during working hours. The right is to take time off during working hours to attend adoption appointments. The term 'working hours' in this context is defined in Ss.57ZJ(12) and 57ZL(10) as 'any time when, in accordance with the employee's contract of employment, the employee is required to be at work'. Equivalent provisions apply in the case of agency workers: in that case, such hours are defined in Ss.57ZN(12) and 57ZP(10) as 'any time when, in accordance with the terms under which the agency worker works temporarily for and under the supervision and direction of the hirer, the agency worker is required to be at work'. It will therefore not be reasonable for the employer/ temporary work agency/hirer to require the employee/agency worker to rearrange his or her working hours or to make up for lost time later. **6.26**

227

6.27 Right to payment for time off

Once an employee or agency worker is permitted to take time off under Ss.57ZJ or 57ZN, he or she is entitled to be paid for it at the appropriate hourly rate – Ss.57ZK(1) and 57ZO(1). Payment must be made for the number of working hours for which the employee or agency worker 'is entitled to be absent' rather than the number of hours that he or she was actually absent.

The right to paid time off only applies when an employee is allowed paid time off 'under S.57ZJ' or, in the case of agency workers, 'under S.57ZN'. This means that he or she must comply with any request from the employer/temporary work agency/hirer to produce a document showing the date and time of the appointment and that it has been arranged by or at the request of the adoption agency and, in the case of joint adopters, a signed declaration stating that he or she has elected to take paid time off in connection with the adoption (see 'Scope of right – conditions' above). If he or she does not do so, the employer/temporary work agency will not be obliged to pay him or her for any time off allowed. However, the employee or worker need only produce these documents if the employer/temporary work agency/hirer actually asks to see them.

6.28 Calculation of pay. Pay is for the number of working hours for which the employee or agency worker is entitled to be absent at the 'appropriate hourly rate' – Ss.57ZK(1) and 57ZO(1). In the context of employment, where the employee is paid a fixed annual salary, he or she should simply be paid as normal. In other cases, the appropriate hourly rate is found by dividing a week's pay by the number or average number of normal working hours in a week – S.57ZK(2) and (3). Equivalent calculation rules apply to agency workers – S.57ZO(2) and (3). The rules governing the calculation of a week's pay are set out in Chapter II of Part XIV of the ERA – see IDS Employment Law Handbook, 'Wages' (2011), Chapter 10, 'A week's pay'. There is no ceiling on the amount of a week's pay for the purposes of calculating paid time off for adoption appointments as there is, for example, in the case of calculating redundancy payments.

There are three ways of ascertaining an employee's 'normal working hours':

- if the number of normal working hours does not vary from week to week, that is the number to be used – S.57ZK(2)

- if the number of normal working hours varies from week to week, take the total number of hours worked during the 12 weeks ending with the last complete week before the day of the adoption appointment and divide by 12 – S.57ZK(3)(a)

- if the number of normal working hours varies from week to week, but the employee has worked for less than 12 weeks, take a number that fairly represents his or her normal working hours in a week – S.57ZK(3)(b).

Regard may be had, as appropriate, to the average number of hours the employee could expect to work under his or her contract and to the average hours worked by employees in comparable jobs – S.57ZK(4).

The calculation date for establishing the rate of payment is the day of the appointment concerned – S.225(3B).

So far as agency workers are concerned, the appropriate hourly rate where **6.29** normal working hours do not vary is calculated by taking the amount of one week's pay and dividing it by the number of normal working hours in a week in accordance with the terms under which the worker works temporarily for and under the supervision and direction of the hirer in force on the date when the time off is taken – S.57ZO(2). However, where the working hours during the temporary assignment vary from week to week, the same calculation as set out in S.57ZK(3)(a) above is applied – see S.57ZO(3).

Note that there is no provision equivalent to S.57ZK(4) with regard to calculating remuneration for agency workers with fewer than 12 weeks' service, as such workers will not have met the qualifying period of 12 weeks' work on which the new entitlement to paid time off for adoption appointments depends.

Rate of pay and set off. Where an employee or agency worker has a **6.30** contractual right to be paid for the time off, he or she is entitled to claim the contractual or statutory rate, whichever is the greater, but no more – S.57ZK(5)/S.57ZO(4). Payment under one head also discharges liability under the other – S.57ZK(6)–(7)/S.57ZO(5)–(6).

Remedies   6.31

An employee or agency worker who is unreasonably denied time off to attend adoption appointments can bring a complaint under the provisions in Part VI of the ERA. However, that is not the only means by which aggrieved individuals can seek redress. If they have been victimised as a result of exercising the right to time off, they may be able to claim discrimination or unlawful detriment or, in the case of employees, automatically unfair dismissal. We consider these remedies below.

Complaints under Part VI ERA. If an employer unreasonably refuses time off **6.32** (whether paid or unpaid) or allows time off but refuses to pay for it (either in whole or in part), the employee may complain to an employment tribunal – S.57ZM(1) ERA. Similar provisions apply to agency workers, save that whereas a complaint can be brought against a temporary work agency both in respect of a failure to permit (paid or unpaid) time off or to pay the worker for any time off taken, a complaint can only be brought against a hirer in respect of a failure to permit time off – S.57ZQ(1) and (2). In other words, a complaint solely concerned with a failure to pay for time off taken can only be brought against the agency.

If the tribunal finds that the employee's or agency worker's complaint is justified, it must make a declaration to that effect – S.57ZM(4)/S.57ZQ(5). It must also award compensation – see 'Compensation' below.

6.33 *Time limits.* Any complaint under S.57ZM or S.57ZQ must be presented within a period of three months beginning with the date of the adoption appointment concerned – S.57ZM(2)(a)/S.57ZQ(3)(a). So, for example, if the appointment was on 10 June, time runs out on 9 September and not, as the unwary often think, on 10 September. However, if it was not reasonably practicable to present the complaint within the three-month time limit, the tribunal may extend the time limit by such further period as it considers reasonable – S.57ZM(2)(b)/S.57ZQ(3)(b). The time limit may also be extended to facilitate early conciliation or cross-border mediation. The law on time limits is explained in IDS Employment Law Handbook, 'Employment Tribunal Practice and Procedure' (2014), Chapter 5, 'Time limits'.

6.34 *Compensation.* If the complaint is of unreasonable refusal to allow paid time off, the tribunal must order the employer to pay the employee an amount that is twice the amount of remuneration he or she would have received for the period of time off requested – S.57ZM(5). If the equivalent complaint is brought by an agency worker, then the tribunal must require the temporary work agency or, if appropriate, the hirer to pay such an amount – S.57ZQ(6). S.57ZQ(10) confers on a tribunal the power to apportion this payment between the temporary work agency and the hirer in such a manner as is 'just and equitable having regard to the extent of each respondent's responsibility for the infringement'.

If the employee's or agency worker's complaint is that the employer or temporary work agency allowed time off but refused to pay for it, either in whole or in part, the tribunal must order the employer or agency to pay the amount due – S.57ZM(6)/S.57ZQ(7).

6.35 Where the complaint is for unreasonably refusing the employee or agency worker unpaid time off as required by S.57ZL or S.57ZP, the tribunal must assess the compensation due according to the following formula:

- A x B x 2, where
- A is the 'appropriate hourly rate' (see 'Right to payment for time off – calculation of pay' above), and
- B is the number of working hours for which the employee would have been entitled to be absent if the request had been granted – S.57ZM(7)–(8)/S.57ZQ(8)–(9).

In the case of an agency worker, the tribunal has the power to apportion this payment between the temporary work agency and the hirer in such a manner as is 'just and equitable having regard to the extent of each respondent's responsibility for the infringement' – S.57ZQ(10).

Unlawful detriment. Section 47C(1) ERA stipulates that an employee 'has the **6.36** right not to be subjected to any detriment by any act, or any deliberate failure to act, by his employer done for a prescribed reason'. Subsection (2) goes on to state that 'a prescribed reason' must be one that is prescribed by regulations and which relates, among other things, to the right to paid or unpaid time off to attend adoption appointments under S.57ZJ or S.57ZL. The prescribed reasons are set out in Reg 28 of the Paternity and Adoption Leave Regulations 2002 SI 2002/2788 ('the PAL Regulations') and provide that an employee has the right not to be subjected to any detriment by any act, or any deliberate failure to act, by the employer because:

- the employee took or sought to take paid or unpaid time off to attend an adoption appointment, or

- the employer believed that the employee was likely to take such time off.

An employee is therefore protected from suffering any detrimental treatment related to the fact that he or she took or requested time off in connection with an expected adoption placement. This is the case regardless of whether the employee is the primary or the secondary adopter; in other words, the legislation protects both those who request paid leave in order to attend an adoption meeting and those who request unpaid leave for the same reason.

Agency workers benefit from more explicit protection in relation to time off in **6.37** order to attend adoption appointments. S.47C(5)(c) and (d) ERA, which was inserted by the Children and Families Act 2014 on 1 October 2014, gives agency workers a right not to be subjected to a detriment by the temporary work agency or the hirer on certain grounds. The grounds are that the agency worker:

- took or sought to take time off for an adoption appointment under S.57ZN or S.57ZP ERA, or

- (in the case of the primary or sole adopter) received or sought to receive remuneration under S.57ZO for time off to attend an adoption appointment.

The enforcement of claims under S.47C(1) and (5) for a refusal to allow time off for adoption meetings is discussed in Chapter 12, 'Detriment and unfair dismissal', under 'Right not to suffer detriment – remedies'.

Automatically unfair dismissal. Section 99 ERA and Reg 29 PAL Regulations **6.38** provide that an employee is regarded as automatically unfairly dismissed if the reason or principal reason for the dismissal (or his or her selection for redundancy) is connected to the fact that the employee took or sought to take paid or unpaid time off under S.57ZJ or S.57ZL ERA, or the employer believed

231

that the employee was likely to take such time off. There is no minimum service requirement for the right to claim automatically unfair dismissal under S.99.

Section 99 and Reg 29 apply to employees. As a result, agency workers are only covered if they are employees employed under a contract of employment, which is generally not the case. The employment status of agency workers is discussed in detail in IDS Employment Law Handbook, 'Atypical and Flexible Working' (2014), Chapter 1, 'Agency workers', under 'Employment status'.

6.39 **Asserting a statutory right.** If an employee is dismissed because he or she has tried to exercise the right to take time off for adoption appointments, the employee may also be able to claim that he or she has been dismissed for asserting a statutory right. Under S.104(1) ERA an employee's dismissal will be automatically unfair if the reason or principal reason for the dismissal was that:

- the employee brought proceedings against the employer to enforce a relevant statutory right, or

- the employee alleged that the employer had infringed a relevant statutory right.

It is immaterial whether the employee actually has the statutory right in question or whether it has been infringed, but the employee's claim to the right must be made in good faith – S.104(1) ERA. Furthermore, it is sufficient that the employee made it reasonably clear to the employer what the right claimed to have been infringed was; it is not necessary actually to specify the right – S.104(3).

6.40 Dismissals for asserting a statutory right are dealt with in detail in IDS Employment Law Handbook, 'Unfair Dismissal' (2010), Chapter 12, 'Dismissal for asserting a statutory right'.

6.41 **Discrimination.** The ERA provisions against unlawful detriment and dismissal protect employees (or agency workers, in the case of unlawful detriment) wanting to take time off work for pre-adoption meetings. Such claims could potentially be accompanied by a claim for unlawful discrimination under the Equality Act 2010 (EqA), which would allow the claimant to seek an award of compensation for injury to feelings (a head of damages not available in a straightforward claim under the ERA). The EqA outlaws discrimination on a number of grounds, including sex, pregnancy and maternity, marriage and civil partnership, and sexual orientation. Several different types of claim could arise in the context of the right to time off to attend adoption appointments. For example, it would amount to direct sex discrimination contrary to S.13 EqA to refuse to allow a man to exercise his statutory right to paid time off for adoption appointments where a woman would not be refused a similar request. A claim would also be likely to succeed where the employer has granted all requests for time off but has subsequently made it clear to a man (but not a woman) taking time off for this reason that his adoption appointments are harming his career prospects. It would similarly amount to direct discrimination, albeit on the ground of sexual orientation, to refuse the right to time off for adoption appointments to a lesbian or gay employee intending to adopt a child but not to a heterosexual employee.

An indirect sex discrimination claim, based on the premise that more women than men are likely to take paid time off for adoption appointments (as they will have the main responsibility for the child), is also a possibility. Indirect discrimination occurs under S.19 EqA where an employer applies to a woman a provision, criterion or practice which it applies or would apply equally to a man but which puts, or would put, women at a particular disadvantage when compared with men, which puts her at that disadvantage, and which the employer cannot show to be a proportionate means of achieving a legitimate aim.

For further discussion of discrimination law in this area, see Chapter 13, **6.42** 'Discrimination and equal pay'. For a more in-depth analysis, see IDS Employment Law Handbook, 'Discrimination at Work' (2012).

Ordinary adoption leave   6.43

Section 75A ERA provides that an employee who satisfies certain conditions is entitled to take ordinary adoption leave (OAL). (As we will see under 'Additional adoption leave' below, these conditions are also pertinent to additional adoption leave (AAL) because the main condition for entitlement to AAL is that the employee has taken OAL.)

Who has the right?   6.44
SAL is available to employees – regardless of their length of service – who:

- are matched with a child for adoption (see 'Conditions of entitlement – adopter' below)

- foster a child with a view to adoption (see 'Foster parents' below), or

- are intended parents in a surrogacy arrangement who have, or have applied or intend to apply for, a parental order (see 'Intended parents in surrogacy arrangement' below).

Employees only. OAL can only be taken by employees and not other types of **6.45** 'worker' or the self-employed. 'Employee' means an individual who has entered into or works under a contract of employment, which is defined as a contract of service or apprenticeship, whether express or implied, and (if express) whether oral or in writing – Reg 2(1) PAL Regulations. These definitions are identical to those that apply for the purposes of unfair dismissal and redundancy under the ERA and reference should be made to IDS Employment Law Handbook, 'Contracts of Employment' (2014), Chapter 2, 'Employment status', for a full

233

discussion of the law in this area. Note that the definition of 'employee' for statutory adoption pay (SAP) purposes is different. The implications of this are discussed later in this chapter under 'Statutory adoption pay – eligible persons'.

Share fishermen and women and the police are excluded from the right to SAL – Ss.199(2) and 200 ERA. However, seafarers employed on ships registered under S.8 of the Merchant Shipping Act 1995 are covered provided that the ship is registered as belonging to a port in Great Britain, that under his or her contract of employment the worker does not work wholly outside Great Britain, and that he or she is ordinarily resident in Great Britain – S.199(7) and (8). Crown employees and parliamentary staff are also covered – Ss.191, 194 and 195, but members of the armed forces are not – S.192 (read with para 16, Sch 2). (Note, however, that similar arrangements to the statutory scheme exist for armed service personnel.)

6.46 *Employee shareholders.* Section 31 of the Growth and Infrastructure Act 2013, which came into force on 1 September 2013, added a new S.205A to the ERA that introduced a new type of employment contract: an 'employee shareholder' contract. Under this type of contract, an individual agrees to waive certain employment rights, including the right to claim ordinary unfair dismissal, in return for at least £2,000 worth of free shares in the employer's company. These shares are subject to a number of favourable tax concessions. The right to take SAL is not one of the rights that an individual must waive in order to become an employee shareholder and such an employee is therefore entitled to take SAL in the normal way. However, an employee shareholder is required to give 16 weeks' notice of his or her intention to return to work during a period of adoption leave (as opposed to the eight weeks' notice that would usually be required) – S.205A(3)(b) (see the section 'Returning to work after adoption leave' below, under 'Notice of return during adoption leave – employee shareholders'). For more information about employee shareholder status, see IDS Employment Law Handbook, 'Atypical and Flexible Working' (2014), Chapter 7, 'Employee shareholders'.

6.47 **Foster parents.** Local authority foster parents who are approved prospective adopters are entitled to claim OAL where a child is placed with them with a view to adoption under S.22C of the Children Act 1989. These placements are commonly known as 'fostering for adoption' placements. Under S.22C of the Children Act 1989, a local authority in England is under a duty to consider a 'fostering for adoption' placement where it is considering adoption as an option for the child's long-term care (whether as the only option, or as one of several) but it does not yet have authorisation to place the child for adoption. The right to adoption leave applies to foster parents who are notified of having been matched with a child on or after 5 April 2015.

The necessary amendments to the PAL Regulations were made by the Paternity and Adoption Leave (Amendment) (No.2) Regulations 2014 SI 2014/3206. As